Programming Android with Kotlin

Achieving Structured Concurrency
with Coroutines

Pierre-Olivier Laurence and
Amanda Hinchman-Dominguez,
with G. Blake Meike and Mike Dunn

Beijing · Boston · Farnham · Sebastopol · Tokyo

Programming Android with Kotlin

by Pierre-Olivier Laurence and Amanda Hinchman-Dominguez, with G. Blake Meike and Mike Dunn

Copyright © 2022 Pierre-Olivier Laurence, Amanda Hinchman-Dominguez, and O'Reilly Media Inc. All rights reserved.

Published by O'Reilly Media, Inc., 1005 Gravenstein Highway North, Sebastopol, CA 95472.

O'Reilly books may be purchased for educational, business, or sales promotional use. Online editions are also available for most titles (*http://oreilly.com*). For more information, contact our corporate/institutional sales department: 800-998-9938 or *corporate@oreilly.com*.

Acquisition Editor: Suzanne McQuade	**Indexer:** WordCo Indexing Services, Inc.
Development Editor: Jeff Bleiel	**Interior Designer:** David Futato
Production Editor: Beth Kelly	**Cover Designer:** Karen Montgomery
Copyeditor: Piper Editorial Consulting, LLC	**Illustrator:** Kate Dullea
Proofreader: Audrey Doyle	

December 2021: First Edition

Revision History for the First Edition
2021-12-03: First Release
2022-05-27: Second Release

See *http://oreilly.com/catalog/errata.csp?isbn=9781492063001* for release details.

978-1-492-06300-1

[LSI]

Table of Contents

Preface. ix

1. Kotlin Essentials. 1
   The Kotlin Type System   2
      Primitive Types   2
      Null Safety   3
      The Unit Type   5
      Function Types   6
      Generics   8
   Variables and Functions   8
      Variables   8
      Lambdas   9
      Extension Functions   10
   Classes   12
      Class Initialization   12
      Properties   14
      lateinit Properties   15
      Lazy Properties   17
      Delegates   18
      Companion Objects   19
      Data Classes   20
      Enum Classes   21
      Sealed Classes   23
   Visibility Modifiers   24
   Summary   26

2. The Kotlin Collections Framework. **29**

Collection Basics 29
   Java Interoperability 30
   Mutability 30
   Overloaded Operators 32
   Creating Containers 33
Functional Programming 34
   Functional Versus Procedural: A Simple Example 35
   Functional Android 36
Kotlin Transformation Functions 37
   The Boolean Functions 37
   Filter Functions 38
   Map 38
   flatMap 40
   Grouping 42
   Iterators Versus Sequences 43
An Example 44
   The Problem 44
   The Implementation 45
Summary 51

3. Android Fundamentals. **53**

The Android Stack 53
   Hardware 54
   Kernel 54
   System Services 55
   Android Runtime Environment 55
   Applications 55
The Android Application Environment 55
   Intents and Intent Filters 57
   Context 59
Android Application Components: The Building Blocks 62
   The Activity and Its Friends 62
   Services 67
   Content Providers 71
   Broadcast Receivers 72
Android Application Architectures 73
   MVC: The Foundation 74
   Widgets 75
   The Local Model 75

Android Patterns   76
  Model–View–Intent   76
  Model–View–Presenter   76
  Model–View–ViewModel   77
Summary   78

4. **Concurrency in Android**. **81**
Thread Safety   82
  Atomicity   82
  Visibility   83
The Android Threading Model   84
Dropped Frames   85
Memory Leaks   87
Tools for Managing Threads   90
  Looper/Handler   91
  Executors and ExecutorServices   93
Tools for Managing Jobs   95
  JobScheduler   96
  WorkManager   98
Summary   99

5. **Thread Safety**. **101**
An Example of a Thread Issue   101
Invariants   103
  Mutexes   104
  Thread-Safe Collections   104
Thread Confinement   107
Thread Contention   108
Blocking Call Versus Nonblocking Call   109
Work Queues   110
Back Pressure   111
Summary   113

6. **Handling Concurrency Using Callbacks**. **115**
Example-of-Purchase Feature   116
Creating the App   118
  View-Model   118
  View   119
  Implement the Logic   123
  Discussion   124
Limitations of the Threading Model   126

Summary   127

7. Coroutines Concepts... 129
    What Exactly Is a Coroutine?   129
        Your First Coroutine   130
        The async Coroutine Builder   133
    A Quick Detour About Structured Concurrency   134
    The Parent-Child Relationship in Structured Concurrency   137
    CoroutineScope and CoroutineContext   138
    Suspending Functions   145
    Suspending Functions Under the Hood   146
    Using Coroutines and Suspending Functions: A Practical Example 150
    Don't Be Mistaken About the suspend Modifier   153
    Summary   154

8. Structured Concurrency with Coroutines......................... 157
    Suspending Functions   157
        Set the Scene   158
        Traditional Approach Using java.util.concurrent.ExecutorService 160
        A Reminder About HandlerThread   163
        Using Suspending Functions and Coroutines   167
        Summary of Suspending Functions Versus Traditional Threading 171
    Cancellation   171
        Coroutine Lifecycle   172
        Cancelling a Coroutine   174
        Cancelling a Task Delegated to a Third-Party Library   176
        Coroutines That Are Cooperative with Cancellation   180
        delay Is Cancellable   182
        Handling Cancellation   183
        Causes of Cancellation   184
    Supervision   187
    supervisorScope Builder   189
    Parallel Decomposition   189
    Automatic Cancellation   191
    Exception Handling   191
        Unhandled Versus Exposed Exceptions   191
        Exposed Exceptions   193
        Unhandled Exceptions   196
    Summary   199
    Closing Thoughts   200

9. Channels. **201**

Channels Overview 202
   Rendezvous Channel 204
   Unlimited Channel 208
   Conflated Channel 209
   Buffered Channel 210
   Channel Producers 211
Communicating Sequential Processes 212
   Model and Architecture 213
   A First Implementation 214
   The select Expression 219
   Putting It All Together 221
   Fan-Out and Fan-In 222
   Performance Test 223
   Back Pressure 224
   Similarities with the Actor Model 225
   Execution Is Sequential Inside a Process ... 226
   Final Thoughts 226
Deadlock in CSP 227
TL;DR 229
Limitations of Channels 230
Channels Are Hot 232
Summary 233

10. Flows. **235**

An Introduction to Flows 236
   A More Realistic Example 237
   Operators 239
   Terminal Operators 239
Examples of Cold Flow Usage 240
   Use Case #1: Interface with a Callback-Based API ... 240
   Use Case #2: Concurrently Transform a Stream of Values ... 245
   What Happens in Case of Error? 247
   Final Thoughts 248
   Use Case #3: Create a Custom Operator 248
   Usage 251
Error Handling 251
   The try/catch Block 252
   Separation of Concern Is Important 254
   Exception Transparency Violation 255

The catch Operator   256
Materialize Your Exceptions   259
Hot Flows with SharedFlow   262
Create a SharedFlow   263
Register a Subscriber   263
Send Values to the SharedFlow   264
Using SharedFlow to Stream Data   264
Using SharedFlow as an Event Bus   270
StateFlow: A Specialized SharedFlow   271
An Example of StateFlow Usage   272
Summary   274

11. **Performance Considerations with Android Profiling Tools.**. **275**
Android Profiler   277
Network Profiler   280
CPU Profiler   286
Energy Profiler   297
Memory Profiler   299
Detecting Memory Leaks with LeakCanary   304
Summary   308

12. **Trimming Down Resource Consumption with Performance Optimizations.**. **311**
Achieving Flatter View Hierarchy with ConstraintLayout   312
Reducing Programmatic Draws with Drawables   316
Minimizing Asset Payload in Network Calls   321
Bitmap Pooling and Caching   321
Reducing Unnecessary Work   323
Using Static Functions   325
Minification and Obfuscation with R8 and ProGuard   326
Summary   327

Index.. . . . . **329**

Preface

JetBrains created Kotlin for two reasons: there was no language that filled all the gaps in Android development using (legacy) Java libraries, and a new language would allow Android development to set trends, rather than just follow them.

In February 2015, Kotlin 1.0 was officially announced. Kotlin is concise, safe, pragmatic, and focused on interoperability with Java code. It can be used everywhere Java is used today: for server-side development, Android apps, desktop or portable clients, IoT device programming, and much, much more. Kotlin gained popularity among Android developers quite rapidly, and Google's decision to adopt Kotlin as the official language of Android development resulted in skyrocketing interest in the language. According to the Android Developers website (*https://developer.android.com/kotlin*), more than 60% of professional Android developers currently use Kotlin.

The learning curve in Android is rather steep: admittedly, it's hard to learn and harder to master. Part of the Android developer "upbringing," for many, is to be exposed over time to unintended interactions between the Android operating system and the application. This book intends to bring those kinds of exposures to readers in depth and up close by examining such problems in Android. We'll talk not only about Kotlin and Java, but also about the concurrency problems that arise when using Android and how Kotlin is able to solve them.

We will sometimes compare Kotlin to Java when we believe doing so provides better insight (especially since most readers are expected to have a Java background). We can demonstrate, with working examples, how to bridge that gap, and how the underlying concepts of most Kotlin operations are more similar to the Java equivalent than not. The tasks will be organized by topic to provide software engineers with a structured decomposition of that mass of information, and they will show how to make an application robust and maintainable.

Additionally, users familiar with Java—including Android developers—will find their learning curve dramatically flatten when we present each of the common tasks in both Java and Kotlin. Where appropriate, we'll discuss the difference and the pitfalls of one or both, but we hope to provide bite-size and easily digestible examples of a task that will "just work," and enable the reader to consume and adapt to the modern paradigm, as well as become aware of the significance of the updated code immediately and instinctively.

While Kotlin is fully interoperable with Java, other Java application development (server-side programming, desktop clients, middleware, etc.) has not caught on to the extent that Android has. This is largely due to the maintainer of Android (Google) strongly "encouraging" its users to make the change. Users are regularly migrating to Kotlin, but even more still fall back to Java for mission-critical work. Our hope is that this book will serve as the lifeline an Android developer needs to feel safe in committing to the advantages and simplicity that Kotlin represents.

Who Should Read This Book

Any of the over six million Android engineers. We believe that virtually every Android engineer could benefit from this book. While a small percentage will be fluent in Kotlin, even they will likely learn something from the information we'll present. But realistically, we're targeting the very large majority who haven't made the transition to Kotlin. This book is also for those who have dipped a toe in but not gained the same level of familiarity with Kotlin that they may have accrued in Java-centric Android development:

Scenario 1

A reader is proficient in Java, heard of this new Kotlin language, and wants to try it out. So they read some online tutorial and start using it and it works great. Soon they realize that this isn't just a new syntax. The idioms aren't the same (e.g., functional programming, coroutines) and a whole new way of developing is now possible. But they lack guidelines, structure. For them, this book is a perfect fit.

Scenario 2

A reader is part of a small team of Java developers. They have discussions about whether they should start including Kotlin in their project. Even if Kotlin is said to be 100% interoperable with Java, some colleagues argue that introducing another language will add complexity to the project. Others suggest it might limit the number of colleagues who will be able to work on the project because of the need to master two languages. The reader could use this book to convince their colleagues, if they can show that the benefits will outweigh the costs.

Scenario 3

An experienced Android developer may have played around with Kotlin or written a feature in it, but still falls back to the home base of Java when things need to get done. This was the scenario we found ourselves in when realizing the book we're pitching now would have made our lives much easier. This is also the state we see most commonly around us—many Android devs have touched Kotlin, and many feel like they understand enough to write it when necessary, but they are either unaware, or simply unconvinced, of the significance of data classes, immutable properties, and structured concurrency. We think this book will turn a curious person into a committed evangelist.

Why We Wrote This Book

There are plenty of books that show how Android works, how Kotlin works, or how concurrency works. Kotlin is becoming wildly popular with Android development for its easy adoption and cleaner syntax, but Kotlin offers Android much more than that: it offers new ways to solve concurrency problems in Android. We wrote this book to provide a unique and specific intersectionality of these topics in great depth. Both Android and Kotlin are rapidly changing, separately and together. Trying to keep up with all the changes can be difficult.

We view this book as a valuable checkpoint in history: showing where Android came from, where it is now, and how it will continue to evolve with Kotlin as the language matures.

Navigating This Book

Sometimes we include code snippets as screenshots instead of regular atlas code formatting. This is particularly useful with coroutines and flows, as suspension points are clearly identifiable. We also get type hints from the IDE.

Chapter 1, "Kotlin Essentials" and Chapter 2, "The Kotlin Collections Framework" cover major notable transitions made with Android in Kotlin. While the information in these chapters is enough to give you a good grounding in Kotlin, further chapters will take a deeper dive into more complex/advanced features. Users familiar with Java or similar syntactic structures will find the translation surprisingly natural.

Chapter 3, "Android Fundamentals" and Chapter 4, "Concurrency in Android" will provide you with a foundation in the Android system in relation to memory and threading. As in any other operating system, concurrency is hard to achieve.

Chapter 5, "Thread Safety" through Chapter 11, "Performance Considerations with Android Profiling Tools" examine common issues surrounding memory and threading, while indicating how the Android framework has evolved over time to grant developers more control around them. In tandem, these chapters show how Kotlin's extensions and language features can help developers write better applications faster.

Chapter 12, "Trimming Down Resource Consumption with Performance Optimizations" explores the use of powerful Android developer tools to examine performance and memory-related analytics under the hood—to be able to see things you never really knew about. This book will provide engineers with professionally developed and curated implementations of the most common tasks seen in native Android development. Many tasks will consist of a real-world problem, followed by the corresponding solution in both Java and Kotlin. When further explanation is required, the solutions will follow a snappy compare-and-contrast model with a focus on brevity and natural language.

Conventions Used in This Book

The following typographical conventions are used in this book:

Italic

Indicates new terms, URLs, email addresses, filenames, and file extensions.

`Constant width`

Used for program listings, as well as within paragraphs to refer to program elements such as variable or function names, databases, data types, environment variables, statements, and keywords.

`Constant width bold`

Shows commands or other text that should be typed literally by the user.

`Constant width italic`

Shows text that should be replaced with user-supplied values or by values determined by context.

This element signifies a tip or suggestion.

This element signifies a general note.

This element indicates a warning or caution.

Using Code Examples

Supplemental material (code examples, exercises, etc.) is available for download at *https://github.com/ProgrammingAndroidWithKotlin*.

If you have a technical question or a problem using the code examples, please send email to *bookquestions@oreilly.com*.

This book is here to help you get your job done. In general, if example code is offered with this book, you may use it in your programs and documentation. You do not need to contact us for permission unless you're reproducing a significant portion of the code. For example, writing a program that uses several chunks of code from this book does not require permission. Selling or distributing examples from O'Reilly books does require permission. Answering a question by citing this book and quoting example code does not require permission. Incorporating a significant amount of example code from this book into your product's documentation does require permission.

We appreciate, but generally do not require, attribution. An attribution usually includes the title, author, publisher, and ISBN. For example: "*Programming Android with Kotlin* by Pierre-Olivier Laurence, Amanda Hinchman-Dominguez, G. Blake Meike, and Mike Dunn (O'Reilly). Copyright 2022 Pierre-Olivier Laurence, Amanda Hinchman-Dominguez, and O'Reilly Media, Inc., 978-1-492-06300-1."

If you feel your use of code examples falls outside fair use or the permission given above, feel free to contact us at *permissions@oreilly.com*.

O'Reilly Online Learning

 For more than 40 years, *O'Reilly Media* has provided technology and business training, knowledge, and insight to help companies succeed.

Our unique network of experts and innovators share their knowledge and expertise through books, articles, and our online learning platform. O'Reilly's online learning platform gives you on-demand access to live training courses, in-depth learning paths, interactive coding environments, and a vast collection of text and video from O'Reilly and 200+ other publishers. For more information, visit *http://oreilly.com*.

How to Contact Us

Please address comments and questions concerning this book to the publisher:

O'Reilly Media, Inc.
1005 Gravenstein Highway North
Sebastopol, CA 95472
800-998-9938 (in the United States or Canada)
707-829-0515 (international or local)
707-829-0104 (fax)

We have a web page for this book, where we list errata, examples, and any additional information. You can access this page at *https://oreil.ly/pak*.

Email *bookquestions@oreilly.com* to comment or ask technical questions about this book.

For news and information about our books and courses, visit *http://oreilly.com*.

Find us on Facebook: *http://facebook.com/oreilly*

Follow us on Twitter: *http://twitter.com/oreillymedia*

Watch us on YouTube: *http://youtube.com/oreillymedia*

Acknowledgments

This book has been greatly strengthened and improved thanks to our technical reviewers, Adnan Sozuan and Andrew Gibel. We give thanks to the folks at O'Reilly for helping to bring us together and giving us all the support we needed to bring this book to life, especially Jeff Bleiel and Zan McQuade.

We thank Roman Elizarov and Jake Wharton for taking the time to speak with us about direction on evolution in concurrency in Kotlin and low-level optics in Android.

We thank our friends, family, and colleagues for support. We thank the Kotlin community, and the individuals who have taken the time to read early drafts and give feedback.

Lastly, we dedicate this book to Mike Dunn: coauthor, colleague, friend, and father. We miss him dearly and hope this book is something he'd be proud of.

CHAPTER 1

Kotlin Essentials

Kotlin was created by the JetBrains team from St. Petersburg, Russia. JetBrains is perhaps best known for the IntelliJ Idea IDE, the basis for Android Studio. Kotlin is now used in a wide variety of environments across multiple operating systems. It has been nearly five years since Google announced support for Kotlin on Android. According to the Android Developers Blog (*https://oreil.ly/PrfQm*), as of 2021, over 1.2 million apps in the Google Play store use Kotlin, including 80% of the top one thousand apps.

If you've picked up this book, we are assuming that you are already an Android developer and that you are familiar with Java.

Kotlin was designed to interoperate with Java. Even its name, taken from an island near St. Petersburg, is a sly allusion to Java, an island in Indonesia. Though Kotlin supports other platforms (iOS, WebAssembly, Kotlin/JS, etc.), a key to Kotlin's broad use is its support for the Java virtual machine (JVM). Since Kotlin can be compiled to Java bytecode, it can run anywhere that a JVM runs.

Much of the discussion in this chapter will compare Kotlin to Java. It's important to understand, though, that Kotlin is not just warmed-over Java with some added bells and whistles. Kotlin is a new and different language with connections to Scala, Swift, and C# that are nearly as strong as its connection with Java. It has its own styles and its own idioms. While it is possible to think Java and write Kotlin, thinking in idiomatic Kotlin will reveal the full power of the language.

We realize that there may be some Android developers who have been working with Kotlin for some time, and who have never written any Java at all. If this sounds like you, you may be able to skim this chapter and its review of the Kotlin language. However, even if you are fairly handy with the language, this may be a good chance to remind yourself of some of the details.

This chapter isn't meant to be a full-fledged primer on Kotlin, so if you are completely new to Kotlin, we recommend the excellent *Kotlin in Action*.[1] Instead, this chapter is a review of some Kotlin basics: the type system, variables, functions, and classes. Even if you are not a Kotlin language expert, it should provide enough of a foundation for you to understand the rest of the book.

As with all statically typed languages, Kotlin's type system is the meta language that Kotlin uses to describe itself. Because it is an essential aspect for discussing Kotlin, we'll start by reviewing it.

The Kotlin Type System

Like Java, Kotlin is a statically typed language. The Kotlin compiler knows the type of every entity that a program manipulates. It can make deductions[2] about those entities and, using those deductions, identify errors that will occur when code contradicts them. Type checking allows a compiler to catch and flag an entire large class of programming errors. This section highlights some of the most interesting features of Kotlin's type system, including the Unit type, functional types, null safety, and generics.

Primitive Types

The most obvious difference between Java's and Kotlin's type systems is that Kotlin has no notion of a *primitive type*.

Java has the types int, float, boolean, etc. These types are peculiar in that they do not inherit from Java's base type, Object. For instance, the statement int n = null; is not legal Java. Neither is List<int> integers;. In order to mitigate this inconsistency, each Java primitive type has a *boxed type* equivalent. Integer, for instance, is the analog of int; Boolean of boolean; and so on. The distinction between primitive and boxed types has nearly vanished because, since Java 5, the Java compiler automatically converts between the boxed and unboxed types. It is now legal to say Integer i = 1.

Kotlin does not have primitive types cluttering up its type system. Its single base type, Any, analogous to Java's Object, is the root of the entire Kotlin type hierarchy.

---

1. Dmitry Jemerov and Svetlana Isakova. *Kotlin in Action*. Manning, 2017.

2. Kotlin officially calls this type inferencing, which uses a partial phase of the compiler (the frontend component) to do type checking of the written code while you write in the IDE. It's a plug-in for IntelliJ! Fun fact: the entirety of IntelliJ and Kotlin is made of compiler plug-ins.

Kotlin's internal representation of simple types is not connected to its type system. The Kotlin compiler has sufficient information to represent, for instance, a 32-bit integer with as much efficiency as any other language. So, writing val i: Int = 1 might result in using a primitive type or a boxed type, depending on how the i variable is used in the code. Whenever possible, the Kotlin compiler will use primitive types.

Null Safety

A second major difference between Java and Kotlin is that *nullability* is part of Kotlin's type system. A nullable type is distinguished from its nonnullable analog by the question mark at the end of its name; for example, String and String?, Person and Person?. The Kotlin compiler will allow the assignment of null to a nullable type: var name: String? = null. It will not, however, permit var name: String = null (because String is not a nullable type).

Any is the root of the Kotlin type system, just like Object in Java. However, there's a significant difference: Any is the base class for all nonnullable classes, while Any? is the base class for all nullable ones. This is the basis of *null safety*. In other words, it may be useful to think of Kotlin's type system as two identical type trees: all nonnullable types are subtypes of Any and all nullable types are subtypes of Any?.

Variables must be initialized. There is no default value for a variable. This code, for instance, will generate a compiler error:

```
val name: String // error! Nonnullable types must be initialized!
```

As described earlier, the Kotlin compiler makes deductions using type information. Often the compiler can figure out the type of an identifier from information it already has. This process is called *type inference*. When the compiler can infer a type, there is no need for the developer to specify it. For instance, the assignment var name = "Jerry" is perfectly legal, despite the fact that the type of the variable name has not been specified. The compiler can infer that the variable name must be a String because it is assigned the value "Jerry" (which is a String).

Inferred types can be surprising, though. This code will generate a compiler error:

```
var name = "Jerry"
name = null
```

The compiler inferred the type String for the variable name, not the type String?. Because String is not a nullable type, attempting to assign null to it is illegal.

It is important to note that a *nullable* type is not the same as its *nonnullable* counterpart. As makes sense, a nullable type behaves as the supertype of the related nonnullable type. This code, for instance, compiles with no problem because a `String` is a `String?`:

```
val name = Jerry
fun showNameLength(name: String?) { // Function accepts a nullable parameter
    // ...
}

showNameLength(name)
```

On the other hand, the following code will not compile at all, because a `String?` is *not* a `String`:

```
val name: String? = null
fun showNameLength(name: String) { // This function only accepts non-nulls
    println(name.length)
}

showNameLength(name)              // error! Won't compile because "name"
                                  // can be null
```

Simply changing the type of the parameter will not entirely fix the problem:

```
val name: String? = null
fun showNameLength(name: String?) { // This function now accepts nulls
    println(name.length)             // error!
}

showNameLength(name)              // Compiles
```

This snippet fails with the error `Only safe (?.) or non-null asserted (!!.) calls are allowed on a nullable receiver of type String?`.

Kotlin requires that nullable variables be handled safely—in a way that cannot generate a null pointer exception. In order to make the code compile, it must correctly handle the case in which `name` is `null`:

```
val name: String? = null
fun showNameLength(name: String?) {
    println(if (name == null) 0 else name.length)
    // we will use an even nicer syntax shortly
}
```

Kotlin has special operators, ?. and ?:, that simplify working with nullable entities:

```kotlin
val name: String? = null
fun showNameLength(name: String?) {
    println(name?.length ?: 0)
}
```

In the preceding example, when `name` is not `null`, the value of `name?.length` is the same as the value of `name.length`. When `name` is `null`, however, the value of `name?.length` is `null`. The expression does not throw a null pointer exception. Thus, the first operator in the previous example, the safe operator `?.`, is syntactically equivalent to:

```kotlin
if (name == null) null else name.length
```

The second operator, the *elvis operator* `?:`, returns the left expression if it is non-null, or the right expression otherwise. Note that the expression on the right-hand side is evaluated only if the left expression is null.

It is equivalent to:

```kotlin
if (name?.length == null) 0 else name.length
```

The Unit Type

In Kotlin, *everything* has a value. Always. Once you understand this, it is not difficult to imagine that even a method that doesn't specifically return anything has a default value. That default value is named `Unit`. `Unit` is the name of exactly one object, the value things have if they don't have any other value. The type of the `Unit` object is, conveniently, named `Unit`.

The whole concept of `Unit` can seem odd to Java developers who are used to a distinction between expressions—things that have a value—and statements—things that don't.

Java's conditional is a great example of the distinction between a *statement* and an *expression* because it has one of each! In Java you can say:

```java
if (maybe) doThis() else doThat();
```

You cannot, however, say:

```
int n = if (maybe) doThis() else doThat();
```

Statements, like the `if` statement, do not return a value. You cannot assign the value of an `if` statement to a variable, because `if` statements don't return anything. The same is true for loop statements, case statements, and so on.

Java's `if` statement, however, has an analog, the *ternary expression*. Since it is an expression, it returns a value and that value can be assigned. This is legal Java (provided both `doThis` and `doThat` return integers):

```
int n = (maybe) ? doThis() : doThat();
```

In Kotlin, there is no need for two conditionals because `if` is an expression and returns a value. For example, this is perfectly legal:

```
val n = if (maybe) doThis() else doThat()
```

In Java, a method with `void` as the return type is like a statement. Actually, this is a bit of a misnomer because `void` isn't a type. It is a reserved word in the Java language that indicates that the method does not return a value. When Java introduced generics, it introduced the type `Void` to fill the void (intended!). The two representations of "nothing," the keyword and the type, however, are confusing and inconsistent: a function whose return type is `Void` must explicitly return `null`.

Kotlin is much more consistent: all functions return a value and have a type. If the code for a function does not return a value explicitly, the function has the value `Unit`.

Function Types

Kotlin's type system supports *function types*. For example, the following code defines a variable, func, whose value is a function, the lambda `{ x -> x.pow(2.0) }`:

```
val func: (Double) -> Double = { x -> x.pow(2.0) }
```

Since `func` is a function that takes one `Double` type argument and returns a `Double`, it's type is `(Double) -> Double`.

In the previous example, we specified the type of `func` explicitly. However, the Kotlin compiler can infer a lot about the type of the variable `func` from the value assigned to it. It knows the return type because it knows the type of pow. It doesn't, however, have enough information to guess the type of the parameter x. If we supply that, though, we can omit the type specifier for the variable:

```
val func = { x: Double -> x.pow(2.0)}
```

 Java's type system cannot describe a function type—there is no way to talk about functions outside the context of the classes that contain them. In Java, to do something similar to the previous example, we would use the functional type Function, like this:

```
Function<Double, Double> func
    = x -> Math.pow(x, 2.0);

func.apply(256.0);
```

The variable func has been assigned an anonymous instance of the type Function whose method apply is the given lambda.

Thanks to function types, functions can receive other functions as parameters or return them as values. We call these *higher-order functions*. Consider a template for a Kotlin type: (A, B) -> C. It describes a function that takes two parameters, one of type A and one of type B (whatever types those may be), and returns a value of type C. Because Kotlin's type language can describe functions, A, B, and C can all, themselves, be functions.

If that sounds rather meta, it's because it is. Let's make it more concrete. For A in the template, let's substitute (Double, Double) -> Int. That's a function that takes two Doubles and returns an Int. For B, let's just substitute a Double. So far, we have ((Double, Double) -> Int, Double) -> C.

Finally, let's say our new functional type returns a (Double) -> Int, a function that takes one parameter, a Double, and returns an Int. The following code shows the complete signature for our hypothetical function:

```
fun getCurve(
    surface: (Double, Double) -> Int,
    x: Double
): (Double) -> Int {
    return { y -> surface(x, y) }
}
```

We have just described a function type that takes two arguments. The first is a function (surface) of two parameters, both Doubles, that returns an Int. The second is a Double (x). Our getCurve function returns a function that takes one parameter, a Double (y), and returns an Int.

The ability to pass functions as arguments into other functions is a pillar of functional languages. Using higher-order functions, you can reduce code redundancy, while not having to create new classes as you would in Java (subclassing Runnable or Function interfaces). When used wisely, higher-order functions improve code readability.

Generics

Like Java, Kotlin's type system supports type variables. For instance:

```
fun <T> simplePair(x: T, y: T) = Pair(x, y)
```

This function creates a Kotlin Pair object in which both of the elements must be of the same type. Given this definition, simplePair("Hello", "Goodbye") and simple Pair(4, 5) are both legal, but simplePair("Hello", 5) is not.

The generic type denoted as T in the definition of simplePair is a type variable: the values it can take are Kotlin types (in this example, String or Int). A function (or a class) that uses a type variable is said to be *generic*.

Variables and Functions

Now that we have Kotlin's type language to support us, we can start to discuss the syntax of Kotlin itself.

In Java the top-level syntactic entity is the class. All variables and methods are members of some class or other, and the class is the main element in a homonymous file.

Kotlin has no such limitations. You can put your entire program in one file, if you like (please don't). You can also define variables and functions outside any class.

Variables

There are two ways to declare a variable: with the keywords val and var. The keyword is required, is the first thing on the line, and introduces the declaration:

```
val ronDeeLay = "the night time"
```

The keyword val creates a variable that is read-only: it cannot be reassigned. Be careful, though! You might think val is like a Java variable declared using the final keyword. Though similar, it is not the same! Although it cannot be reassigned, a val definitely can change value! A val variable in Kotlin is more like a Java class's field, which has a getter but no setter, as shown in the following code:

```
val surprising: Double
    get() = Math.random()
```

Every time `surprising` is accessed, it will return a different random value. This is an example of a property with no *backing field*. We'll cover properties later in this chapter. On the other hand, if we had written `val rand = Random()`, then `rand` wouldn't change in value and would be more like a `final` variable in Java.

The second keyword, `var`, creates a familiar mutable variable: like a little box that holds the last thing that was put into it.

In the next section, we will move on to one of Kotlin's features as a functional language: *lambdas*.

Lambdas

Kotlin supports function literals: lambdas. In Kotlin, lambdas are always surrounded by curly braces. Within the braces, the argument list is to the left of an arrow, `->`, and the expression that is the value of executing the lambda is to the right, as shown in the following code:

```
{ x: Int, y: Int -> x * y }
```

By convention, the returned value is the value of the last expression in the body of the lambda. For example, the function shown in the following code is of type `(Int, Int) -> String`:

```
{ x: Int, y: Int -> x * y; "down on the corner" }
```

Kotlin has a very interesting feature that allows actually extending the language. When the last argument to a function is another function (the function is higher-order), you can move the lambda expression passed as a parameter out of the parentheses that normally delimit the actual parameter list, as shown in the following code:

```
// The last argument, "callback", is a function
fun apiCall(param: Int, callback: () -> Unit)
```

This function would typically be used like this:

```
apiCall(1, { println("I'm called back!")})
```

But thanks to the language feature we mentioned, it can also be used like this:

```
apiCall(1) {
    println("I'm called back!")
}
```

This is much nicer, isn't it? Thanks to this feature, your code can be more readable. A more advanced usage of this feature are DSLs.[3]

Extension Functions

When you need to add a new method to an existing class, and that class comes from a dependency whose source code you don't own, what do you do?

In Java, if the class isn't `final`, you can subclass it. Sometimes this isn't ideal, because there's one more type to manage, which adds complexity to the project. If the class is `final`, you can define a static method inside some utility class of your own, as shown in the following code:

```
class FileUtils {
    public static String getWordAtIndex(File file, int index) {
        /* Implementation hidden for brevity */
    }
}
```

In the previous example, we defined a function to get a word in a text file, at a given index. On the use site, you'd write `String word = getWordAtIndex(file, 3)`, assuming you make the static import of `FileUtils.getWordAtIndex`. That's fine, we've been doing that for years in Java, and it works.

In Kotlin, there's one more thing you can do. You have the ability to define a new method on a class, even though it isn't a real member-function of that class. So you're not really extending the class, but on the use site it feels like you added a method to the class. How is this possible? By defining an *extension function*, as shown in the following code:

---

3. DSL stands for *domain-specific language*. An example of a DSL built in Kotlin is the Kotlin Gradle DSL.

```
// declared inside FileUtils.kt
fun File.getWordAtIndex(index: Int): String {
    val context = this.readText()  // 'this' corresponds to the file
    return context.split(' ').getOrElse(index) { "" }
}
```

From inside the declaration of the extension function, this refers to the receiving type instance (here, a File). You only have access to public and internal attributes and methods, so private and protected fields are inaccessible—you'll understand why shortly.

On the use site, you would write val word = file.getWordAtIndex(3). As you can see, we invoke the getWordAtIndex() function on a File instance, as if the File class had the getWordAtIndex() member-function. That makes the use site more expressive and readable. We didn't have to come up with a name for a new utility class: we can declare extension functions directly at the root of a source file.

Let's have a look at the decompiled version of getWordAtIndex:

```
public class FileUtilsKt {
    public static String getWordAtIndex(
            File file, int index
    ) {
        /* Implementation hidden for brevity */
    }
}
```

When compiled, the generated bytecode of our extension function is the equivalent of a static method which takes a File as its first argument. The enclosing class, FileUtilsKt, is named after the name of the source file (*FileUtils.kt*) with the "kt" suffix.

That explains why we can't access private fields in an extension function: we are just adding a static method that takes the receiving type as a parameter.

There's more! For class attributes, you can declare *extension properties*. The idea is exactly the same—you're not really extending a class, but you can make new attributes accessible using the dot notation, as shown in the following code:

```
// The Rectangle class has width and height properties
val Rectangle.area: Double
    get() = width * height
```

Notice that this time we used `val` (instead of `fun`) to declare the extension property. You would use it like so: `val area = rectangle.area`.

Extension functions and extension properties allow you to extend classes' capabilities, with a nice dot-notation usage, while still preserving separation of concern. You're not cluttering existing classes with specific code for particular needs.

Classes

Classes in Kotlin, at first, look a lot like they do in Java: the `class` keyword, followed by the block that defines the class. One of Kotlin's killer features, though, is the syntax for the constructor and the ability to declare properties within it. The following code shows the definition of a simple `Point` class along with a couple of uses:

```
class Point(val x: Int, var y: Int? = 3)

fun demo() {
    val pt1 = Point(4)
    assertEquals(3, pt1.y)
    pt1.y = 7
    val pt2 = Point(7, 7)
    assertEquals(pt2.y, pt1.y)
}
```

Class Initialization

Notice that in the preceding code, the constructor of `Point` is embedded in the declaration of the class. It is called the *primary constructor*. `Point`'s primary constructor declares two class properties, x and y, both of which are integers. The first, x, is read-only. The second, y, is mutable and nullable, and has a default value of 3.

Note that the `var` and `val` keywords are very significant! The declaration `class Point(x: Int, y: Int)` is *very* different from the preceding declaration because it does not declare any member properties. Without the keywords, identifiers x and y are simply arguments to the constructor. For example, the following code will generate an error:

```
class Point(x: Int, y: Int?)

fun demo() {
    val pt = Point(4)
    pt.y = 7 // error!  Variable expected
}
```

The Point class in this example has only one constructor, the one defined in its declaration. Classes are not limited to this single constructor, though. In Kotlin, you can also define both secondary constructors and initialization blocks, as shown in the following definition of the Segment class:

```
class Segment(val start: Point, val end: Point) {
    val length: Double = sqrt(
            (end.x - start.x).toDouble().pow(2.0)
                + (end.y - start.y).toDouble().pow(2.0))

    init {
        println("Point starting at $start with length $length")
    }

    constructor(x1: Int, y1: Int, x2: Int, y2: Int) :
            this(Point(x1, y1), Point(x2, y2)) {
        println("Secondary constructor")
    }
}
```

There are some other things that are of interest in this example. First of all, note that a secondary constructor must delegate to the primary constructor, the : this(...), in its declaration. The constructor may have a block of code, but it is required to delegate, explicitly, to the primary constructor, first.

Perhaps more interesting is the order of execution of the code in the preceding declaration. Suppose one were to create a new Segment, using the secondary constructor. In what order would the print statements appear?

Well! Let's try it and see:

```
>>> val s = Segment(1, 2, 3, 4)

Point starting at Point(x=1, y=2) with length 2.8284271247461903
Secondary constructor
```

This is pretty interesting. The init block is run before the code block associated with secondary constructor! On the other hand, the properties length and start have been initialized with their constructor-supplied values. That means that the primary constructor must have been run even before the init block.

In fact, Kotlin guarantees this ordering: the primary constructor (if there is one) is run first. After it finishes, init blocks are run in declaration order (top to bottom). If the new instance is being created using a secondary constructor, the code block associated with that constructor is the last thing to run.

Properties

Kotlin variables, declared using `val` or `var` in a constructor, or at the top level of a class, actually define a *property*. A property, in Kotlin, is like the combination of a Java field and its getter (if the property is read-only, defined with `val`), or its getter and setter (if defined with `var`).

Kotlin supports customizing the accessor and mutator for a property and has special syntax for doing so, as shown here in the definition of the class `Rectangle`:

```
class Rectangle(val l: Int, val w: Int) {
    val area: Int
        get() = l * w
}
```

The property `area` is *synthetic*: it is computed from the values for the length and width. Because it wouldn't make sense to assign to `area`, it is a `val`, read-only, and does not have a `set()` method.

Use standard "dot" notation to access the value of a property:

```
val rect = Rectangle(3, 4)
assertEquals(12, rect.area)
```

In order to further explore custom property getters and setters, consider a class that has a hash code that is used frequently (perhaps instances are kept in a `Map`), and that is quite expensive to calculate. As a design decision, you decide to cache the hash code, and to set it when the value of a class property changes. A first try might look something like this:

```
// This code doesn't work (we'll see why)
class ExpensiveToHash(_summary: String) {

    var summary: String = _summary
        set(value) {
            summary = value     // unbounded recursion!!
            hashCode = computeHash()
        }

    // other declarations here...
    var hashCode: Long = computeHash()

    private fun computeHash(): Long = ...
}
```

The preceding code will fail because of unbounded recursion: the assignment to sum mary is a call to summary.set()! Attempting to set the value of the property inside its own setter won't work. Kotlin uses the special identifier field to address this problem. The following shows the corrected version of the code:

```
class ExpensiveToHash(_summary: String) {

    var summary: String = _summary
        set(value) {
            field = value
            hashCode = computeHash()
        }

    //  other declarations here...
    var hashCode: Long = computeHash()

    private fun computeHash(): Long = ...
}
```

The identifier field has a special meaning only within the custom getter and setter, where it refers to the *backing field* that contains the property's state.

Notice, also, that the preceding code demonstrates the idiom for initializing a property that has a custom getter/setter with a value provided to the class constructor. Defining properties in a constructor parameter list is really handy shorthand. If a few property definitions in a constructor had custom getters and setters, though, it could make the constructor really hard to read.

When a property with a custom getter and setter must be initialized from the constructor, the property is defined, along with its custom getter and setter, in the body of the class. The property is initialized with a parameter from the constructor (in this case, _summary). This illustrates, again, the importance of the keywords val and var in a constructor's parameter list. The parameter _summary is just a parameter, not a class property, because it is declared without either keyword.

lateinit Properties

There are times when a variable's value is not available at the site of its declaration. An obvious example of this for Android developers is a UI widget used in an Activ ity or Fragment. It is not until the onCreate or onCreateView method runs that the variable, used throughout the activity to refer to the widget, can be initialized. The button in this example, for instance:

```
class MyFragment: Fragment() {
    private var button: Button? = null // will provide actual value later
}
```

The variable must be initialized. A standard technique, since we can't know the value, yet, is to make the variable nullable and initialize it with null.

The first question you should ask yourself in this situation is whether it is really necessary to define this variable at this moment and at this location. Will the button reference really be used in several methods or is it really only used in one or two specific places? If the latter, you can eliminate the class global altogether.

However, the problem with using a nullable type is that whenever you use button in your code, you will have to check for nullability. For example: button?.setOnClickListener { .. }. A couple of variables like this and you'll end up with a lot of annoying question marks! This can look particularly cluttered if you are used to Java and its simple dot notation.

Why, you might ask, does Kotlin prevent me from declaring the button using a non-null type when you are *sure* that you will initialize it before anything tries to access it? Isn't there a way to relax the compiler's initialization rule just for this button?

It's possible. You can do exactly that using the lateinit modifier, as shown in the following code:

```
class MyFragment: Fragment() {
    private lateinit var button: Button // will initialize later
}
```

Because the variable is declared lateinit, Kotlin will let you declare it without assigning it a value. The variable must be mutable, a var, because, by definition, you will assign a value to it, later. Great—problem solved, right?

We, the authors, thought exactly that when we started using Kotlin. Now, we lean toward using lateinit only when absolutely necessary, and using nullable values instead. Why?

When you use lateinit, you're telling the compiler, "I don't have a value to give you right now. But I'll give you a value later, I promise." If the Kotlin compiler could talk, it would answer, "Fine! You say you know what you're doing. If something goes wrong, it's on you." By using the lateinit modifier, you disable Kotlin's null safety for your variable. If you forget to initialize the variable or try to call some method on it before it's initialized, you'll get an UninitializedPropertyAccessException, which is essentially the same as getting a NullPointerException in Java.

Every single time we've used `lateinit` in our code, we've been burned eventually. Our code might work in all of the cases we'd foreseen. We've been certain that we didn't miss anything... and we were wrong.

When you declare a variable `lateinit` you're making assumptions that the compiler cannot prove. When you or other developers refactor the code afterward, your careful design might get broken. Tests might catch the error. Or not.[4] In our experience, using `lateinit` always resulted in runtime crashes. How did we fix that? By using a nullable type.

When you use a nullable type instead of `lateinit`, the Kotlin compiler will force you to check for nullability in your code, exactly in the places that it might be null. Adding a few question marks is definitely worth the trade-off for more robust code.

Lazy Properties

It's a common pattern in software engineering to put off creating and initializing an object until it is actually needed. This pattern is known as *lazy initialization*, and is especially common on Android, since allocating a lot of objects during app startup can lead to a longer startup time. Example 1-1 is a typical case of lazy initialization in Java.

Example 1-1. Java lazy initialization

```
class Lightweight {
    private Heavyweight heavy;

    public Heavyweight getHeavy() {
        if (heavy == null) {
            heavy = new Heavyweight();
        }
        return heavy;
    }
}
```

The field `heavy` is initialized with a new instance of the class `Heavyweight` (which is, presumably, expensive to create) only when its value is first requested with a call, for example, to `lightweight.getHeavy()`. Subsequent calls to `getHeavy()` will return the cached instance.

---

4. You can check whether the `lateinit` button property is initialized using `this::button.isInitialized`. Relying on developers to add this check in all the right places doesn't solve the underlying issue.

In Kotlin, lazy initialization is a part of the language. By using the directive by lazy and providing an initialization block, the rest of the lazy instantiation is implicit, as shown in Example 1-2.

Example 1-2. Kotlin lazy initialization

```
class Lightweight {
    val heavy by lazy { // Initialization block
        Heavyweight()
    }
}
```

We will explain this syntax in greater detail in the next section.

Notice that the code in Example 1-1 isn't thread-safe. Multiple threads calling Lightweight's getHeavy() method simultaneously might end up with different instances of Heavyweight.

By default, the code in Example 1-2 is thread-safe. Calls to Lightweight::getHeavy() will be synchronized so that only one thread at a time is in the initialization block.

Fine-grained control of concurrent access to a lazy initialization block can be managed using LazyThreadSafetyMode.

A Kotlin lazy value will not be initialized until a call is made at runtime. The first time the property heavy is referenced, the initialization block will be run.

Delegates

Lazy properties are an example of a more general Kotlin feature, called *delegation*. A declaration uses the keyword by to define a delegate that is responsible for getting and setting the value of the property. In Java, one could accomplish something similar with, for example, a setter that passed its argument on as a parameter to a call to a method on some other object, the delegate.

Because Kotlin's lazy initialization feature is an excellent example of the power of idiomatic Kotlin, let's take a minute to unpack it.

The first part of the declaration in Example 1-2 reads val heavy. This is, we know, the declaration of a read-only variable, heavy. Next comes the keyword by, which introduces a delegate. The keyword by says that the next identifier in the declaration is an expression that will evaluate to the object that will be responsible for the value of heavy.

The next thing in the declaration is the identifier `lazy`. Kotlin is expecting, an expression. It turns out that `lazy` is just a function! It is a function that takes a single argument, a lambda, and returns an object. The object that it returns is a `Lazy<T>` where T is the type returned by the lambda.

The implementation of a `Lazy<T>` is quite simple: the first time it is called it runs the lambda and caches its value. On subsequent calls it returns the cached value.

Lazy delegation is just one of many varieties of *property delegation*. Using keyword by, you can also define *observable properties* (see the Kotlin documentation for delegated properties (*https://oreil.ly/6lTab*)). Lazy delegation is, though, the most common property delegation used in Android code.

Companion Objects

Perhaps you are wondering what Kotlin did with static variables. Have no fear; Kotlin uses *companion objects*. A companion object is a *singleton object* always related to a Kotlin class. Although it isn't required, most often the definition of a companion object is placed at the bottom of the related class, as shown here:

```
class TimeExtensions {
    // other code

    companion object {
        const val TAG = "TIME_EXTENSIONS"
    }
}
```

Companion objects can have names, extend classes, and inherit interfaces. In this example, `TimeExtension`'s companion object is named `StdTimeExtension` and inherits the interface `Formatter`:

```
interface Formatter {
    val yearMonthDate: String
}

class TimeExtensions {
    // other code

    companion object StdTimeExtension : Formatter {
        const val TAG = "TIME_EXTENSIONS"
        override val yearMonthDate = "yyyy-MM-d"
    }
}
```

When referencing a member of a companion object from outside a class that contains it, you must qualify the reference with the name of the containing class:

```
val timeExtensionsTag = TimeExtensions.StdTimeExtension.TAG
```

A companion object is initialized when Kotlin loads the related class.

Data Classes

There is a category of classes so common that, in Java, they have a name: they are called *POJOs*, or plain old Java objects. The idea is that they are simple representations of structured data. They are a collection of data members (fields), most of which have getters and setters, and just a few other methods: equals, hashCode, and toString. These kinds of classes are so common that Kotlin has made them part of the language. They are called *data classes*.

We can improve our definition of the Point class by making it a data class:

```
data class Point(var x: Int, var y: Int? = 3)
```

What's the difference between this class, declared using the data modifier, and the original, declared without it? Let's try a simple experiment, first using the original definition of Point (without the data modifier):

```
class Point(var x: Int, var y: Int? = 3)

fun main() {
    val p1 = Point(1)
    val p2 = Point(1)
    println("Points are equals: ${p1 == p2}")
}
```

The output from this small program will be "Points are equals: false". The reason for this perhaps unexpected result is that Kotlin compiles p1 == p2 as p1.equals(p2). Since our first definition of the Point class did not override the equals method, this turns into a call to the equals method in Point's base class, Any. Any's implementation of equals returns true only when an object is compared to itself.

If we try the same thing with the new definition of Point as a data class, the program will print "Points are equals: true". The new definition behaves as intended because a data class automatically includes overrides for the methods equals, hashCode, and toString. Each of these automatically generated methods depends on all of a class's properties.

For example, the data class version of Point contains an equals method that is equivalent to this:

```kotlin
override fun equals(o: Any?): Boolean {
    // If it's not a Point, return false
    // Note that null is not a Point
    if (o !is Point) return false

    // If it's a Point, x and y should be the same
    return x == o.x && y == o.y
}
```

In addition to providing default implementations of equals and hashCode, a data class also provides the copy method. Here's an example of its use:

```kotlin
data class Point(var x: Int, var y: Int? = 3)
val p = Point(1)         // x = 1, y = 3
val copy = p.copy(y = 2)  // x = 1, y = 2
```

Kotlin's data classes are a perfect convenience for a frequently used idiom.

In the next section, we examine another special kind of class: *enum classes*.

Enum Classes

Remember when developers were being advised that enums were too expensive for Android? Fortunately, no one is even suggesting that anymore: use enum classes to your heart's desire!

Kotlin's enum classes are very similar to Java's enums. They create a class that cannot be subclassed and that has a fixed set of instances. Also as in Java, enums cannot subclass other types but can implement interfaces and can have constructors, properties, and methods. Here are a couple of simple examples:

```kotlin
enum class GymActivity {
    BARRE, PILATES, YOGA, FLOOR, SPIN, WEIGHTS
}

enum class LENGTH(val value: Int) {
    TEN(10), TWENTY(20), THIRTY(30), SIXTY(60);
}
```

Enums work very well with Kotlin's when expression. For example:

```
fun requiresEquipment(activity: GymActivity) = when (activity) {
    GymActivity.BARRE -> true
    GymActivity.PILATES -> true
    GymActivity.YOGA -> false
    GymActivity.FLOOR -> false
    GymActivity.SPIN -> true
    GymActivity.WEIGHTS -> true
}
```

When the when expression is used to assign a variable, or as an expression body of a function as in the previous example, it must be *exhaustive*. An exhaustive when expression is one that covers every possible value of its argument (in this case, activity). A standard way of assuring that a when expression is exhaustive is to include an else clause. The else clause matches any value of the argument that is not explicitly mentioned in its case list.

In the preceding example, to be exhaustive, the when expression must accommodate every possible value of the function parameter activity. The parameter is of type GymActivity and, therefore, must be one of that enum's instances. Because an enum has a known set of instances, Kotlin can determine that all of the possible values are covered as explicitly listed cases and permit the omission of the else clause.

Omitting the else clause like this has a really nice advantage: if we add a new value to the GymActivity enum, our code suddenly won't compile. The Kotlin compiler detects that the when expression is no longer exhaustive. Almost certainly, when you add a new case to an enum, you want to be aware of all the places in your code that have to adapt to the new value. An exhaustive when expression that does not include an else case does exactly that.

What happens if a when statement need not return a value (for instance, a function in which the when statement's value is not the value of the function)?

If the when statement is not used as an expression, the Kotlin compiler doesn't force it to be exhaustive. You will, however, get a lint warning (a yellow flag, in Android Studio) that tells you that it is recommended that a when expression on enum be exhaustive.

There's a trick that will force Kotlin to interpret any when statement as an expression (and, therefore, to be exhaustive). The extension function defined in Example 1-3 forces the when statement to return a value, as we see in Example 1-4. Because it must have a value, Kotlin will insist that it be exhaustive.

Example 1-3. Forcing when to be exhaustive

```
val <T> T.exhaustive: T
    get() = this
```

Example 1-4. Checking for an exhaustive when

```
when (activity) {
    GymActivity.BARRE -> true
    GymActivity.PILATES -> true
}.exhaustive // error!  when expression is not exhaustive.
```

Enums are a way of creating a class that has a specified, static set of instances. Kotlin provides an interesting generalization of this capability, the *sealed class*.

Sealed Classes

Consider the following code. It defines a single type, Result, with exactly two sub-types. Success contains a value; Failure contains an Exception:

```
interface Result
data class Success(val data: List<Int>) : Result
data class Failure(val error: Throwable?) : Result
```

Notice that there is no way to do this with an enum. All of the values of an enum must be instances of the same type. Here, though, there are two distinct types that are sub-types of Result.

We can create a new instance of either of the two types:

```
fun getResult(): Result = try {
    Success(getDataOrExplode())
} catch (e: Exception) {
    Failure(e)
}
```

And, again, a when expression is a handy way to manage a Result:

```
fun processResult(result: Result): List<Int> = when (result) {
    is Success -> result.data
    is Failure -> listOf()
```

```
        else -> throw IllegalArgumentException("unknown result type")
    }
```

We've had to add an else branch again, because the Kotlin compiler doesn't know that Success and Failure are the only Result subclasses. Somewhere in your program, you might create another subclass of result Result and add another possible case. Hence the else branch is required by the compiler.

Sealed classes do for types what enums do for instances. They allow you to announce to the compiler that there is a fixed, known set of subtypes (Success and Failure in this case) for a certain base type (Result, here). To make this declaration, use the keyword sealed in the declaration, as shown in the following code:

```
sealed class Result
data class Success(val data: List<Int>) : Result()
data class Failure(val error: Throwable?) : Result()
```

Because Result is *sealed*, the Kotlin compiler knows that Success and Failure are the only possible subclasses. Once again, we can remove the else from a when expression:

```
fun processResult(result: Result): List<Int> = when (result) {
    is Success -> result.data
    is Failure -> listOf()
}
```

Visibility Modifiers

In both Java and Kotlin, visibility modifiers determine the scope of a variable, class, or method. In Java, there are three visibility modifiers:

private
    References are only visible to the class that they are defined within, and from the outer class if defined in an inner class.

protected
    References are visible to the class that they are defined within, or any subclasses of that class. In addition, they are also visible from classes in the same package.

public
    References are visible anywhere.

Kotlin also has these three visibility modifiers. However, there are some subtle differences. While you can only use them with class-member declarations in Java, you can use them with class-member *and* top-level declarations in Kotlin:

private
> The declaration's visibility depends on where it is defined:
>
> - A class member declared as private is visible only in the *class* in which it is defined.
>
> - A top-level private declaration is visible only in the *file* in which it is defined.

protected
> Protected declarations are visible only in the class in which they are defined, and the subclasses thereof.

public
> References are visible anywhere, just like in Java.

In addition to these three different visibilities, Java has a fourth, *package-private*, making references only visible from classes that are within the same package. A declaration is package-private when it has no visibility modifiers. In other words, this is the default visibility in Java.

Kotlin has no such concept.[5] This might be surprising, because Java developers often rely on package-private visibility to hide implementation details from other packages within the same module. In Kotlin, packages aren't used for visibility scoping at all—they're just namespaces. Therefore, the default visibility is different in Kotlin—it's *public*.

The fact that Kotlin doesn't have package-private visibility has quite a significant impact on how we design and structure our code. To guarantee a complete encapsulation of declarations (classes, methods, top-level fields, etc.), you can have all these declarations as private within the same file.

Sometimes it's acceptable to have several closely related classes split into different files. However, those classes won't be able to access siblings from the same package unless they are public or internal. What's internal? It's the fourth visibility modifier supported by Kotlin, which makes the reference visible anywhere within the containing *module*.[6] From a module standpoint, internal is identical to public. However, internal is interesting when this module is intended as a library—for

---

5. At least, as of Kotlin 1.5.20. As we write these lines, Jetbrains is considering adding a package-private visibility modifier to the language.

6. A module is a set of Kotlin files compiled together.

example, it's a dependency for other modules. Indeed, `internal` declarations aren't visible from modules that import your library. Therefore, `internal` is useful to hide declarations from the outside world.

 The `internal` modifier isn't meant for visibility scoping inside the module, which is what package-private does in Java. This isn't possible in Kotlin. It is possible to restrict visibility a little more heavy-handedly using the `private` modifier.

Summary

Table 1-1 highlights some of the key differences between Java and Kotlin.

Table 1-1. Differences between Java and Kotlin features

Feature	Java	Kotlin
File contents	A single file contains a single top-level class.	A single file can hold any number of classes, variables, or functions.
Variables	Use `final` to make a variable immutable; variables are mutable by default. Defined at the class level.	Use `val` to make a variable read-only, or `var` for read/write values. Defined at the class level, or may exist independently outside of a class.
Type inferencing	Data types are required. `Date date = new Date();`	Data types can be inferred, like `val date = Date()`, or explicitly defined, like `val date: Date = Date()`.
Boxing and unboxing types	In Java, data primitives like `int` are recommended for more expensive operations, since they are less expensive than boxed types like `Integer`. However, boxed types have lots of useful methods in Java's wrapper classes.	Kotlin doesn't have primitive types out of the box. Everything is an object. When compiled for the JVM, the generated bytecode performs automatic unboxing, when possible.
Access modifiers	Public and protected classes, functions, and variables can be extended and overridden.	As a functional language, Kotlin encourages immutability whenever possible. Classes and functions are final by default.
Access modifiers in multi-module projects	Default access is package-private.	There is no package-private, and default access is public. New `internal` access provides visibility in the same module.
Functions	All functions are methods.	Kotlin has function types. Function data types look like, for example, `(param: String) -> Boolean`.
Nullability	Any non-primitive object can be null.	Only explicitly nullable references, declared with the `?` suffix on the type, can be set to null: `val date: Date? = new Date()`.
Statics versus constants	The `static` keyword attaches a variable to a class definition, rather than an instance.	There is no `static` keyword. Use a private `const` or a `companion` object.

Congratulations, you just finished a one-chapter covering Kotlin's essentials. Before we start talking about applying Kotlin to Android, we need to discuss Kotlin's built-in library: collections and data transformations. Understanding the underlying functions of data transformations in Kotlin will give you the necessary foundation needed to understand Kotlin as a functional language.

CHAPTER 2

The Kotlin Collections Framework

In the preceding chapter we offered an overview of the syntax of the Kotlin language. As with any language, syntax is a foundation but, really, no more than that. When it comes to getting actual work done, syntax alone won't carry the water. To do that you need expressions and idioms that are easy to assemble into useful code, and that are as easy for other developers to understand and modify.

One important aspect of nearly every modern language is its *collections framework*: ways of grouping objects, and libraries of functions that manipulate them.

At the time it was introduced, Java's collection framework was state of the art. Today, more than 20 years later, the basic data structures provided by newer languages have not changed much. All of the containers that we're familiar with from the Java framework (or even the earliest versions of the C++ `stdlib`) are still there: `Iterable`, `Collection`, `List`, `Set`, and `Map` (to use their Java names). In response to broad acceptance of functional styles of programming, however, collections frameworks for modern languages like Swift and Scala usually provide a set of common, higher-order functions that operate on the collections: `filter`, `map`, `flatmap`, `zip`, and more. You will, indeed, find these functions in the collections framework from the Kotlin Standard Library.

In this chapter, we will first visit the collections themselves and a few interesting extensions that the Kotlin language empowers. After that, we will dig into some of the powerful higher-order functions that operate on the collections.

Collection Basics

Kotlin's collections framework embeds the data structures from the Java Collections Framework as a subset. It wraps the basic Java classes with some new features and adds functional transformations that operate on them.

Let's start this deep dive into the collections library with a quick look at some of the extensions to the data structures themselves.

Java Interoperability

Because seamless interoperablity with Java is a central goal of the Kotlin language, Kotlin collection data types are based on their Java counterparts. Figure 2-1 illustrates the relationship.

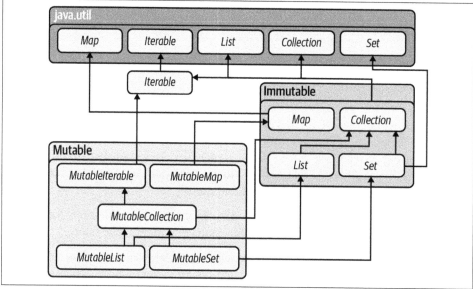

Figure 2-1. The Kotlin collection type hierarchy and its relation to Java.

By making Kotlin collection types subtypes of their Java analogs, Kotlin preserves all of functionality of the Java Collections Framework. For the most part, Kotlin extends, but does not alter the Java framework. It just adds the new, functional methods.

There is one significant exception: mutability.

Mutability

It is, perhaps, only logical that a language that embeds mutability in its syntax would also embed mutability in its collection system.

Kotlin defines two distinct type hierarchies in its collections framework, one for collections that are mutable and one for collections that are not. This can be seen in Example 2-1.

Example 2-1. Mutable and Immutable Lists

```
val mutableList = mutableListOf(1, 2, 4, 5)
val immutableList = listOf(1, 2, 4, 5)
mutableList.add(4)      // compiles

// doesn't compile: ImmutableList has no `add` method.
immutableList.add(2)
```

 Mutable is the opposite of *immutable*. A mutable object can be changed and an immutable one cannot. The distinction is critical when trying to optimize code. Since they cannot change, immutable objects can be shared safely among multiple threads. A mutable object, however, must be made explicitly thread-safe if it is to be shared. Thread safety requires locking or copying, which may be expensive.

Unfortunately, Kotlin cannot guarantee the immutablity of its immutable collections. Immutable collections simply do not have mutator functions (add, remove, put, etc.). Especially when a Kotlin collection is passed to Java code—where Kotlin's immutability constraints are not enforced by the type system—there can be no assurance that the contents of the collection will not change.

Note that the mutability of a collection is not related to the mutability of the object that the collection contains. As a very simple example, consider the following code:

```
val deeplist = listOf(mutableListOf(1, 2), mutableListOf(3, 4))

// Does not compile: "Unresolved reference: add"
deeplist.add(listOf(3))

deeplist[1][1] = 5      // works
deeplist[1].add(6)      // works
```

The variable `deeplist` is a `List<MutableList<Int>>`. It is and always will be a list of two lists. The contents of the lists that `deeplist` contains, however, can grow, shrink, and change.

The creators of Kotlin are actively investigating all things immutable. The prototype `kotlinx.collections.immutable` library is intended to be a set of truly immutable collections. To use them in your own Android/Kotlin project, add the following dependency to your `build.gradle` file:

```
implementation \
'org.jetbrains.kotlinx:kotlinx-collections-immutable:$IC_VERSION'
```

While the *Kotlinx Immutable Collections Library* uses state-of-the-art algorithms and optimizes them so that they are very fast compared to other JVM implementations of immutable collections, these true immutable collections are still an order of magnitude slower than their mutable analogs. Currently, there's nothing to be done about it. However, many modern developers are willing to sacrifice some performance for the safety that immutability brings, especially in the context of concurrency.[1]

Overloaded Operators

Kotlin supports a disciplined ability to overload the meanings of certain infix operators, in particular, + and -. Kotlin's collections framework makes good use of this capability. To demonstrate, let's look at a naive implementation of a function to convert a List<Int> to a List<Double>:

```
fun naiveConversion(intList: List<Int>): List<Double> {
    var ints = intList
    var doubles = listOf<Double>()
    while (!ints.isEmpty()) {
        val item = ints[0]
        ints = ints - item
        doubles = doubles + item.toDouble()
    }
    return doubles
}
```

Don't do this. The only thing that this example does efficiently is demonstrate the use of the two infix operators + and -. The former adds an element to a list and the latter removes an element from it.

The operand to the left of a + or - operator can define the behavior of that operator. Containers, when they appear to the left of a + or -, define two implementations for each of those two operators: one when the right-hand operand is another container and the other when it is not.

Adding a noncontainer object to a container creates a new container that has all of the elements from the left-hand operand (the container) with the new element (the right-hand operand) added. Adding two containers together creates a new container that has all of the elements from both.

---

1. Roman Elizarov; email interview on Kotlin Collections Immutable Library. Oct. 8, 2020.

Similarly, subtracting an object from a container creates a new container with all but the first occurrence of the left-hand operand. Subtracting one container from another produces a new container that has the elements of the left-hand operand, with *all* occurrences of *all* the elements in the right-hand operand removed.

The + and - operators preserve order when the underlying container is ordered. For instance:

```
(listOf(1, 2) + 3)
    .equals(listOf(1, 2, 3))      // true
(listOf(1, 2) + listOf(3, 4))
    .equals(listOf(1, 2, 3, 4)) // true
```

Creating Containers

Kotlin does not have a way to express container literals. There is no syntactic way, for instance, of making a `List` of the numbers 8, 9, and 54. Nor is there a way of making a `Set` of the strings "Dudley" and "Mather." Instead, there are handy methods for creating containers that are nearly as elegant. The code in Example 2-1 showed two simple examples of creating lists. There are also ...`Of` methods for creating mutable and immutable lists, sets, and maps.

Creating literal maps requires knowing a clever trick. The `mapOf` function takes a list of `Pairs` as its argument. Each of the pairs provides a key (the pair's first value) and a value (the pair's second value). Recall that Kotlin supports an extended set of infix operators. Among these operators is `to`, which creates a new `Pair` with its left operand as the first element and its right operand as the second element. Combine these two features and you can, conveniently, build a `Map` like this:

```
val map = mapOf(1 to 2, 4 to 5)
```

The type of the content of a container is expressed using a generic syntax very similar to Java's. The type of the variable map in the preceding code, for instance, is `Map<Int, Int>`, a container that maps `Int` keys to their `Int` values.

The Kotlin compiler is quite clever about inferring the types of the contents of containers created with their factory methods. Obviously in this example:

```
val map = mutableMapOf("Earth" to 3, "Venus" to 4)
```

the type of `map` is `MutableMap<String, Int>`. But what about this?

```
val list = listOf(1L, 3.14)
```

Kotlin will choose the nearest type in the type hierarchy tree that is an ancestor of all of the elements of the container (this type is called the *upper bound type*). In this case it will choose Number, the nearest ancestor of both Long and Double. The variable list has the inferred type List<Number>.

We can add a String, though, as in the following:

```
val list = mutablelistOf(1L, 3.14, "e")
```

The only type that is an ancestor to all of the elements, a Long, a Double, and a String, is the root of the Kotlin type hierarchy, Any. The type of the variable list is MutableList<Any>.

Once again, though, recall from Chapter 1 that the type Any is not the same as the type Any?. The following will not compile (assuming the definition from the preceding example):

```
list.add(null)   // Error: Null cannot be a value of a non-null type Any
```

In order to allow the list to contain null, we'd have to specify its type explicitly:

```
val list: MutableList<Any?> = mutablelistOf(1L, 3.14, "e")
```

We can create collections now. So, what do we do with them?

Functional Programming

We operate on them! Nearly all of the operations that we will discuss here are based on the paradigm of functional programming. In order to understand their context and motivation, let's review the paradigm.

Object-oriented programming (OOP) and *functional programming* (FP) are both paradigms for software design. Software architects understood the promise of functional programming soon after its invention in the late 1950s. Early functional programs tended to be slow, though, and it's only recently that the functional style has been able to challenge a more pragmatic imperative model for performance. As programs get more complex and difficult to understand, as concurrency becomes inevitable, and as compiler optimization improves, functional programming is changing from a cute academic toy into a useful tool that every developer should be able to wield.

Functional programming encourages *immutability*. Unlike the functions in code, mathematical functions don't change things. They don't "return" anything. They simply have a value. Just as "4" and "2 + 2" are names for the same number, a given function evaluated with given parameters is simply a name (perhaps a verbose name!) for its value. Because mathematical functions do not change, they are not affected by time. This is immensely useful when working in a concurrent environment.

Though different, FP and OOP paradigms can coexist. Java was, certainly, designed as an OO language, and Kotlin, fully interoperable, can duplicate Java algorithms nearly word for word. As we proclaimed in the preceding chapter, though, the true power of Kotlin lies in its extensible functional programming capabilities. It's not uncommon for folks to start out writing "Java in Kotlin." As they start to feel more comfortable, they tend to gravitate toward more idiomatic Kotlin, and much of that involves applying the power of FP.

Functional Versus Procedural: A Simple Example

The following code shows a procedural way of working with a collection:

```
fun forAll() {
    for (x in collection) { doSomething(x) }
}
```

In the example, a `for` loop iterates over a list. It selects an element from `collection` and assigns it to the variable `x`. It then calls the method `doSomething` on the element. It does this for each element in the list.

The only constraint on the collection is that there must be a way to fetch each of its elements exactly once. That capability is precisely what is encapsulated by the type `Iterable<T>`.

The functional paradigm is certainly less complicated: no extra variables and no special syntax. Just a single method call:

```
fun forAll() = collection.forEach(::doSomething)
```

The `forEach` method takes a function as its argument. That argument, `doSomething` in this case, is a function that takes a single parameter of the type contained in `collection`. In other words, if `collection` is a list of `Strings`, `doSomething` must be `doSomething(s: String)`. If `collection` is a `Set<Freeptootsie>`, then `doSomething` must be `doSomething(ft: Freeptootsie)`. The `forEach` method calls its argument (`doSomething`) with each element in `collection` as its parameter.

This might seem like an insignificant difference. It is not. The `forEach` method is a much better separation of concerns.

An `Iterable<T>` is stateful, ordered, and time dependent. Anyone who has ever had to deal with a `ConcurrentModificationException` knows it is entirely possible that the state of an iterator may not match the state of the collection over which it is iterating. While Kotlin's `forEach` operator is not completely immune to `ConcurrentModificationException`, those exceptions occur in code that is actually concurrent.

More importantly, the mechanism that a collection uses to apply a passed function to each of its elements is entirely the business of the collection itself. In particular, there is no intrinsic contract about the order in which the function will be evaluated on the collection's elements.

A collection could, for instance, divide its elements into groups. It could farm each of these groups out to a separate processor and then reassemble the results. This approach is particularly interesting at a time when the number of cores in a processor is increasing rapidly. The `Iterator<T>` contract cannot support this kind of parallel execution.

Functional Android

Android has a quirky history with functional programming. Because its virtual machine has nothing to do with Java's, improvements in the Java language have not necessarily been available to Android developers. Some of the most important changes in Java, including lambdas and method references, were not supported in Android for quite a while after they appeared in Java 8.

Although Java could compile these new features and DEX (Android's bytecode) could even represent them (though, perhaps, not efficiently), the Android toolchain couldn't convert the representations of these features—the compiled Java bytecode—into the DEX code that could be run on an Android system.

The first attempt to fill the gap was a package called *RetroLambda*. Other add-on library solutions followed, sometimes with confusing rules (e.g., with the Android Gradle Plugin [AGP] 3.0+, if you wanted to use the Java Streams API you had to target, at a minimum, Android API 24).

All of these constraints are now gone with Kotlin on Android. Recent versions of the AGP will support functional programming even on older versions of Android. You can now use the full Kotlin collection package on any supported platform.

Kotlin Transformation Functions

In this section, you will see how Kotlin brings functional capabilities to collections to provide elegant and safe ways of manipulating them. Just as in the previous chapter we didn't visit all of Kotlin's syntax, we will not in this chapter attempt to visit all of Kotlin's library functions. It isn't necessary to memorize them all. It is essential, though, for idiomatic and effective use of Kotlin, to get comfortable with a few key transforms and to get a feel for how they work.

The Boolean Functions

A convenient set of collection functions return a `Boolean` to indicate whether the collection has—or does not have—a given attribute. The function `any()`, for instance, will return `true` when a collection contains at least one element. If used with a predicate, as in `any { predicate(it) }`, any will return `true` if the predicate evaluates true for any element in the collection:

```
val nums = listOf(10, 20, 100, 5)
val isAny = nums.any()                   // true
val isAnyOdd = nums.any { it % 1 > 0 } // true
val isAnyBig = nums.any { it > 1000}    // false
```

 When a lambda takes only a single argument and the Kotlin compiler can figure that out using type inferencing (it usually can), you can omit the parameter declaration and use the implicit parameter named `it`. The preceding example uses this shortcut twice, in the definitions of the predicates to the any method.

Another boolean function, `all { predicate }`, returns `true` only if every element in the list matches the predicate:

```
val nums = listOf(10, 20, 100, 5)
val isAny = nums.all { it % 1 > 0 } // false
```

The opposite of any is none. Without a predicate, `none()` returns `true` only if there are no elements in a collection. With a predicate, `none { predicate }` returns `true` only if the predicate evaluates to true for none of the elements in the collection. For example:

```
val nums = listOf(10, 20, 100, 5)
val isAny = nums.none()               // false
val isAny4 = nums.none { it == 4 }    // true
```

Filter Functions

The basic `filter` function will return a new collection containing only the elements of the original collection that match the given predicate. In this example, for instance, the variable `numbers` will contain a list with the single value `100`:

```
val nums = listOf(10, 20, 100, 5)
val numbers = nums.filter { it > 20 }
```

The `filterNot` function is the reverse. It returns elements that do *not* match the predicate. In this example, for instance, the variable `numbers` will contain three elements, 10, 20, and 5: the elements of `nums` that are not greater than 20:

```
val nums = listOf(10, 20, 100, 5)
val numbers = nums.filterNot { it > 20 }
```

A beautifully convenient special case of `filterNot` is the function `filterNotNull`. It removes all of the `null`s from a collection:

```
val nums = listOf(null, 20, null, 5)
val numbers = nums.filterNotNull() // { 20, 5 }
```

In this example, the variable `numbers` will be a list containing two elements, 20 and 5.

Map

The *map* function applies its argument to each element in a collection and returns a collection of the resulting values. Note that it does not mutate the collection to which it is applied; it returns a new, resulting, collection.

Here is the definition of the `map` function, for the `Array` type:

```
inline fun <T, R> Array<out T>.map(transform: (T) -> R): List<R>
```

Let's unpack this.

Starting at the left, map is an inline function. The "fun" part should be clear by now. But what about "inline."

The keyword inline tells the Kotlin compiler to copy the bytecode for a function directly into the binary whenever the method is called, instead of generating a transfer to a single compiled version. When the number of instructions necessary to call a function is a substantial percentage of the total number necessary to run it, an inline function makes sense as a trade-off of space for time. Sometimes, too, it can remove the overhead of the extra object allocation that some lambda expressions require.

Next, <T, R> are the two, free, type variables used in the function definition. We'll get back to them.

Next is the description of the receiver, Array<out T>. This map function is an extension function on the Array type: it is a function on an array whose elements are of type T (or one of T's superclasses, e.g., Any).

Next is the map's parameter. The parameter is a function named *transform*. Transform is a function transform: (T) -> R: it takes as its argument something of type T and returns something of type R. Well! That's interesting! The array to which the function will be applied is full of objects of type T! The function can be applied to the elements of the array.

Finally, there is map's return. It is a List<R>, a list whose elements are of type R. An R is what you get if you apply transform to an elements of the array (a T).

It all works out. Calling map on an array with a function that can be applied to the elements of the array will return a new List that contains the results of the application of the function to each of the elements in the array.

Here's an example that returns a list of starting dates for employee records that have those starting dates stored as strings:

```kotlin
data class Hire(
    val name: String,
    val position: String,
    val startDate: String
)

fun List<Hire>.getStartDates(): List<Date> {
    val formatter
        = SimpleDateFormat("yyyy-MM-d", Locale.getDefault())
    return map {
        try {
            formatter.parse(it.startDate)
        } catch (e: Exception) {
            Log.d(
                "getStartDates",
```

```
                "Unable to format first date. $e")
            Date()
        }
    }
}
```

Perhaps you're wondering: "What happens if the transform function doesn't return a value?" Ah! But Kotlin functions *always* have a value!

For example:

```
val doubles: List<Double?> = listOf(1.0, 2.0, 3.0, null, 5.0)
val squares: List<Double?> = doubles.map { it?.pow(2) }
```

In this example, the variable `squares` will be the list [1.0, 4.0, 9.0, null, 25.0]. Because of the conditional operator, `?.`, in the transform function, the function's value is the square of its argument, if that argument is not null. If the argument is null, however, the function has the value `null`.

There are several variations on the `map` function in the Kotlin library. One of them, `mapNotNull`, addresses situations like this:

```
val doubles: List<Double?> = listOf(1.0, 2.0, 3.0, null, 5.0)
val squares: List<Double?> = doubles.mapNotNull { it?.pow(2) }
```

The value of the variable `squares` in this example is [1.0, 4.0, 9.0, 25.0].

Another variant of `map` is `mapIndexed`. `mapIndexed` also takes a function as its argument. Unlike `map`, though, `mapIndexed`'s functional argument takes an element of the collection as its second parameter (not its first and only parameter, as did `map`'s argument). `mapIndexed`'s functional argument takes, as its first parameter, an `Int`. The `Int` is the ordinal that gives the position in the collection of the element that is its second paramter: 0 for the first element, 1 for the second, and so on.

There are mapping functions for most collection-like objects. There are even similar functions for `Maps` (though they are not subtypes of `Collection`): the functions `Map::mapKeys` and `Map::mapValues`.

flatMap

The thing that makes the `flatMap` function hard to understand is that it may seem abstract and not particularly useful. It turns out that, although it is abstract, it is quite useful.

Let's start with an analogy. Suppose you decide to reach out to the members of your old high school debate team. You don't know how to get in touch anymore. You do remember, though, that you have yearbooks for all four years you were in the school and that each yearbook has a picture of the debate team.

You decide to divide the process of contacting members into two steps. First you will examine each photo of the team and try to identify each person depicted there. You will make a list of the people you identify. You will then combine the four lists into a single list of all debate-team members.

That's flatmapping! It's all about containers. Let's generalize.

Suppose you have some kind of container of something. It is a CON<T>. In the yearbook example, CON<T> was four photographs, a Set<Photo>. Next you have a function that maps T -> KON<R>. That is, it takes an element of CON and turns it into a new kind of container, a KON, whose elements are of type R. In the example, this was you identifying each person in one of the photos, and producing a list of names of people in the photo. KON is a paper list and R is the name of a person.

The result of the flatMap function in the example is the consolidated list of names.

The flatmap on CON<T> is the function:

```
fun <T, R> CON<T>.flatMap(transform: (T) -> KON<R>): KON<R>
```

Note, just for comparison, how flatMap is different from map. The map function, for the container CON, using the same transform function, has a signature like this:

```
fun <T, R> CON<T>.map(transform: (T) -> KON<R>): CON<KON<R>>
```

The flatMap function "flattens" away one of the containers.

While we're on the subject, let's take a look at an example of the use of flatMap that is very common:

```
val list: List<List<Int>> = listOf(listOf(1, 2, 3, 4), listOf(5, 6))
val flatList: List<Int> = list.flatMap { it }
```

The variable flatList will have the value [1, 2, 3, 4, 5, 6].

This example can be confusing. Unlike the previous example, which converted a set of photographs to lists of names and then consolidated those lists, in this common example the two container types CON and KON are the same: they are List<Int>. That can make it difficult to see what's actually going on.

Just to prove that it works, though, let's go through the exercise of binding the quantities in this somewhat baffling example to the types in the function description. The function is applied to a List<List<Int>>, so T must be a List<Int>. The transform function is the identity function. In other words, it is (List<Int>) -> List<Int>: it returns its parameter. This means that KON<R> must also be a List<Int> and R must be an Int. The flatMap function, then, will return a KON<R>, a List<Int>.

It works.

Grouping

In addition to filtering, the Kotlin Standard Library provides another small set of transformation extension functions that group elements of a collection. The signature for the groupBy function, for instance, looks like this:

```
inline fun <T, K> Array<out T>
    .groupBy(keySelector: (T) -> K): Map<K, List<T>>
```

As is often the case, you can intuit this function's behavior just by looking at the type information. groupBy is a function that takes an Array of things (Array in this case: there are equivalents for other container types). For each of the things, it applies the keySelector method. That method, somehow, labels the thing with a value of type K. The return from the groupBy method is a map of each of those labels to a list of the things to which the keySelector assigned that label.

An example will help:

```
val numbers = listOf(1, 20, 18, 37, 2)
val groupedNumbers = numbers.groupBy {
    when {
        it < 20 -> "less than 20"
        else -> "greater than or equal to 20"
    }
}
```

The variable groupedNumbers now contains a Map<String, List<Int>>. The map has two keys, "less than 20" and "greater than or equal to 20." The value for the first key is the list [1, 18, 2]. The value for the second is [20, 37].

Maps that are generated from grouping functions will preserve the order of the elements in the original collection, in the lists that are the values of the keys of the output map.

Iterators Versus Sequences

Suppose you are going to paint your desk. You decide that it will look much nicer if it is a nice shade of brown instead of that generic tan. You head down to the paint store and discover that there are around 57 colors that might be just the thing.

What you do next? Do you buy samples of each of the colors to take home? Almost certainly not! Instead, you buy samples of two or three that seem promising and try them. If they turn out not to be all your heart desires, you go back to the store and buy three more. Instead of buying samples of all the candidate colors and iterating over them, you create a process that will let you get the next candidate colors, given the ones you have already tried.

A sequence differs from an iterator in a similar way. An iterator is a way of getting each element from an existing collection exactly once. The collection exists. All the iterator needs to do is order it.

A sequence, on the other hand, is not necessarily backed by a collection. Sequences are backed by *generators*. A generator is a function that will provide the next item in the sequence. In this example, if you need more paint samples, you have a way of getting them: you go back to the store and buy more. You don't have to buy them all and iterate over them. You just need to buy a couple because you know how to get more. You can stop when you find the right color, and with luck, that will happen before you pay for samples of all of the possible colors.

In Kotlin, you might express your search for desk paint like this:

```
val deskColor = generateSequence("burnt umber") {
    buyAnotherPaintSample(it)
}.first { looksGreat(it) }

println("Start painting with ${deskColor}!")
```

This algorithm is efficient. On average, desk painters using it will buy only 28 paint samples instead of 57.

Because sequences are lazy—only generating the next element when it is needed—they can be very, very useful in optimizing operations, even on collections with fixed content. Suppose, for instance, that you have a list of URLs, and you want to know which one is a link to a page that contains an image of a cat. You might do it like this:

```
val catPage = listOf(
    "http://ragdollies.com",
    "http://dogs.com",
    "http://moredogs.com")
```

```
        .map { fetchPage(it) }
        .first { hasCat(it) }
```

That algorithm will download all of the pages. If you do the same thing using a sequence:

```
val catPage = sequenceOf(
    "http://ragdollies.com",
    "http://dogs.com",
    "http://moredogs.com")
    .map { fetchPage(it) }
    .first { hasCat(it) }
```

only the first page will be downloaded. The sequence will provide the first URL, the map function will fetch it, and the first function will be satisfied. None of the other pages will be downloaded.

Be careful, though! Don't ask for all of the elements of an infinite collection! This code, for instance, will eventually produce an OutOfMemory error:

```
val nums = generateSequence(1) { it + 1 }
    .map { it * 7 }                  // that's fine
    .filter { it mod 10000 = 0 }     // still ok
    .asList()                        // FAIL!
```

An Example

Let's make all this concrete with an example.

We just met several of the handy functions that Kotlin's Standard Library provides for manipulating collections. Using those functions, you can create robust implementations of complex logic. To illustrate that, we'll take an example inspired by a real application used in an aircraft engine factory.

The Problem

Bandalorium Inc. builds aircraft engines. Each engine part is uniquely identifiable by its serial number. Each part goes through a rigorous quality control process that records numerical measurements for several of the part's critical attributes.

An attribute for an engine part is any measurable feature. For example, the outside diameter of a tube might be an attribute. The electrical resistance of some wire might be another. A third might be a part's ability to reflect a certain color of light. The only requirement is that measuring the attribute must produce a single numerical value.

One of the things that Bandalorium wants to track is the precision of its production process. It needs to track the measurements of the parts it produces and whether they change over time.

The challenge, then, is:

Given a list of measurements for attributes of parts produced during a certain interval (say, three months), create a CSV (comma-separated value) report similar to the one shown in Figure 2-2. As shown, the report should be sorted by the time that the measurement was taken.

	A	B	C	D	E
1	Date	Serial	AngleOfAttack	ChordLength	PaintColor
2	27-07-2020 15:15:00	HC14	15.08	0.71	7,951,688.0
3	27-07-2020 15:25:00	HC13	15.11	0.69	-
4	27-07-2020 15:35:00	HC12	15.05	0.7	-
5	27-07-2020 15:45:00	HC11	15.1	0.68	2201331.0

Figure 2-2. Example of CSV ouput.

If we might make a suggestion—now would be a great time to put this book aside for a moment and consider how you would approach this problem. Maybe just sketch enough high-level code to feel confident that you can solve it.

The Implementation

In Kotlin, we might represent an attribute like this:

```kotlin
data class Attr(val name: String, val tolerance: Tolerance)

enum class Tolerance {
    CRITICAL,
    IMPORTANT,
    REGULAR
}
```

The name is a unique identifier for the attribute. An attribute's tolerance indicates the significance of the attribute to the quality of the final product: critical, important, or just regular.

Each attribute probably has lots of other associated information. There is, surely, a record of the units of measurement (centimeters, joules, etc.), a description of its acceptable values, and perhaps the procedure used to measure it. We will ignore those features for this example.

A measurement of an attribute for a specific engine part includes the following:

- The serial number of the part being measured
- A timestamp giving the time at which the measurement was made
- The measured value

A measurement, then, might be modeled in Kotlin like this:

```
data class Point(
    val serial: String,
    val date: LocalDateTime,
    val value: Double)
```

Finally, we need a way to connect a measurement to the attribute it measures. We model the relationship like this:

```
data class TimeSeries(val points: List<Point>, val attr: Attr)
```

The TimeSeries relates a list of measurements to the Attrs that they measure.

First, we build the header of the CSV file: the column titles that comprise the first line (see Example 2-2). The first two columns are named date and serial. The other column names are the distinct names of the attributes in the dataset.

Example 2-2. Making the header

```
fun createCsv(timeSeries: List<TimeSeries>): String {
    val distinctAttrs = timeSeries
        .distinctBy { it.attr } ❶
        .map { it.attr }        ❷
        .sortedBy { it.name }   ❸

    val csvHeader = "date;serial;" +
        distinctAttrs.joinToString(";") { it.name } +
        "\n"

    /* Code removed for brevity */
}
```

❶ Use the distinctBy function to get a list of TimeSeries instances that have distinct values for the attr attribute.

❷ We have a list of distinct `TimeSeries` from the previous step and we only want the `attr`, so we use the `map` function.

❸ Finally, we sort alphabetically using `sortedBy`. It wasn't required but why not?

Now that we have the list of distinct characteristics, formatting the header is straightforward using the `joinToString` function. This function transforms a list into a string by specifying a string separator to insert between each element of the list. You can even specify a prefix and/or a postfix if you need to.

 It is often useful to be able to find the types of the returns from collection transformation functions. In Example 2-2, for instance, if you activate type hints, you'll only get the inferred type of the whole chain (the type of the variable `distinctAttrs`). There is a nice IntelliJ/Android Studio feature that can help!

1. Click on `distinctCharacs` in the source code.

2. Hit Ctrl + Shift + P. You'll see a drop-down window appear.

```
val distinctCharacs : List<Charac> =
    pointAndCharacList.distinctBy { it.charac }.map { it.charac }.sortedBy { it.name }
val csvHeader : String                        Expressions              n ";") { it.name } +
    pointAndCharacList
        pointAndCharacList.distinctBy { it.charac }
val rows : String = poipointAndCharacList.distinctBy{it.charac}.map{it.charac}        .map { (date : LocalDate
    val bySerial : Map<pointAndCharacList.distinctBy{it.charac}.map{it.charac}.sortedBy{it.name}al }
```

3. Select the step you want and the inferred type will appear before your eyes!

```
List<PointAndCharac>
va                       List<Charac> =
    pointAndCharacList.distinctBy { it.charac }.map { it.charac }.sortedBy { it.name }
val csvHeader : String = "date;serial;" + distinctCharacs.joinToString( separator ";") { it.name } +
```

After building the header, we build the content of the CSV file. This is the most technical and interesting part.

The rest of the CSV file that we are trying to reproduce sorts the data by date. For each given date, it gives a part's serial number and then that part's measurement for each attribute of interest. That's going to take some thought because, in the model we've created, those things are not directly related. A `TimeSeries` contains only data for a single attribute and we will need data for multiple attributes.

A common approach in this situation is to merge and flatten the input data into a more convenient data structure, as shown in Example 2-3.

Example 2-3. Merge and flatten the data

```
fun createCsv(timeSeries: List<TimeSeries>): String {
    /* Code removed for brevity */

    data class PointWithAttr(val point: Point, val attr: Attr)

    // First merge and flatten so we can work with a list of PointWithAttr
    val pointsWithAttrs = timeSeries.flatMap { ts ->
        ts.points.map { point -> PointWithAttr(point, ts.attr) }

    /* Code removed for brevity */
}
```

In this step, we associate each `Point` with its corresponding `Attr`, in a single `PointAndAttr` object. This is much like joining two tables in SQL.

The `flatMap` function transforms a list of `TimeSeries` objects. Internally, the function applied by `flatMap` uses the `map` function, `series.points.map { ... }`, to create a list of `PointAndAttrs` for each point in the `TimeSeries`. If we had used `map` instead of `flatMap`, we would have produced a `List<List<PointAndAttr>>`. Remember, though, that `flatMap` flattens out the top layer of the container, so the result here is a `List<PointAndAttr>`.

Now that we have "spread" the attribute information into every `Point`, creating the CSV file is fairly straightforward.

We'll group the list of `pointWithAttrs` by date to create a `Map<LocalDate, List<PointWithAttr>`. This map will contain a list of `pointWithAttrs` for each date. Since the example seems to have a secondary sort (by the part's serial number), we'll have to group each of the lists in the previously grouped `Map` by serial number. The rest is just string formatting, as shown in Example 2-4.

Example 2-4. Create data rows

```
fun createCsv(timeSeries: List<TimeSeries>): String {
    /* Code removed for brevity */

    val rows = importantPointsWithAttrs.groupBy { it.point.date }   ❶
        .toSortedMap()                                              ❷
        .map { (date, ptsWithAttrs1) ->
            ptsWithAttrs1
                .groupBy { it.point.serial }                        ❸
                .map { (serial, ptsWithAttrs2) ->
                    listOf(                                         ❹
                        date.format(DateTimeFormatter.ISO_LOCAL_DATE),
```

```
                        serial
                ) + distinctAttrs.map { attr ->
                    val value = ptsWithAttrs2.firstOrNull { it.attr == attr }
                    value?.point?.value?.toString() ?: ""
                }
            }.joinToString(separator = "") {          ❺
                it.joinToString(separator = ";", postfix = "\n")
            }
        }.joinToString(separator = "")


    return csvHeader + rows                           ❻
}
```

❶ Group by date, using the groupBy function.

❷ Sort the map (by date). It's not mandatory, but a sorted CSV is easier to read.

❸ Group by serial number.

❹ Build the list of values for each line.

❺ Format each line and assemble all those lines using the joinToString function.

❻ Finally, return the header and the rows as a single String.

Now, let's suppose that you get an additional request to report only on attributes that are CRITICAL or IMPORTANT. You just have to use the filter function, as shown in Example 2-5.

Example 2-5. Filter critical and important samples

```
fun createCsv(timeSeries: List<TimeSeries>): String {
    /* Code removed for brevity */

    val pointsWithAttrs2 = timeSeries.filter {
        it.attr.tolerance == Tolerance.CRITICAL
                || it.attr.tolerance == Tolerance.IMPORTANT
    }.map { series ->
        series.points.map { point ->
            PointWithAttr(point, series.attr)
        }
    }.flatten()

    /* Code removed for brevity */
```

```
        return csvHeader + rows
    }
```

That's it!

To test that code, we can use a predefined input and check that the output matches your expectations. We won't show a full-blown set of unit tests here—just an example of CSV output, as shown in Example 2-6.

Example 2-6. Demonstrate the application

```
fun main() {
    val dates = listOf<LocalDateTime>(
        LocalDateTime.parse("2020-07-27T15:15:00"),
        LocalDateTime.parse("2020-07-27T15:25:00"),
        LocalDateTime.parse("2020-07-27T15:35:00"),
        LocalDateTime.parse("2020-07-27T15:45:00")
    )
    val seriesExample = listOf(
        TimeSeries(
            points = listOf(
                Point("HC11", dates[3], 15.1),
                Point("HC12", dates[2], 15.05),
                Point("HC13", dates[1], 15.11),
                Point("HC14", dates[0], 15.08)
            ),
            attr = Attr("AngleOfAttack", Tolerance.CRITICAL)
        ),
        TimeSeries(
            points = listOf(
                Point("HC11", dates[3], 0.68),
                Point("HC12", dates[2], 0.7),
                Point("HC13", dates[1], 0.69),
                Point("HC14", dates[0], 0.71)
            ),
            attr = Attr("ChordLength", Tolerance.IMPORTANT)
        ),
        TimeSeries(
            points = listOf(
                Point("HC11", dates[3], 0x2196F3.toDouble()),
                Point("HC14", dates[0], 0x795548.toDouble())
            ),
            attr = Attr("PaintColor", Tolerance.REGULAR)
        )
    )
    val csv = createCsv(seriesExample)
    println(csv)
}
```

If you use the `csv` string as the content of a file with the ".csv" extension, you can open it using your favorite spreadsheet tool. Figure 2-3 shows what we got using FreeOffice.

	A	B	C	D	E
1	**Date**	**Serial**	**AngleOfAttack**	**ChordLength**	**PaintColor**
2	27-07-2020 15:15:00	HC14	15.08	0.71	7,951,688.0
3	27-07-2020 15:25:00	HC13	15.11	0.69	-
4	27-07-2020 15:35:00	HC12	15.05	0.7	-
5	27-07-2020 15:45:00	HC11	15.1	0.68	2201331.0

Figure 2-3. Final output.

Using functional programming to transform data, as in this example, is particularly robust. Why? By combining Kotlin's null safety and functions from the Standard Library, you can produce code which has either few or no side effects. Throw in any list of `PointWithAttr` you can imagine. If even one `Point` instance has a `null` value, the code won't even compile. Anytime the result of transformation returns a result which can be null, the language forces you to account for that scenario. Here we did this in step 4, with the `firstOrNull` function.

It's always a thrill when your code compiles and does exactly what you expect it to do on the first try. With Kotlin's null safety and functional programming, that happens a lot.

Summary

As a functional language, Kotlin employs great ideas like mapping, zipping, and other functional transformations. It even allows you to create your own data transformations with the power of higher-order functions and lambdas:

- Kotlin collections include the entire Java collections API. In addition, the library provides all the common functional transformations like mapping, filtering, grouping, and more.
- Kotlin supports inline functions for more performant data transformations.
- The Kotlin collections library supports sequences, a way of working with collections that are defined by intention instead of extension. Sequences are appropriate when getting the next element is very expensive, or even on collections of unbounded size.

If you've ever used languages like Ruby, Scala, or Python, perhaps some of this feels familiar to you. It should! Kotlin's design is based on many of the same principles that drove the development of those languages.

Writing your Android code in a more functional way is as easy as using data transformation operations offered with the Kotlin Standard Library. Now that you are familiar with Kotlin syntax and the spirit of functional programming in Kotlin, the next chapter focuses on the Android OS and other programming fundamentals. Android development turned toward Kotlin as an official language back in 2017, so Kotlin has heavily influenced Android's evolution in recent years. It will continue to do so in the coming years.

CHAPTER 3

Android Fundamentals

The first two chapters of this book were a whirlwind review of the Kotlin language. This chapter will review the environment in which we will use Kotlin: Android.

Android is an operating system, like Windows and MacOS. Unlike those two systems, Android is a Linux-based OS, like Ubuntu and Red Hat. Unlike Ubuntu and Red Hat, though, Android has been very heavily optimized for mobile devices—battery-powered mobile devices, in particular.

The most significant of these optimizations concerns what it means to be an application. In particular, as we will see, Android apps have much more in common with web applications than they do with familiar desktop applications.

But we'll get to that in a moment. First, let's look in a little more detail at the Android environment. We'll look at the operating system as a stack—kind of a layer cake.

The Android Stack

Figure 3-1 shows one way of looking at Android: as a stack of components. Each layer in the stack has a specific task and provides specific services; each uses the features of the layers beneath it.

Walking up from the bottom, the layers are:

- Hardware
- Kernel
- System services
- Android Runtime Environment
- Applications

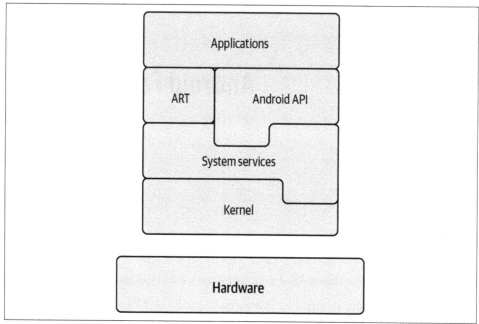

Figure 3-1. The Android stack.

Hardware

Beneath the Android stack, of course, is hardware: a piece of warm silicon. While the hardware is not part of the Android stack, it is important to recognize that the hardware for which Android was designed imposes some fairly tough constraints on the system. By far, the most significant of these constraints is power. Most common operating systems just assume an infinite power supply. The Android systems cannot.

Kernel

The Android operating system depends on the Linux kernel. A kernel is responsible for providing the basic services that developers expect: a filesystem, threads and processes, network access, interfaces to hardware devices, and so on. Linux is free and open source and, thus, a popular choice for hardware and device manufacturers.

Because it is based on Linux, Android bears some similarity to the common Linux distributions: Debian, Centos, etc. In the layers above the kernel, however, the similarity diminishes. While most common Linux distributions are based heavily on the GNU family of system software (and should, properly, be called GNU/Linux), Android's system software is quite a bit different. It is, in general, not possible to run common Linux applications directly on an Android system.

System Services

The system services layer is big and complex. It includes a wide variety of utilities, from code that runs as part of the kernel (drivers or kernel modules), and long-running applications that manage various housekeeping tasks (daemons), to libraries that implement standard functions like cryptography and media presentation.

This layer includes several system services that are unique to Android. Among them are Binder, Android's essential interprocess communication system; ART, which has replaced Dalvik as Android's analog of the Java VM; and Zygote, Android's application container.

Android Runtime Environment

The layer above the system services is the implementation of the *Android Runtime Environment*. The Android Runtime Environment is the collection of libraries that you use from your application by including them with import statements: *android.view*, *android.os*, and so on. They are the services provided by the layers below, made available to your application. They are interesting because they are implemented using two languages: usually Java and C or C++.

The part of the implementation that your application imports is likely to be written in Java. The Java code, however, uses the *Java Native Interface* (JNI) to invoke native code, usually written in C or C++. It is the native code that actually interacts with the system services.

Applications

Finally, at the top of the stack are Android applications. Applications, in the Android universe, are actually part of the stack. They are made up of individually addressable components that other applications can "call." The Dialer, Camera, and Contacts programs are all examples of Android applications that are used as services by other applications.

This is the environment in which an Android application executes. So let's get back to looking at the anatomy of an application itself.

The Android Application Environment

Android applications are programs translated from a source language (Java or Kotlin) into a transportable intermediate language, DEX. The DEX code is installed on a device and interpreted by the ART VM, when the application is run.

Nearly every developer is familiar with the standard application environment. The operating system creates a "process"—a sort of virtual computer that appears to belong entirely to the application. The system runs the application code in the process, where it appears to have its own memory, its own processors, and so on, completely independent of other applications that might be running on the same device. The application runs until it, itself, decides to stop.

That's not how Android works. Android doesn't really think in terms of applications. For instance, Android apps don't contain the equivalent of Java's public static void main method, the method used to start typical Java applications. Instead, Android apps are libraries of components. The Android runtime, Zygote, manages processes, lifecycles, and so on. It calls an application's components only when it needs them. This makes Android apps, as hinted earlier, very similar to web applications: they are an assemblage of components deployed into a container.

The other end of the lifecycle, terminating an application, is perhaps even more interesting. On other operating systems, abruptly stopping an application (kill -9 or "Force Quit") is something that happens rarely and only when the application misbehaves. On Android, it is the most common way for an application to be terminated. Nearly every running app will eventually be terminated abruptly.

As with most web app frameworks, components are implemented as subclasses of template base classes. Component subclasses override the methods that are called by the framework in order to provide application-specific behavior. Often, the superclass has important work to do when one of these template methods is called. In those cases, the overriding method in the subclass must call the superclass method that it overrides.

Android supports four types of components:

- Activity
- Service
- Broadcast receiver
- Content provider

Just as in a web app, the implementations of these components must be registered in a manifest: an XML file. Android's manifest file is called, perhaps unsurprisingly, *AndroidManifest.xml*. The Android container parses this file as part of loading an application. The application components (not some overarching application) are the basic units of the Android app. They are individually addressable and may be published individually for use by other applications.

So, how does an application target an Android component? With an Intent.

Intents and Intent Filters

In Android, components are started with `Intents`. An `Intent` is a small packet that names the component that it targets. It has some extra room in which it can indicate a specific action that it would like the receiving component to take and a few parameters to the request. One can think of an intent as a function call: the name of the class, the name of a particular function within that class, and the parameters to the call. The intent is delivered by the system to the target component. It is up to the component to perform the requested service.

It is interesting to note that, in keeping with its component-oriented architecture, Android doesn't actually have any way of starting an application. Instead, clients start a component, perhaps the `Activity` that is registered as main for an application whose icon a user just tapped on the Launcher page. If the application that owns the activity is not already running, it will be started as a side effect.

An intent can name its target explicitly, as shown here:

```
context.startActivity(
    Intent(context, MembersListActivity::class.java)))
```

This code fires an `Intent` at the `Activity` `MembersListActivity`. Note that the call, `startActivity` here, must agree with the type of the component being started: an `Activity` in this case. There are other, similar methods for firing intents at other kinds of components (`startService` for a `Service`, and so on).

The `Intent` fired by this line of code is called an *explicit intent* because it names a specific, unique class, in a unique application (identified by a `Context`, discussed in a moment), to which the `Intent` is to be delivered.

Because they identify a unique, specific target, explicit intents are faster and more secure than implicit ones. There are places that the Android system, for reasons related to security, requires the use of explicit intents. Even when they are not required, explicit intents should be preferred whenever possible.

Within an application, a component can always be reached with an explicit intent. A component from another application that is publicly visible can also always be reached explicitly. So why ever use an implicit intent? Because implicit intents allow dynamic resolution of a request.

Imagine that the email application you've had on your phone for years allows editing messages with an external editor. We now can guess that it does this by firing an intent that might look something like this:

```
val intent = Intent(Intent.ACTION_EDIT))
intent.setDataAndType(textToEditUri, textMimeType);
startActivityForResult(intent, reqId);
```

The target specified in this intention is *not* explicit. The `Intent` specifies neither a `Context` nor the fully qualified name of a component within a context. The intent is *implicit* and Android will allow any component at all to register to handle it.

Components register for implicit intents using an `IntentFilter`. In fact, the "Awesome Code Editor" that you happen to have installed just 15 minutes ago registers for exactly the intent shown in the preceding code, by including an `IntentFilter` like this in its manifest:

```
<manifest ...>
  <application
    android:label="@string/awesome_code_editor">
    ...>
    <activity
      android:name=".EditorActivity"
      android:label="@string/editor">
      <intent-filter>
        <action
          android:name="android.intent.action.EDIT" />
        <category
          android:name="android.intent.category.TEXT" />
      </intent-filter>
    </activity>
  </application>
</manifest>
```

As you can see, the intent filter matches the intent that the email application fires.

When Android installs the Awesome Code Editor application it parses the application manifest and notices that the `EditorActivity` claims to be able to handle an `EDIT` action for the category `android.intent.category.TEXT` (see more in the Android Developers documentation (*https://oreil.ly/oJNkY*)). It remembers that fact.

The next time your email program requests an editor, Android will include Awesome Code Editor in the list of editors it offers for your use. You have just upgraded your email program simply by installing another application. Talk about awesome!

Android gradually increased restrictions on the use of implicit intents in recent releases. Because they can be intercepted by any randomly installed application, despite their power, implicit intents are not secure. Recent versions of Android have imposed strict new constraints on their use. In particular, as of v30, it is not possible to register for many implicit intents in the manifest.

Context

Because Android components are just subsystems run in a larger container, they need some way of referring to the container so that they can request services from it. From within a component, the container is visible as a Context. Contexts come in a couple of flavors: component and application. Let's have a look at each of them.

Component context

We've already seen a call like this:

```
context.startActivity(
    Intent(context, MembersListActivity::class.java)))
```

This call uses a Context twice. First, starting an Activity is a function that a component requests from the framework, the Context. In this case, it called the Context method startActivity. Next, in order to make the intent explicit, the component must identify the unique package that contains the component it wants to start. The Intent's constructor uses the context passed as its first argument to get a unique name for the application to which the context belongs: this call starts an Activity that belongs to this application.

The Context is an abstract class that provides access to various resources, including:

- Starting other components
- Accessing system services
- Accessing SharedPreferences, resources, and files

Two of the Android components, Activity and Service, are themselves Contexts. In addition to being Contexts, they are also components that the Android container expects to manage. This can lead to problems, all of which are variations on the code shown in Example 3-1.

Example 3-1. Do NOT do this!

```kotlin
class MainActivity : AppCompatActivity() {
  companion object {
    var context: Context? = null;
  }

  override fun onCreate() {
    if (context == null) {
      context = this  // NO!
    }
  }
  // ...
}
```

Our developer has decided that it would be really handy to be able to say things like `MainActivity.context.startActivity(...)` anywhere in their application. In order to do that, they've stored a reference to an `Activity` in a global variable, where it will be accessible for the entire life of the application. What could go wrong?

There are two things that could go wrong, one bad and the other horrible. Bad is when the Android framework knows that the `Activity` is no longer needed, and would like to free it up for garbage collection, but it cannot do so. The reference in that companion object will prevent the `Activity` from being released, for the entire lifetime of the application. The `Activity` has been leaked. `Activitys` are large objects and leaking their memory is no small matter.

The second (far worse) thing, that could go wrong is that a call to a method on the cached `Activity` could fail catastrophically. As we will explain shortly, once the framework decides that an `Activity` is no longer being used, it discards it. It is done with it and will never use it again. As a result, the object may be put into an inconsistent state. Calling methods on it may lead to failures that are both difficult to diagnose and reproduce.

While the problem in that bit of code is pretty easy to see, there are variants that are much more subtle. The following code may have a similar problem:

```kotlin
override fun onCreate(savedInstanceState: Bundle?) {
  super.onCreate(savedInstanceState)
  // ...
  NetController.refresh(this::update)
}
```

It is harder to see, but the callback `this::update` is a reference to a method on `this`, the `Activity` that contains this `onCreate` method. Once `onCreate` completes, the

`NetController` holds a reference to this `Activity` that does not honor its lifecycle and can incur either of the problems described earlier.

Application context

There is another kind of context. When Android starts an application, it usually creates a singleton instance of the `Application` class. That instance is a `Context` and, though it has a lifecycle, that lifecycle is essentially congruent with the lifecycle of the application. Because it is long-lived, it is quite safe to hold references to it in other long-lived places. This code, similar to the dangerous code shown earlier, is fairly safe because the `context` to which it stores a reference is the `ApplicationContext`:

```
class SafeApp : Application() {
  companion object {
    var context: Context? = null;
  }

  override fun onCreate() {
    if (context == null) {
      context = this
    }
  }
  // ...
}
```

Be sure to remember that, in order for the Android system to use the custom subclass of `Application` instead of its default, the `SafeApp` class must be registered in the manifest, like this:

```
<manifest ...>
  <application
    android:name=".SafeApp"
    ...>
    ...
  </application>
</manifest>
```

Now, when the framework creates the `ApplicationContext` it will be an instance of `SafeApp` instead of the instance of `Application` that it would have used otherwise.

There is another way to get the `ApplicationContext` as well. Calling the method `Context.getApplicationContext()` on any context at all, including the `ApplicationContext` itself, will always return the long-lived application context. But here's the bad news: the `ApplicationContext` is not a magic bullet. An `ApplicationContext` is not an `Activity`. Its implementations of `Context` methods behave differently from those of `Activity`. For instance, and probably most annoying, you cannot launch `Activity` from an `ApplicationContext`. There is a `startActivity` method on `ApplicationContext`, but it simply generates an error message in all but a very limited set of circumstances.

Android Application Components: The Building Blocks

Finally, we can narrow our focus to the components themselves, the essence of an application.

The lifecycles of Android application components are managed by the Android framework, which creates and destroys them according to its needs. Note that this absolutely includes instantiation! Application code must *never* create a new instance of a component.

Recall that there are four types of components:

- Activity
- Service
- Broadcast receiver
- Content provider

Remember, also, that the following descriptions are nothing more than brief overviews, perhaps calling attention to potential pitfalls or features of interest. The Android Developers documentation (*https://oreil.ly/PJABc*) is extensive, complete, and authoritative.

The Activity and Its Friends

An `Activity` component manages a single page of an application's UI. It is Android's analog of a web application servlet. It uses Android's rich library of "widgets" to draw a single, interactive page. Widgets (buttons, text boxes, and the like) are the basic UI elements, and they combine a screen representation with the input collection that gives the widgets behavior. We'll discuss them in detail shortly.

As mentioned previously, it is important to understand that an `Activity` is not an application! Activities are ephemeral and guaranteed to exist only while the page that they manage is visible. When that page becomes invisible, either because the application presents a different page or because the user, for instance, takes a phone call, there is no guarantee that Android will preserve either the `Activity` instance or any of the state that it represents.

Figure 3-2 shows the state machine that controls the lifecycle of an `Activity`. The methods—shown as state transitions—come in pairs and are the bookends of the four states that an `Activity` may assume: *destroyed, created, started,* and *running.* The methods are called strictly in order. After a call to `onStart`, for instance, Android will make only one of two possible calls: `onResume`, to enter the next state, or `onStop`, to revert to the previous state.

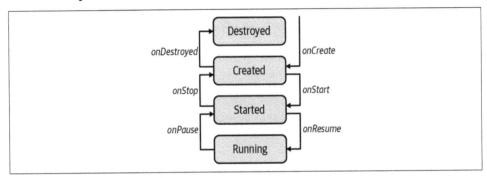

Figure 3-2. The `Activity` lifecycle.

The first pair of bookends are `onCreate` and `onDestroy`. Between them, an `Activity` is said to be *created.* When Android instantiates a new `Activity`, it calls its `onCreate` method nearly immediately. Until it does so, the `Activity` is in an inconsistent state and most of its functions will not work. Note, in particular, that most of an `Activity`'s functionality is, inconveniently, not available from its constructor.

The `onCreate` method is the ideal place to do any initialization that an `Activity` needs to do only once. This almost always includes setting up the view hierarchy (usually by inflating an XML layout), installing view controllers or presenters, and wiring up text and touch listeners.

`Activity`s, similarly, should not be used after the call to their `onDestroy` method. The `Activity` is, again, in an inconsistent state and the Android framework will make no further use of it. (It will not, for instance, call `onCreate` to revivify it.) Beware, though: the `onDestroy` method is not necessarily the best place to perform essential finalization! Android calls `onDestroy` only on a best-effort basis. It is entirely possible that an application will be terminated before all of an `Activity`s'. `onDestroy` methods have completed.

An `Activity` can be destroyed from within its own program by calling its `finish()` method.

The next pair of methods are `onStart` and `onStop`. The former, `onStart`, will only ever be called on an `Activity` that is in the created state. It moves the `Activity` to its on-deck state, called *started.* A started `Activity` may be partially visible behind a dialog or another app that only incompletely fills the screen. In started state, an `Activity` should be completely painted but should not expect user input. A well-written `Activity` will not run animations or other resource-hogging tasks while it is in the started state.

The `onStop` method will only be called on a started `Activity`. It returns it to the created state.

The final pair of methods are `onResume` and `onPause`. Between them, an `Activity`'s page is in focus on the device and the target of user input. It is said to be *running*. Again, these methods will only be called on an `Activity` that is in the started or running state, respectively.

Along with `onCreate`, `onResume` and `onPause` are the most important in the lifecycle of an `Activity`. They are where the page comes to life, starting, say, data updates, animations, and all of the other things that make a UI feel responsive.

 It is a good practice to respect the pairing of these methods: a beginning method and an end method. If you start something running in the beginning method of the pair, stop it in the end method of the same pair. Trying to start, say, network polling in `onResume` and stop it in `onStop` is a recipe for hard-to-find bugs.

Fragments

`Fragments` are an afterthought added to Android's stable of component-like features only at version 3 (Honeycomb, 2011). They can feel a bit "bolted on." They were introduced as a way of making it possible to share UI implementations across screens with shapes and sizes so different that it affects navigation: in particular, phones and tablets.

`Fragments` are not `Contexts`. Though they hold a reference to an underlying `Activity` for most of their lifecycle, `Fragments` are not registered in the manifest. They are instantiated in application code and cannot be started with `Intents`. They are also quite complex. Compare Figure 3-3, the state diagram for a `Fragment`, to that of an `Activity`!

A thorough discussion of how (or, for that matter, even whether) to use `Fragments` is well outside the scope of this book. Briefly, however, one might think of a `Fragment` as something like an *iframe* on a web page: almost an `Activity` embedded in an `Activity`. They are complete, logical UI units that can be assembled in different ways to form a page.

As shown, `Fragments` have lifecycles that are similar to (though more complex than) those of an `Activity`. However, a `Fragment` is only useful when it is attached to an `Activity`. This is the main reason that a `Fragment` lifecycle is more complex: its state can be affected by changes in the state of the `Activity` to which it is attached.

Also, just as an `Activity` is programmatically accessible in the inconsistent state before its `onCreate` method is called, so a `Fragment` is programmatically accessible before it is attached to an `Activity`. `Fragments` must be used with great care before their `onAttach` and `onCreateView` methods have been called.

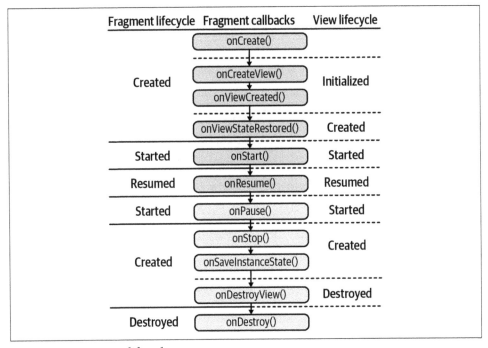

Figure 3-3. Fragment lifecycle.

The back stack

Android supports a navigation paradigm sometimes called *card-deck* navigation. Navigating to a new page stacks that page on top of the previous page. When a user presses a back button the current page is popped from the stack to reveal the one that previously held the screen. This paradigm is fairly intuitive for most human users: push new cards on top; pop them off to get back to where you were.

In Figure 3-4, the current `Activity` is the one named SecondActivity. Pushing the back button will cause the `Activity` named MainActivity to take the screen.

Note that, unlike a web browser, Android does not support *forward* navigation. Once the user pushes the back button, there is no simple navigational device that will allow them to return to the popped page. Android uses this fact to infer that it can destroy SecondActivity (in this case), should it need the resources.

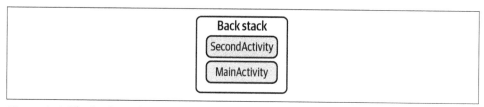

Figure 3-4. The back stack stores an Activity's pages in last in, first out (LIFO) order.

Fragments can also go on the back stack as part of a fragment transaction, as shown in Figure 3-5.

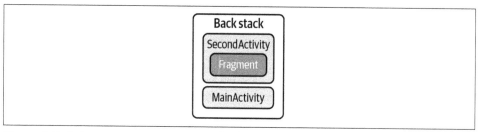

Figure 3-5. A Fragment transaction, on the back stack, will be reverted before the Activity that contains it is popped.

Adding a fragment to the back stack can be particularly useful when combined with tagging, as shown in the following code:

```
// Add the new tab fragment
supportFragmentManager.beginTransaction()
    .replace(
        R.id.fragment_container,
        SomeFragment.newInstance())
    .addToBackStack(FRAGMENT_TAG)
    .commit()
```

This code creates a new instance of SomeFragment and adds it to the back stack, tagged with the identifier FRAGMENT_TAG (a string constant). As shown in the following code, you can use supportFragmentManager to pop *everything* off the back stack, all the way to the tag:

```
manager.popBackStack(
    FRAGMENT_TAG,
    FragmentManager.POP_BACK_STACK_INCLUSIVE)
```

When the back stack is empty, pushing the back button returns the user to the Launcher.

Services

A `Service` is an Android component that is, almost exactly, an `Activity` with no UI. That may sound a bit odd, given that an `Activity`'s sole reason for existence is that it manages the UI!

Android was designed for hardware that is much different from that which is common now. The first Android phone, the HTC Dream, was announced in September of 2008. It had very little physical memory (192 MB) and did not support virtual memory at all. It could run no more than a handful of applications simultaneously. Android's designers needed a way to know when an application was not doing useful work so that they could reclaim its memory for other uses.

It's easy to figure out when an `Activity` is not doing useful work. It has only one job: to manage a visible page. If applications were composed only of `Activitys`, it would be easy to tell when one was no longer useful and could be terminated. When none of an application's `Activitys` are visible, the application is not doing anything useful and can be reclaimed. It's that simple.

The problem comes when an application needs to perform long-running tasks that are not attached to any UI: monitoring location, synchronizing a dataset over the network, and so on. While Android is definitely prejudiced toward "if the user can't see it, why do it?" it grudgingly acknowledges the existence of long-running tasks and invented `Services` to handle them.

While `Services` still have their uses, much of the work that they were designed to do, back on earlier versions of Android with its more limited hardware, can now be done using other techniques. Android's `WorkManager` is a terrific way to manage repeating tasks. There are also other, simpler and more maintainable ways of running tasks in the background, on a worker thread. Something as simple as a singleton class may be sufficient.

Service components still exist, though, and still have important roles to play.

There are, actually, two different kinds of `Service`: *bound* and *started*. Despite the fact that the `Service` base class is, confusingly, the template for both, the two types are completely orthogonal. A single `Service` can be either or both.

Both types of `Service` have `onCreate` and `onDestroy` methods that behave exactly as they do for an `Activity`. Since a `Service` has no UI, it does not need any of an `Activity`'s other templated methods.

Services do have other templated methods, though. Which of them a specific `Service` implements depends on whether it is started or bound.

Started Services

A *started* Service is initiated by sending it an Intent. While it is possible to create a started service that returns a value, doing so is inelegantly complex and probably indicative of a design that could be improved. For the most part, started services are fire-and-forget: something like "put this in the database" or "send this out to the net."

To start a service, send it an intent. The intent must name the service, probably explicitly by passing the current context and the service class. If the service provides multiple functions, of course, the intent may also indicate which of them it is intended to invoke. It might also supply parameters appropriate for the call.

The service receives the intent as the argument to a call from the Android framework, to the method Service.onStart. Note that this is not done in the "background"! The onStart method runs on the main/UI thread. The onStart method parses the Intent content and processes the contained request appropriately.

A well-behaved started Service will call Service.stopSelf() whenever it completes its work. This call is similar to Activity.finish(): it lets the framework know that the Service instance is no longer performing useful work and can be reclaimed. Modern versions of Android actually pay very little attention to whether a service has stopped itself or not. Services are suspended and, possibly even terminated, using less voluntary criteria (see the Android Developers documentation (*https://oreil.ly/yGloh*)).

Bound Services

A *bound* Service is Android's IPC mechanism. Bound services provide a communication channel between a client and a server that is process agnostic: the two ends may or may not be part of the same application. Bound services—or at least the communication channels they provide—are at the very heart of Android. They are the mechanism through which applications send tasks to system services.

A bound service, itself, actually does very little. It is just the factory for a Binder, a half-duplex IPC channel. While a complete description of the Binder IPC channels and their use is beyond the scope of this book, their structure will be familiar to users of any of the other common IPC mechanisms. Figure 3-6 illustrates the system.

Typically, a service provides a *proxy* that looks like a simple function call. The proxy *marshals* an identifier for the requested service (essentially, the function name) and its parameters, by converting them to data that can be transmitted over the connection: usually aggregates of very simple data types like integers and strings. The marshaled data is communicated, in this case via the Binder kernel module, to a *stub* provided by the bound service that is the target of the connection.

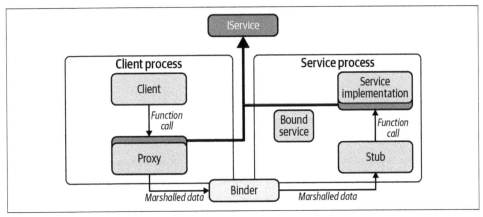

Figure 3-6. Binder IPC.

The stub *unmarshals* the data, converting it back into a function call to the service implementation. Notice that the proxy function and the service implementation function have the same signature: they implement the same interface (IService, as shown in Figure 3-6).

Android makes *extensive* use of this mechanism in the implementation of system services. Functions that are actually calls to remote processes are a fundamental part of Android.

An instance of the class `ServiceConnection` represents a connection to a bound service. The following code demonstrates its use:

```kotlin
abstract class BoundService<T : Service> : ServiceConnection {
    abstract class LocalBinder<out T : Service> : Binder() {
        abstract val service: T?
    }

    private var service: T? = null

    protected abstract val intent: Intent?

    fun bind(ctxt: Context) {
        ctxt.bindService(intent, this, Context.BIND_AUTO_CREATE)
    }

    fun unbind(ctxt: Context) {
        service = null
        ctxt.unbindService(this)
    }

    override fun onServiceConnected(name: ComponentName, binder: IBinder) {
        service = (binder as? LocalBinder<T>)?.service
        Log.d("BS", "bound: ${service}")
```

```
        }
        override fun onServiceDisconnected(name: ComponentName) {
            service = null
        }
    }
```

A subclass of BoundService provides the type of the service that will be bound, and an Intent that targets it.

The client side initiates a connection using the bind call. In response, the framework initiates a connection to the remote bound service object. The remote framework calls the bound service's onBind method with the intent. The bound service creates and returns an implementation of IBinder that is also an implementation of the interface the client requested. Note that this is often a reference to the bound service itself. In other words, the Service is often not only the factory but also the implementation.

The service side uses the implementation provided by the bound service to create the remote-side stub. It then notifies the client side that it's ready. The client-side framework creates the proxy and then finally calls the ServiceConnection's onServiceConnected method. The client now holds a live connection to the remote service. Profit!

As one might guess from the presence of an onServiceDisconnected method, a client can lose the connection to a bound service at any time. Though the notification is usually immediate, it is definitely possible for a client call to a service to fail even before it receives a disconnect notification.

Like a started service, bound service code does not run in the background. Unless explicitly made to do otherwise, bound service code runs on the application's main thread. This can be confusing, though, because a bound service might run on the main thread of a *different* application.

If the code in a service implementation must run on a background thread, it is the service implementation that is responsible for arranging that. Client calls to a bound service, while asynchronous, cannot control the thread on which the service itself runs.

Services, like every other component, must be registered in the application manifest:

```
<manifest xmlns:android="http://schemas.android.com/apk/res/android">
  <application...>
    <service android:name=".PollService"/>
  </application>
</manifest>
```

Content Providers

A `ContentProvider` is a REST-like interface to data held by an application. Because it is an API, not simply direct access to data, a `ContentProvider` can exercise very fine-grained control over what it publishes and to whom it publishes it. External applications get access to a `ContentProvider` using a Binder IPC interface, through which the `ContentProvider` can obtain information about the querying process, the permissions it holds, and the type of access it requests.

Early Android applications often shared data simply by putting it into publicly accessible files. Even then, Android encouraged the use of `ContentProviders` instead. More recent versions of Android, in the interests of security, have made it difficult to share files directly, making `ContentProviders` more relevant.

Android Jetpack

While `ContentProviders` provide access to stored data, you must have some kind of data store from which to read and write the data. Android Jetpack offers the Room persistence library as an option. As described in its official documentation, Room provides "an abstraction layer to allow for more robust access while harnessing the full power of SQLite."

For more information on how to save data in a local database using Room, check out the Android Developers documentation (*https://oreil.ly/9OwGH*).

One particularly interesting capability of a `ContentProvider` is that it can pass an open file to another program. The requesting program need not have any way to access the file directly using a file path. The `ContentProvider` can construct the file it passes in any way that it wants. By passing an open file, though, the `ContentProvider` moves itself out of the loop. It gives the requesting program direct access to the data. Neither the `ContentProvider` nor any other IPC mechanism remains between the client and the data. The client simply reads the file just as if it had opened that file itself.

An application publishes a `ContentProvider`, as usual, by declaring it in the application manifest:

```
<application...>
  <provider
    android:name="com.oreilly.kotlin.example.MemberProvider"
    android:authorities="com.oreilly.kotlin.example.members"
    android:readPermission="com.oreilly.kotlin.example.members.READ"/>
</application>
```

This XML element says that the application contains the class named `com.oreilly.kotlin.example.MemberProvider`, which has to be a subclass of `android.content.ContentProvider`. The element declares that `MemberProvider` is the authority for any requests for data from the URL *content://com.oreilly.kotlin .example.members*. Finally, the declaration mandates that requesting applications must hold the permission "com.oreilly.kotlin.example.members.READ" in order to get any access at all and that even then they will get only read access.

`ContentProviders` have exactly the API one would expect from a REST interface:

`query()`
This fetches data from a particular table.

`insert()`
This inserts a new row within a content provider and returns the content URI.

`update()`
This updates the fields of an existing row and returns the number of rows updated.

`delete()`
This deletes existing rows and returns the number of rows deleted.

`getType()`
This returns the MIME data type for the given Content URI.

The `ContentProvider` for `MemberProvider` would probably implement only the first of these methods, because it is read-only.

Broadcast Receivers

The original concept for a `BroadcastReceiver` was as a kind of data bus. Listeners could subscribe in order to get notification of events that were of interest. As the system has come of age, however, `BroadcastReceivers` have proved to be too expensive and too prone to security problems to be used pervasively. They remain mostly a tool used by the system to signal applications of important events.

Perhaps the most common use of a `BroadcastReceiver` is as a way of starting an application, even if there has been no user request to do so.

The `Intent android.intent.action.BOOT_COMPLETED` is broadcast by the Android system once the OS is stable, after a system restart. An application could register to receive this broadcast, like this:

```
<receiver android:name=".StartupReceiver">
    <intent-filter>
        <action android:name="android.intent.action.BOOT_COMPLETED"/>
```

```
    </intent-filter>
  </receiver>
```

If an application does this, its `StartupReceiver` will be started, to receive the `BOOT_COMPLETED` Intent broadcast when the OS is rebooted. As noted earlier, a side effect of starting the `StartupReceiver` is that the application that contains the receiver is also started.

Applications have used this as a way of creating a *daemon*: an app that is always running. While a hack and fragile (even in early Android, behavior changed from version to version), this trick worked well enough that many, many applications used it. Even as Android version 26 introduced some fairly radical changes in background process management (`BroadcastReceivers` cannot be registered for implicit broadcasts in their manifests; they must instead register them dynamically using `Context.registerReceiver`), developers continue to find ways to use it.

 There are exceptions to the Android 26 implicit intent rule. Receiving SMS messaging, changing locale, detecting USB devices, and a few other intents are *permitted*, and applications may register for them, in their manifests. `ACTION_USB_ACCESSORY_ATTACHED`, `ACTION_CONNECTION_STATE_CHANGED`, and our dear old friend `ACTION_BOOT_COMPLETED` are among the permitted intents. For more, check out the Android Developers documentation (*https://oreil.ly/PMNhM*).

`Activity`, `Service`, `ContentProvider`, and `BroadcastReceiver` are the four components that are the essential building blocks of an Android application. As Android has grown and improved, it has introduced new abstractions that obscure these basic mechanisms. A modern Android application may use only one or two of these building blocks directly, and many developers will never code a `ContentProvider` or a `BroadcastReceiver`.

The essential lesson here, which bears repeating, is that an Android app is not an "application" in the traditional sense. It is more like a web application: a collection of components that provide services to a framework when requested to do so.

Android Application Architectures

So far, in this chapter we've discussed the Android system architecture. While understanding that architecture is essential for any serious Android developer, it is not sufficient for understanding how to write resilient, bug-free Android programs. As evidence of this, one need only look at the many tools and abstractions that have been tried and abandoned over the years of Android's existence. Time and experience, though, have honed the Android playbook and made the path to a robust, maintainable application much easier to follow.

MVC: The Foundation

The original pattern for applications with a UI was called Model–View–Controller (MVC). The innovation that the pattern introduced was a guarantee that the view—what was rendered on the screen—was always consistent. It did this by insisting on a unidirectional cycle for data flow.

It all starts with the user. They see something on the screen (the *View*: I told you it was a cycle!) and, in response to what they see, take some action. They touch the screen, type something, speak, whatever. They do something that will change the state of the application.

Their input is fielded by the *Controller*. The Controller has two responsibilities. First, it orders the user's input. For any given user event—say, tapping the "stop" button—all other user events happen either before that tap or after it. No two events are ever processed at the same time.

The implication that the Controller is single-threaded is one of the most important aspects of the original MVC pattern. Prior multi-threaded strategies (including Java's Abstract Window Toolkit [AWT]) often produced a nightmare of deadlocks as messages traveling in opposite directions—from the user and to the user—tried to seize the same locks in different orders.

The Controller's second responsibility is to translate user input into operations on a *Model*.

The Model is the business logic of an application. It probably combines some kind of persistent data store and perhaps a network connection with rules for combining and interpreting the input from the Controller. In the ideal MVC architecture, it is the only component that holds the current state of the application.

The Model, again, ideally is allowed to send only one message to the View: "things have changed." When the View receives such a message it does its job. It requests the application state from the Model, interprets it, and renders it on the screen. What it renders is always a consistent snapshot of the Model. At this point, the user can see the new state and take new actions in response. The cycle continues.

While the MVC pattern was fairly revolutionary when it was introduced, there is room for improvement.

Widgets

As we mentioned earlier in the context of the `Activity` component, a widget is a single class that combines a View component with a Controller component. After the preceding discussion of the MVC pattern and its emphasis on separating the two, it may seem odd to find classes like `Button`, `TextBox`, and `RadioButton` that clearly combine the two.

Widgets do not break MVC architecture. There is still, in each widget, distinct View and Controller code. The Controller portion of a widget never talks directly to the View, and the View does not receive events from the Controller. The sections are independent; they are just bundled together into a single handy container.

Combining the two functions just seems fairly obvious. What is the use of the image of a button, that can be placed anywhere on the screen, if it doesn't respond to clicks? It just makes sense that the renderer for the UI components, and the mechanism that handles input for it, be part of the same component.

The Local Model

With the advent of the Web, browsers, and the long delay required for an entire MVC cycle, developers began to see the need for keeping the state of the screen as a separate, UI-Local Model. Developers have, over time, referred to this component using several names, depending on other features of the design pattern in which it is being used. To avoid confusion, we will refer to it, for the rest of this chapter, as the *Local Model*.

The use of a Local Model gives rise to a new pattern that is sort of a two-layer MVC— it has even been referred to as the "Figure Eight" pattern. When the user takes an action, the Controller updates the Local Model instead of the Model, because a Model update may be a network connection away. The Local Model is not business logic. It represents, as simply as possible, the state of the View: which buttons are on, which are off, what text is in which box, and the color and length of the bars in the graph.

The Local Model does two things in response to an action. First it notifies the View that things have changed so that the View can rerender the screen from the new Local Model state. In addition, though, with code that is analogous to the simple MVC's Controller, the Local Model forwards the state changes to the Model. In response, the Model eventually notifies—this time the Local Model—that there has been an update and that the Local Model should sync itself. This probably results in a second request that the View update itself.

Android Patterns

In Android, regardless of the pattern, an `Activity` object—or possibly its cousin, a `Fragment`—takes the role of the View. This is more or less mandated by the structure of the `Activity` object: it is the thing that owns the screen and it is the thing that has access to the widgets that comprise the view. Over time, though, as is appropriate for an MVC-based UI, `Activity` objects have gotten simpler and simpler. In a modern Android application, it is likely that an `Activity` will do little more than inflate the view, delegate events inbound from the user to the Local Model, and observe Local Model state that is of interest, redrawing itself in response to updates.

Model–View–Intent

One of the oldest versions of MVC adopted by the Android community was called Model–View–Intent. The pattern decouples the `Activity` from a Model by using `Intents` and their payloads. While this structure produces excellent component isolation, it can be quite slow and the code for constructing the `Intents` quite bulky. Although it is still used successfully, newer patterns have largely supplanted it.

Model–View–Presenter

A goal for all of these MVC-based patterns is to loosen the coupling among the three components and to make information flow unidirectionally. In a naive implementation, though, the View and the Local Model each hold a reference to the other. Perhaps the View gets an instance of the Local Model from some sort of factory and then registers with it. Though subtle—and regardless of the apparent direction in which information flows—holding a reference to an object of a specific type is coupling.

Over the past few years, there have been several refinements to the MVC pattern in an attempt to reduce this coupling. While these refinements have often resulted in better code, the distinctions among them, and the very names used to identify them, have not always been clear.

One of the earliest refinements replaces the View and Local Model references to each other with references to interfaces. The pattern is often called Model–View–Presenter (MVP). In implementations of this pattern, the Local Model holds a reference, not to the View `Activity`, but simply to the implementation of some interface. The interface describes the minimal set of operations that the Local Model can expect from its peer. It has, essentially, no knowledge that the View is a View: it sees only operations for updating information.

The View proxies user input events to its Presenter. The Presenter, as described earlier, responds to the events, updating Local Model and Model state as necessary. It then notifies the View that it needs to redraw itself. Because the Presenter knows exactly what changes have taken place, it may be able to request that the View update only affected sections, instead of forcing a redraw of the entire screen.

The most important attribute of this architecture, however, is that the Presenter (this architecture's name for the Local Model) can be unit tested. Tests need only mock the the interface that the View provides to the Presenter to completely isolate it from the View. Extremely thin views and testable Presenters lead to much more robust applications.

But it is possible to do even better than this. The Local Model might hold no references to the View at all!

Model–View–ViewModel

Google, with its introduction of Jetpack, supports an architecture called Model–View–ViewModel (MVVM). Because it's supported, internally, by the modern Android framework, it is the most common and most discussed pattern for modern Android apps.

In the MVVM pattern, as usual, either an `Activity` or a `Fragment` takes the role of the View. The View code will be as simple as it is possible to make it, often contained entirely within the `Activity` or `Fragment` subclass. Perhaps some complex views will need separate classes for image rendering or a `RecyclerView`. Even these, though, will be instantiated and installed in the view, directly by the `Activity` or `Fragment`.

The ViewModel is responsible for wiring together the commands necessary to update the View and the backend Model. The novel feature of this pattern is that a single interface, `Observable`, is used to transmit changes in the state of the Local Model to the View.

Instead of the multiple Presenter interfaces used in the MVP pattern, the ViewModel represents viewable data as a collection of `Observables`. The View simply registers as an observer for these observables and reacts to notifications of changes in the data they contain.

The Jetpack library calls these `Observables` `LiveData`. A `LiveData` object is an observable data holder class with a single generified interface that notifies subscribers of changes in the underlying data.

Like MVP, MVVM makes mocking and unit testing easy. The important new feature that MVVM introduces is lifecycle awareness.

The keen reader will have noticed that the version of the MVP pattern described earlier does *exactly* the thing we warned against in Example 3-1: it stores the reference to an `Activity`, an object with an Android-controlled lifecycle, in a long-lived object!

Applications are left to their own devices to make sure the reference doesn't outlive the target object.

The Jetpack-supported implementation of the MVVM pattern dramatically reduces this problem. In its implementation, the only references to the View are the subscriptions to the LiveData observables. The LiveData objects identify Fragment and Activity observers, and unregister them, automatically when their lifecycle ends.

Applications built with JetPack's version of MVVM can be quite elegant. For a broad variety of applications, the View will contain a single, simple, declarative method that draws the screen. It will register that method as an observer for ViewModel observables. The ViewModel translates user input into calls to the backend Model and updates its observables in response to notifications from the Model. It's that simple.

Summary

Congratulations, you've successfully covered an intimidating amount of information in a very short chapter!

Remember that much of this material is foundational. It is not important that you master all of the information presented here. In fact, it's quite possible that you will never touch, for instance, a ContentProvider or a BroadcastReceiver. Use what is practical for you, and approach mastering items only as they become useful.

Here are some key points to take with you:

- An Android app is not an "application" in the traditional sense. It is more like a web application: a collection of components that provide services to a framework, when requested to do so.

- The Android OS is a very specialized Linux distribution. Each application is treated as an individual "user" and has its own private file storage.

- Android has four kinds of components. They are: Activitys, Services, ContentProviders, and BroadcastReceiver. Activitys, Services, and the ContentProviders must be registered and possibly given permission within the Android manifest:

  — Activitys are the UI of an Android application. They start their lifecycle at onCreate, are live to user interaction after onResume, and may be interrupted (onPause) at any time.

  — Fragments are complex beasts with lifecycles all their own. They can be used to organize independent UI containers, within a UI page.

  — Services can be started services and/or bound. API 26 started introducing restrictions for background use of services, so the general rule is that if the user interacts with a task in any way, a service ought to be made into a fore-ground service.

— Unless a `BroadcastReceiver` is using implicit intent that is explicitly allowed by the system with the action, it is probably necessary to register the broadcast receiver dynamically from application code.

- Use the `Activity Context` carefully. Activities have a lifecycle that is not under the control of your application. A reference to an `Activity` *must* respect the actual lifecycle of the Activity.

- General software architectures in Android, like MVI, MVP, and MVVM, are designed to keep `Fragments` and `Activitys` lean and encourage better separation of concern and testing and while being "lifecycle-aware."

Now that we've reviewed the ground rules and explored the playing field, our journey to achieving structured coroutines in Kotlin officially starts. In the following chapter, we begin to apply this foundation to examining memory and threading in Android. Understanding the details of Android's organization will reveal the issues that the coming chapters set out to solve.

CHAPTER 4

Concurrency in Android

This chapter does not focus specifically on Kotlin. Instead, it will introduce some of the issues that surround *concurrent programming* and that the rest of the book addresses. It will also introduce a few tools, already available to Android developers, for managing concurrent tasks.

Concurrent programming has a reputation as kind of a dark art: something that is done by self-proclaimed wizards and that novices touch at their peril. Certainly, writing correct concurrent programs can be quite challenging. This is particularly true because errors in concurrent programs don't always show up right away. It is nearly impossible to test for concurrency bugs and they can be extremely difficult to reproduce, even when they are known to exist.

A developer concerned about the hazards of concurrent programming would do well to remember these three things:

- Nearly everything you do, every day, *except* programming, is concurrent. You get along quite nicely in a concurrent environment. It is programming, where things happen in order, that is odd.

- If you are trying to understand the issues that concurrent programming presents, you are on the right path. Even an incomplete understanding of concurrency is better than copying sample code and crossing your fingers.

- Concurrent programming is just how Android works. Anything other than the most trivial Android application will require concurrent execution. Might as well get on with it and figure out what it's all about!

Before getting into specifics, let's define some terms.

The first term is *process*. A process is memory that an application can use, and one or more threads of execution. The memory space belongs to the process—no other processes can affect it.[1] An application usually runs as a single process.

That, of course, introduces the second term: *thread*. A thread is a sequence of instructions, executed one at a time, in order.

And this leads us to the term that, to some extent, drives the rest of this book: *thread safe*. A set of instructions is thread-safe if, when multiple threads execute it, no possible ordering of the instructions executed by the threads can produce a result that could not be obtained if each of the threads executed the code completely, in some order, one at a time. That's a little hard to parse, but it just says that the code produces the same results whether the multiple threads execute it all at the same time or, serially, one at a time. It means that running the program produces predictable results.

So how does one make a program thread-safe? There are lots and lots of ideas about this. We would like to propose one that is clear, relatively easy to follow, and always correct. Just follow one, fairly clear, fairly simple rule. We'll state the rule in a few pages. First, though, let's discuss in more detail what thread safety means.

Thread Safety

We've already said that thread-safe code cannot produce a result, when executed by multiple threads at the same time, that could not have been produced by some ordering of the threads executing one at a time. That definition, though, is not very useful in practice: no one is going to test all possible execution orders.

Perhaps we can get a handle on the problem by looking at some common ways that code can be *thread-unsafe*.

Thread-safety failures can be divided into a few categories. Two of the most important are *atomicity* and *visibility*.

Atomicity

Nearly all developers understand problems of atomicity. This code is not thread-safe:

```
fun unsafe() { globalVar++ }
```

Multiple threads executing this code can interfere with each other. Each thread executing this code might read the same value for globalVar—say, 3. Each might increment that value to get 4, and then each might update globalVar to have the value 4.

---

1. It is possible for processes to share some memory (as with Binder), but they do so in very controlled ways.

Even if 724 threads executed the code, globalVar might, when all were through executing, have the value 4.

There is no possible way that each of those 724 threads could execute that code serially and have globalVar end up as 4. Because the result of executing the code concurrently can be different from any possible result generated by serial execution, this code is not thread-safe, according to our definition.

To make the code thread-safe, we need to make the read, increment, and write operations on the variable globalVar, together, *atomic*. An atomic operation is one that cannot be interrupted by another thread. If the read, increment, and write operations are atomic, then no two threads can see the same value of globalVar, and the program is guaranteed to behave as expected.

Atomicity is easy to understand.

Visibility

Our second category of thread-safety errors, visibility, is much more difficult to apprehend. This code is also not thread-safe:

```
var shouldStop = false

fun runner() {
    while (!shouldStop) { doSomething() }
}

fun stopper() { shouldStop = true }
```

A thread running the function runner may never stop, even though another thread runs stopper. The thread running runner may never notice that the value of shouldStop has changed to true.

The reason for this is optimization. Both the hardware (using registers, multilayer caches, etc.) and the compiler (using hoisting, reordering, etc.) do their very best to make your code run fast. In order to do this, the instructions that the hardware actually executes may not look much like the Kotlin source at all. In particular, while you think that shouldStop is a single variable, the hardware probably has at least two representations for it: one in a register and one in main memory.

You definitely want that! You would not want the loops in your code to depend on access to main memory instead of using caches and registers. Fast memory optimizes your code because it has access times that are several orders of magnitude faster than main memory.

To make the example code work, though, you have to explain to the compiler that it cannot keep the value of shouldStop in local memory (a register or cache). If, as proposed, there are multiple representations of shouldStop in different kinds of hardware memory, the compiler must be sure that the value kept in the fast, local representation of shouldStop is pushed to memory that is visible to all threads. This is called *publishing* the value.

@Synchronized is the way to do that. Synchronization tells the compiler that it must make sure that any side effects of the code executed within the synchronized block are visible to all other threads, before the executing thread leaves the block.

Synchronization, then, is not so much about hardware, or tricky and complicated criteria for what must be protected and what need not be. Synchronization is a contract between the developer and the compiler. If you don't synchronize code, the compiler is free to make any optimization that it can prove safe, based on serial execution. If there is other code somewhere, running on a different thread, that makes the compiler's proof invalid, you must synchronize the code.

So, here's the rule. If you want to write code that is thread-safe, you just have to follow this one short, clear rule. Paraphrasing from Java's bible of parallel programming, *Java Concurrency in Practice* (*https://oreil.ly/4zx8L*):[2] Whenever more than one thread accesses a given state variable, and one of them might write to it, they all must coordinate their access to it using synchronization.

Note, by the way, that that quote does not distinguish between read access and write access for synchronization. Unless it is guaranteed that *nobody* will mutate the shared state, all access, read or write, must be synchronized.

The Android Threading Model

As noted in Chapter 3, one of the implications of an MVC architecture is a single-threaded UI (the View and Controller). Although a multithreaded UI seems very tempting (surely a thread for the View and a thread for the Controller would work…), attempts to build them were abandoned back in the 1970s, when it became clear that they, inevitably, ended in a snarl of deadlocks.

Since the general adoption of MVC, the standard UI design is a queue serviced by a single thread (in Android, the *Main-*, or *UI-thread*). As illustrated in Figure 4-1, events—both those that originate with a user (clicks, taps, typing, etc.) and those that originate in the model (animation, requests to redraw/update the screen, etc.)—are enqueued and eventually processed in order by the single UI thread.

---

2. Goetz et al., 2006. *Java Concurrency in Practice*. Boston: Addison-Wesley.

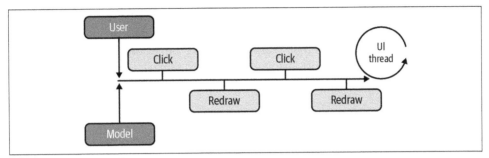

Figure 4-1. UI thread.

This is exactly how Android's UI works. An application's main thread (the application process's original thread) becomes its UI thread. As part of initialization, the thread enters a tight loop. For the rest of the life of the application, it removes tasks from the canonical UI queue one by one and executes them. Because UI methods are always run on a single thread, UI components make no attempt to be thread-safe.

That sounds great, right? A single-threaded UI and no worries about thread safety. There's a problem, though. To understand it, we'll have to switch out of our developer hats and talk a bit about the experience of the end users of Android devices. In particular, we'll need to look into some details of video display.

 Threads are said to *deadlock* when each holds a resource that the other requires: neither can make forward progress. For instance, one thread might hold the widget that displays a value and require the container that holds the value to be displayed. At the same time, another thread might hold the container and require the widget. Deadlocks can be avoided if all threads always seize resources in the same order.

Dropped Frames

We know, from long experience with motion pictures and TV, that the human brain can be tricked into perceiving motion as continuous, even when it is not. A series of still images shown rapidly, one after the other, can appear to the observer to be smooth, uninterrupted motion. The rate at which the images are displayed is known as the *frame rate*. It is measured in *frames per second* (fps).

The standard frame rate for movies is 24 fps. That has worked quite well for the entire Golden Age of Hollywood. Older televisions used a frame rate of 30 fps. As you might imagine, faster frame rates do an even better job of tricking the brain than slow ones. Even if you can't exactly put your finger on what you are sensing, if you watch a high frame rate video next to one with a lower frame rate, you will likely notice a difference. The faster one will feel "smoother."

Many Android devices use a frame rate of 60 fps. This translates to redrawing the screen once approximately every 16 milliseconds (ms). That means that the UI thread, the single thread handling UI tasks, must have a new image available, ready to be drawn on the screen every 16 ms. If producing the image takes longer than that, and the new image is not ready when the screen is redrawn, we say that the frame has been dropped.

It will be another 16 ms before the screen is redrawn again and a new frame becomes visible. Instead of 60 fps, a dropped frame lowers the frame rate to 30 fps, close to the threshold at which the human brain notices it. Just a few dropped frames can give a UI a choppy feeling that is sometimes called "jank."

Consider the queue of tasks shown in Figure 4-2, at Android's standard render rate of 60 fps.

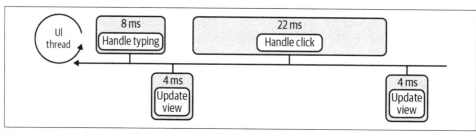

Figure 4-2. Tasks queued for the UI thread.

The first task, handling character input from the user, takes 8 ms to execute. The next task, updating the view, is part of an animation. In order to look smooth, the animation needs to be updated at least 24 times per second. The third task, though, handling a user click, takes 22 ms. The last task in the diagram is the next frame of the animation. Figure 4-3 shows what the UI thread sees.

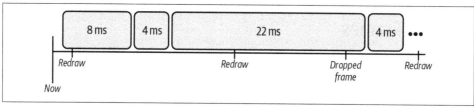

Figure 4-3. A dropped frame.

The first task completes in 8 ms. The animation draws a frame to the display buffer in 4 ms. The UI thread then starts to handle the click. A couple of milliseconds into handling the click, the hardware redraw takes place and the animation's frame is now visible on the screen.

Unfortunately, 16 ms later, the task to handle the click is still not complete. The task to draw the next frame of the animation, which is queued behind it, has not been processed. When the redraw happens, the contents of the display buffer are exactly as they were during the previous redraw. The animation frame has been dropped.

 Computer displays are usually managed using one or more display buffers. A *display buffer* is an area of memory in which user code "draws" the things that will be visible on the screen. Occasionally, at the *refresh interval* (approximately 16 ms for a 60 fps display), user code is briefly locked out of the buffer. The system uses the contents of the buffer to render the screen and then releases it back to the user code for further updates.

A few milliseconds later, when the click handling task is complete, the animation task gets its chance to update the display buffer. Even though the display buffer now contains the next frame of the animation, the screen will not be redrawn for several milliseconds. The frame rate for the animation has been cut in half, to 30 fps, dangerously close to visible flicker.

Some newer devices, like Google's Pixel 4, have the ability to refresh the screen at much higher frame rates. With a frame rate that is, for instance, twice as high (120 fps), even if the UI thread misses two frames in a row, it still only has to wait an extra 8 ms for the next redraw. The interval between the two renderings in this case is only around 24 ms; much better than the 32 ms cost of dropping a frame at 60 fps.

Though increased frame rate may help, an Android developer must be vigilant and make sure that an application drops as few frames as possible. If an app is in the middle of an expensive computation and that computation takes longer than expected to complete, it will miss the redraw time slot and drop the frame, and the application will feel janky.

This scenario is the reason why it is absolutely necessary to deal with concurrency in Android applications. Put simply, the UI is single-threaded and the UI thread must never be occupied for more than a few milliseconds

The only possible solution for a nontrivial application is to pass time-consuming work—database storage and retrieval, network interactions, and long-running computations—to some other thread.

Memory Leaks

We've already dealt with one complexity introduced by concurrency: thread safety. Android's component-based architecture adds a second, equally dangerous complexity: *memory leaks*.

A memory leak occurs when the object can't be freed (garbage-collected) even though it's no longer useful. At worst, memory leaks could result in an OutOfMemoryError, and an application crash. Even if things don't get that bad, though, running short on memory can force more frequent garbage collections that again cause "jank."

As discussed in Chapter 3, Android applications are particularly susceptible to memory leaks because the lifecycles of some of the most frequently used components—Activitys, Fragments, Services, and so on—are not under the control of the application. Instances of those components can all too easily turn into dead weight.

This is particularly true in a multithreaded environment. Consider offloading a task to a worker thread like this:

```kotlin
override fun onViewCreated(
    view: View,
    savedInstanceState: Bundle?
) {
    // DO NOT DO THIS!
    myButton.setOnClickListener {
        Thread {
            val status = doTimeConsumingThing()
            view.findViewById<TextView>(R.id.textview_second)
                .setText(status)
        }
            .start()
    }
}
```

The idea of moving the time-consuming work off the UI thread is a noble one. Unfortunately, the preceding code has several flaws. Can you spot them?

First, as mentioned earlier in this chapter, Android UI components are not thread-safe and cannot be accessed or modified from outside the UI thread. The call to set Text in this code, from a thread other than the UI thread, is incorrect. Many Android UI components detect unsafe uses like this, and throw exceptions if they occur.

One way to address this problem is to return results to the UI thread using one of the Android toolkit methods for safe thread dispatch, as shown here. Note that this code *still* has flaws!

```kotlin
override fun onViewCreated(
    view: View,
    savedInstanceState: Bundle?
) {
    // DO NOT DO THIS EITHER!
    myButton.setOnClickListener {
        Thread {
```

```
          val status = doTimeConsumingThing()
          view.post {
              view.findViewById<TextView>(R.id.textview_second)
                  .setText(status)
          }
      }
          .start()
    }
}
```

That fixes the first issue (the UI method, setText, is now called from the Main thread) but the code is still not correct. Though the vagaries of the language make it hard to see the problem, it is that the thread, newly created in the ClickListener, holds an implicit reference to an Android-managed object. Since doTimeConsuming Thing is a method on an Activity (or Fragment), the thread, newly created in the click listener, holds an *implicit* reference to that Activity, as shown in Figure 4-4.

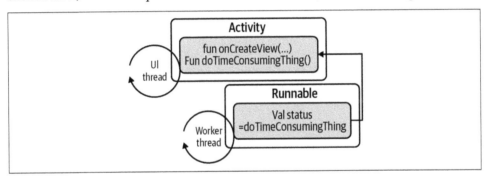

Figure 4-4. A leaked activity.

It might be more obvious if the call to doTimeConsumingThing were written as this.doTimeConsumingThing. If you think about it, though, it is clear that there is no way to call the method doTimeConsumingThing on some object (in this case, an instance of an Activity) without holding a reference to that object. Now the Activity instance cannot be garbage-collected as long as the Runnable running on the worker thread holds a reference to it. If the thread runs for any significant amount of time, Activity memory has leaked.

This issue is considerably more difficult to address than the last. One approach assumes that tasks that are guaranteed to hold such an implicit reference for only a very short period of time (less than a second) may not cause a problem. The Android OS itself occasionally creates such short-lived tasks.

ViewModels and LiveData ensure that your UI always renders the freshest data, and does it safely. Combined with Jetpack's viewModelScope and coroutines—both to be introduced shortly—all these things make it easier to control cancellation of background tasks that are no longer relevant, and ensure memory integrity and thread safety. Without the libraries, we'd have to correctly address all of these concerns ourselves.

Android Jetpack

Careful design using Jetpacks' lifecycle-aware, observable LiveData containers, as described in Chapter 3, can help to eliminate both memory leaks and the danger of using an Android component that has completed its lifecycle.

Tools for Managing Threads

There is, actually, a third flaw in the code we just discussed; a deep design flaw.

Threads are very expensive objects. They are large, they affect garbage collection, and switching context among them is far from free. Creating and destroying threads, as the code in the example does, is quite wasteful, ill-advised, and likely to affect application performance.

Spawning more threads in no way makes an application able to accomplish more work: a CPU has only so much power. Threads that are not executing are simply an expensive way of representing work that is not yet complete.

Consider, for instance, what would happen if a user mashed myButton, from the previous example. Even if the operations that each of the generated threads performed were fast and thread-safe, creating and destroying those threads would slow the app to a crawl.

A best practice for applications is a thread policy: an application-wide strategy based on the number of threads that is actually useful, that controls how many threads are running at any given time. A smart application maintains one or more pools of threads, each with a particular purpose, and each fronted by a queue. Client code, with work to be done, enqueues tasks to be executed by the pool threads and, if necessary, recovers the task results.

The next two sections introduce two threading primitives available to Android developers, the Looper/Handler and the Executor.

Looper/Handler

The `Looper/Handler` is a framework of cooperating classes: a `Looper`, a `MessageQueue` and the `Messages` enqueued on it, and one or more `Handlers`.

A `Looper` is simply a Java `Thread` that is initialized by calling the methods `Looper.prepare()` and `Looper.start()` from its `run` method, like this:

```
var looper = Thread {
    Looper.prepare()
    Looper.loop()
}
looper.start()
```

The second method, `Looper.loop()`, causes the thread to enter a tight loop in which it checks its `MessageQueue` for tasks, removes them one by one, and executes them. If there are no tasks to be executed, the thread sleeps until a new task is enqueued.

If you find yourself thinking that this sounds vaguely familiar, you are right. Android's UI thread is simply a `Looper` created from the application process's main thread.

A `Handler` is the mechanism used to enqueue tasks on a `Looper`'s queue, for processing. You create a `Handler` like this:

```
var handler = new Handler(someLooper);
```

The main thread's `Looper` is always accessible using the method `Looper.get MainLooper`. Creating a `Handler` that posts tasks to the UI thread, then, is as simple as this:

```
var handler = new Handler(Looper.getMainLooper);
```

In fact, this is exactly how the `post()` method, shown in the preceding example, works.

`Handlers` are interesting because they handle both ends of the `Looper`'s queue. In order to see how this works, let's follow a single task through the `Looper/Handler` framework.

There are several `Handler` methods for enqueuing a task. Here are two of them:

- `post(task: Runnable)`
- `send(task: Message)`

These two methods define two slightly different ways of enqueuing a task: sending messages and posting Runnables. Actually, the `Handler` always enqueues a `Message`. For convenience, though, the `post...()` group of methods attach a `Runnable` to the `Message` for special handling.

In this example we use the method `Handler.post(task: Runnable)` to enqueue our task. The `Handler` obtains a `Message` object from a pool, attaches the `Runnable`, and adds the `Message` to the end of the `Looper`'s `MessageQueue`.

Our task is now awaiting execution. When it reaches the head of the queue, the `Looper` picks it up and, interestingly, hands it right back to the exact same `Handler` that enqueued it. The same `Handler` instance that enqueues a task is always the instance that runs it.

This can seem a bit perplexing until you realize that the `Handler` code that submitted the task might be running on any application thread. The `Handler` code that processes the task, however, is *always* running on the `Looper`, as shown in Figure 4-5.

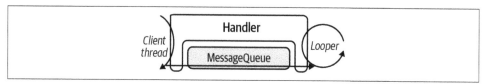

Figure 4-5. Looper/Handler.

The `Handler` method called by the `Looper` to handle a task first checks to see if the `Message` contains a `Runnable`. If it does—and because we used one of the `post...()` methods, our task does—the `Handler` executes the `Runnable`.

If we'd used one of the `send...()` methods, the `Handler` would have passed the `Message` to its own overridable method, `Handler.handleMessage(msg: Message)`. A subclass of `Handler` would, in that method, use the `Message` attribute `what` to decide which particular task it should perform, and the attributes `arg1`, `arg2`, and `obj` as task parameters.

The `MessageQueue` is, actually, a sorted queue. Each `Message` includes, as one of its attributes, the earliest time at which it may be executed. In the preceding two methods, `post` and `send`, simply use the current time (the message will be processed "now," immediately).

Two other methods, though, allow tasks to be enqueued to be run at some time in the future:

- `postDelayed(runnable, delayMillis)`
- `sendMessageDelayed(message, delayMillis)`

Tasks created using these methods will be sorted into the `MessageQueue` to be executed at the indicated time.

 As noted, a `Looper` can only make a best effort at running a task at the requested time. While it will never run a delayed task before its time, if another task hogs the thread the task may run late.

`Looper/Handlers` are a fantastically versatile and efficient tool. The Android system makes extensive use of them, particularly the `send...()` calls, which do not do any memory allocation.

Note that a `Looper` can submit tasks to itself. Tasks that execute and then reschedule themselves after a given interval (using one of the `...Delayed()` methods) are one of the ways that Android creates animations.

Also note that because a `Looper` is single-threaded, a task that is only run on one particular `Looper` need not be thread-safe. There is no need for synchronization or ordering when a task, even a task that is run asynchronously, is run only on a single thread. As mentioned earlier, the entire Android UI framework, which runs only on the UI Looper, depends on this assumption.

Executors and ExecutorServices

Java introduced `Executors` and `ExecutorServices` in Java 5, as part of a new Concurrency Framework. The new framework provided several higher-level concurrency abstractions that allowed developers to leave behind many of the details of threads, locks, and synchronization.

An `Executor` is, as its name suggests, a utility that executes tasks submitted to it. Its contract is the single method `execute(Runnable)`.

Java provides several implementations of the interface, each with a different execution strategy and purpose. The simplest of these is available using the method `Executors.newSingleThreadExecutor`.

A single-threaded executor is very similar to the `Looper/Handler` examined in the previous section: it is an unbounded queue in front of a single thread. New tasks are enqueued onto the queue and then removed and executed in order on the single thread that services the queue.

Looper/Handlers and single-threaded Executors each have their own advantages. For instance, a Looper/Handler is heavily optimized, to avoid object allocation. On the other hand, a single-threaded Executor will replace its thread if that thread is aborted by a failing task.

A generalization of the single-threaded Executor is the FixedThreadPoolExecutor: instead of a single thread, its unbounded queue is serviced by a fixed number of threads. Like the single-threaded Executor, a FixedThreadPoolExecutor will replace threads when tasks kill them. A FixedThreadPoolExecutor does not guarantee task order, though, and will execute tasks simultaneously, hardware permitting.

The single-threaded scheduled Executor is Java's equivalent of the Looper/Handler. It's similar to a single-threaded Executor except that, like the Looper/Handler, its queue is sorted by execution time. Tasks are executed in time order, not submission order. As with the Looper/Handler, of course, long-running tasks can prevent subsequent tasks from being executed on time.

If none of these standard execution utilities meets your needs, you can create a custom instance of ThreadPoolExecutor, specifying details like the size and ordering of its queue, number of threads in its thread pool and how they are created, and what happens when the pool's queue is full.

There is one more type of Executor that deserves special attention—the ForkJoinPool. Fork-join pools exist because of the observation that sometimes a single problem can be broken down into multiple subproblems which can be executed concurrently.

A common example of this kind of problem is adding two same-size arrays together. The synchronous solution is to iterate, $i = 0 \ .. \ n - 1$, where n is the size of the array, and at each i to compute $s[i] = a1[i] + a2[i]$.

There is a clever optimization that is possible, though, if the task is divided into pieces. In this case, the task can be subdivided into n` subtasks, each of which computes $s[i] = a1[i] + a2[i]$ for some i.

Note that an execution service creating subtasks it expects to process *itself* can enqueue the subtasks on a thread-local queue. Since the local queue is used predominantly by the single thread, there is almost never contention for the queue locks. Most of the time, the queue belongs to the thread—it alone puts things on and takes them off. This can be quite an optimization.

Consider a pool of these threads, each with its own fast, local queue. Suppose that one of the threads finishes all of its work and is about to idle itself, while at the same time another pool thread has a queue of 200 subtasks to execute. The idle thread steals the work. It grabs the lock for the busy thread's queue, grabs half of the subtasks, puts them in its own queue, and goes to work on them.

The work-stealing trick is most useful when concurrent tasks spawn their own sub-tasks. As we will see, it turns out that Kotlin coroutines are exactly such tasks.

Tools for Managing Jobs

Just as there can be economies of scale in the production of, say, cars, there are important optimizations that require the large-scale view of a system. Consider the use of the radio on a mobile phone.

When an application needs to interact with a remote service, the phone, normally in battery-saving mode, must power up its radio, connect to a nearby tower, negotiate a connection, and then transmit its message. Because connection negotiation is over-head, the phone holds the connection open for a while. The assumption is that, when one network interaction takes place, it is likely that others will follow. When more than a minute or so goes by without any use of the network, though, the phone goes back to its quiescent, battery-saving state.

Given this behavior, imagine what happens when several applications phone home, each at a different time. When the first app sends its ping, the phone powers its radio up, negotiates the connection, transmits a message for the app, waits a bit, and then goes back to sleep. Just as it goes back to sleep, though, the next application tries to use the network. The phone has to power back up, renegotiate a connection, and so on. If there are more than a handful of applications doing this, the phone radio is at full power essentially all the time. It is also spending a lot of that time renegotiating a network connection that it dropped just a few seconds ago.

No single application can prevent this kind of problem. It requires a system-wide view of battery and network use to coordinate multiple apps (each with its own requirements) and to optimize battery life.

Android 8.0 (API 26+) introduced limits on application resource consumption. Included in these limitations are the following:

- An application is in the foreground only when it has a visible activity or is running a foreground service. Bound and started Services no longer prevent an application from being killed.
- Applications cannot use their manifest to register for implicit broadcasts. There are also limitations on sending broadcasts.

These constraints can make it difficult for an application to perform "background" tasks: synching with a remote, recording location, and so on. In most cases, the constraints can be mitigated using the JobScheduler or Jetpack's WorkManager.

Whenever medium to large tasks have to be scheduled more than a few minutes in the future, it is a best practice to use one of these tools. Size matters: refreshing an animation every few milliseconds, or scheduling another location check in a couple of seconds, is probably a fine thing to do with a thread-level scheduler. Refreshing a database from its upstream every 10 minutes is definitely something that should be done using the JobScheduler.

JobScheduler

The JobScheduler is Android's tool for scheduling tasks—possibly repeating tasks— in the future. It is quite adaptable and, in addition to optimizing battery life, provides access to details of system state that applications used to have to infer from heuristics.

A JobScheduler job is, actually, a bound service. An application declares a special service in its manifest to make it visible to the Android system. It then schedules tasks for the service using JobInfo.

When the JobInfo's conditions are met, Android binds the task service, much as we described in "Bound Services" on page 68. Once the task has been bound, Android instructs the service to run and passes any relevant parameters.

The first step in creating a JobScheduler task is registering it in the application manifest. That is done as shown here:

```
<service
    android:name=".RecurringTask"
    android:permission="android.permission.BIND_JOB_SERVICE"/>
```

The important thing in this declaration is the permission. Unless the service is declared with *exactly* the android.permission.BIND_JOB_SERVICE permission, the JobScheduler will not be able to find it.

Note that the task service is not visible to other applications. This is not a problem. The JobScheduler is part of the Android system and can see things that normal applications cannot.

The next step in setting up a JobScheduler task is scheduling it, as shown here, in the method schedulePeriodically:

```
const val TASK_ID = 8954
const val SYNC_INTERVAL = 30L
const val PARAM_TASK_TYPE = "task"
const val SAMPLE_TASK = 22158

class RecurringTask() : JobService() {
    companion object {
        fun schedulePeriodically(context: Context) {
            val extras = PersistableBundle()
            extras.putInt(PARAM_TASK_TYPE, SAMPLE_TASK)

            (context.getSystemService(Context.JOB_SCHEDULER_SERVICE)
                as JobScheduler)
                .schedule(
                    JobInfo.Builder(
                        TASK_ID,
                        ComponentName(
                            context,
                            RecurringTask::class.java
                        )
                    )
                        .setPeriodic(SYNC_INTERVAL)
                        .setRequiresStorageNotLow(true)
                        .setRequiresCharging(true)
                        .setExtras(extras)
                        .build()
                )
        }
    }

    override fun onStartJob(params: JobParameters?): Boolean {
        // do stuff
        return true;
    }

    override fun onStopJob(params: JobParameters?): Boolean {
        // stop doing stuff
        return true;
    }
}
```

This particular task will be run every SYNC_INTERVAL seconds but only if there is sufficient space on the device and if it is currently attached to an external power source. These are only two of the wide variety of attributes available for scheduling a task. The granularity and flexibility of scheduling is, perhaps, the JobScheduler's most appealing quality.

Note that JobInfo identifies the task class to be run in much the same way that we identified the target for an Intent back in Chapter 3.

The system will call the task's onStartJob method based on the criteria set in the JobInfo when the task is eligible to run. This is why the JobScheduler exists. Because it knows the schedules and requirements for all scheduled tasks, it can optimize scheduling, globally, to minimize the impact, especially on the battery.

Beware! The onStartJob method is run on the main (UI) thread. If, as is very likely, the scheduled task is something that will take more than a few milliseconds, it must be scheduled on a background thread, using one of the techniques described previously.

If onStartJob returns true, the system will allow the application to run until either it calls jobFinished or the conditions described in the JobInfo are no longer satisfied. If, for instance, the phone running the RecurringTask in the previous example was unplugged from its power source, the system would immediately call the running task's onStopJob() method to notify it that it should stop.

When a JobScheduler task receives a call to onStopJob() it must stop. The documentation suggests that the task has a little bit of time to tidy up and terminate cleanly. Unfortunately, it is quite vague about exactly how much time is a "little bit." It is quite dire, though, in its warning that "You are solely responsible for the behavior of your application upon receipt of this message; your app will likely start to misbehave if you ignore it."

If onStopJob() returns false, the task will not be scheduled again, even if the criteria in its JobInfo are met: the job has been cancelled. A recurring task should always return true.

WorkManager

The WorkManager is an Android Jetpack library that wraps the JobScheduler. It allows a single codebase to make optimal use of modern versions of Android—those that support the JobScheduler—and still work on legacy versions of Android that do not.

While the services provided by the WorkManager, as well as its API, are similar to those provided by the JobScheduler that it wraps, they are one more step away from the details of implementation, and one abstraction more concise.

Where the JobScheduler encodes the difference between a task that repeats periodically and one that runs once in the Boolean return from the onStopJob method, the WorkManager makes it explicit; there are two types of tasks: a OneTimeWorkRequest and a PeriodicWorkRequest.

Enqueuing a work request always returns a token, a WorkRequest that can be used to cancel the task, when it is no longer necessary.

The WorkManager also supports the construction of complex task chains: "run this and that in parallel, and run the other when both are done." These task chains might even remind you of the chains we used to transform collections in Chapter 2.

The WorkManager is the most fluent and concise way to both guarantee that the necessary tasks are run (even when your application is not visible on the device screen) and to do so in a way that optimizes battery use.

Summary

In this chapter we introduced Android's threading model, and some concepts and tools to help you use it effectively. To summarize:

- A thread-safe program is one that behaves, no matter how concurrent threads execute it, in a way that could be reproduced if the same threads executed it serially.
- In the Android threading model, the UI thread is responsible for the following:
  — Drawing the view
  — Dispatching events resulting from user interaction with the UI
- Android programs use multiple threads in order to ensure that the UI thread is free to redraw the screen without dropping frames.
- Java and Android provide several language-level threading primitives:
  — A Looper/Handler is a queue of tasks serviced by a single, dedicated thread.
  — Executors and ExecutionServices are Java constructs for implementing an application-wide thread-management policy.
- Android offers the architectural components JobScheduler and WorkManager to schedule tasks efficiently.

The following chapters will turn to more complex topics in Android and concurrency. In them we will explore how Kotlin makes managing concurrent processes clearer and easier and less error-prone.

CHAPTER 5

Thread Safety

With the introduction of the *java.util.concurrent* package in Java 5, threads became commonly used to improve the performance of complex applications. In graphical (or *headed*) applications, they improve responsiveness by reducing the load on the main thread that processes information to render *views*—programmed components the user can see and interact with on-screen. When a thread is created within a program that has a concept of a main or UI thread, it's referred to as a *background thread*. These background threads often receive and process user interaction events, like gestures and text input; or other forms of data retrieval, like reading from a server; or local stores, like a database or filesystem. On the server side, backend applications using threads have better throughput by leveraging the multiple cores of modern CPUs.

However, using threads has its own risks, as you will see in this chapter. Thread safety can be seen as a set of techniques and good practices to circumvent those risks. Those techniques include *synchronization*, *mutexes*, and *blocking* versus *nonblocking*. Higher-level concepts like thread confinement are also important.

The goal of this chapter is to introduce you to some important thread-safety concepts that will be used in the following chapters. However, we won't cover thread safety extensively. For example, we won't explain *object publication* or provide details about the Java memory model. These are advanced topics that we encourage you to learn after you understand the concepts explained in this chapter.

An Example of a Thread Issue

To understand what thread safety is, we'll pick a simple example of a thread-safety issue. When a program runs several threads concurrently, each thread has the potential to do things *at the same time* as other running threads. But it doesn't necessarily mean this will happen. When it does happen, you need to prevent one thread from accessing an object that is being mutated by another thread, because it could read an inconsistent state of the object. The same goes for simultaneous mutations. Ensuring that only one thread at a time can access a block of code is called *mutual exclusion*. Take the following, for example:

```kotlin
class A {
    var aList: MutableList<Int> = ArrayList()
    private set

    fun add() {
        val last = aList.last()  // equivalent of aList[aList.size - 1]
        aList.add(last + 1)
    }

    init {
        aList.add(1)
    }
}
```

The add() method takes the last element of the list, adds 1, and appends the result into the list. What would be the expected behavior if two threads attempted to simultaneously execute add()?

When the first thread references the last element, the other thread might have had time to execute the entire aList.add(last + 1) line.[1] In this case, the first thread reads 2 for the last element and will append 3 to the list. The resulting list would be [1, 2, 3]. Another scenario is possible. If the second thread didn't have time to append a new value, then the two threads will read the same value for the last element. Assuming that the rest of the execution runs without hiccups, we get the result [1, 2, 2]. One more hazard may happen: if the two threads try to append the new element to the list at exactly the same time, an ArrayIndexOutOfBoundsException will be thrown.

Depending on the interleaving of the threads, the result may be different. There's no guarantee that we'll get a result at all. Those are symptoms of a class or function that's not thread-safe, which may not behave correctly when accessed from multiple threads.

---

1. Actually, interleaving of threads can happen between lines of bytecode, not just between lines of normal Java.

So, what could we do to fix this potential misbehavior? We have three options:

1. Don't share state across threads.
2. Share immutable state across threads.
3. Change our implementation so that multiple threads can use our class and get predictable results.

There are multiple strategies for approaching some kind of thread safety, each with its own strengths and caveats, so it is important for a developer to be able to evaluate their options and choose one that best fits the needs of a threading issue.

The first option is relatively obvious. When threads can work on completely independent datasets, there's no risk of accessing the same memory addresses.

The second option is making use of immutable objects and collections. Immutability is a very effective way to design robust systems. If a thread can't mutate an object, there's simply no risk of reading inconsistent state from another thread. In our example, we could make the list immutable, but then threads wouldn't be able to append elements to it. This doesn't mean that this principle can't be applied here. In fact, it can—but we'll come back to it later in this chapter. We have to mention that there's a potential downside with using immutability. In essence, it requires more memory because of object copying. For example, whenever a thread needs to work with another thread's state, a copy of the state object is performed. When done repeatedly and at a high pace, immutability can increase the memory footprint—which may be an issue (especially on Android).

The third option could be described like so: "Any thread which executes the add method happens before any subsequent add accesses from other threads." In other words, add accesses happen serially, with no interleaving. If your implementation enforces the aforementioned statement, then there won't be thread-safety issues—the class is said to be thread-safe. In the world of concurrency, the previous statement is called an *invariant*.

Invariants

To properly make a class or a group of classes thread-safe, we have to define invariants. An invariant is an assertion that should always be true. No matter how threads are scheduled, the invariant shall not be violated. In the case of our example, it could be expressed like this (from the standpoint of a thread):

> When I'm executing the add method, I'm taking the last element of the list and when I'm appending it to the list, I'm sure that the inserted element is greater than the previous one by a difference of 1.

Mathematically, we could write:

$$list[n] = list[n-1] + 1$$

We've seen from the beginning that our class wasn't thread-safe. Now we can say so because when executed in a multithreaded environment, the invariant is sometimes violated or our program just crashes.

So, what can we do to enforce our invariants? Actually, this is a complex matter, but we'll cover some of the most common techniques:

- Mutexes
- Thread-safe collections

Mutexes

Mutexes allow you to prevent concurrent access of a state—which can be a block of code or just an object. This mutual exclusion is also called *synchronization*. An Object called a *mutex* or *lock* guarantees that when taken from a thread, no other thread can enter the section guarded by this lock. When a thread attempts to acquire a lock held by another thread, it's blocked—it cannot proceed with its execution until the lock is released. This mechanism is relatively easy to use, which is why it's often the go-to response of developers when facing this situation. Unfortunately, this is also like opening a Pandora's box to problems like deadlocks, race conditions, etc. These problems that can arise from improper synchronization are so numerous that drawing a complete picture is way beyond the scope of this book. However, later in the book we will discuss some of them, like deadlocks in communicating sequential processes.

Thread-Safe Collections

Thread-safe collections are collections that can be accessed by multiple threads while keeping their state consistent. The Collections.synchronizedList is a useful way to make a List thread-safe. It returns a List that wraps access to the List passed as a parameter, and regulates concurrent access with an internal lock.

At first sight, it looks interesting. So you could be tempted to use it:

```
class A {
    var list =
        Collections.synchronizedList<Int>(object : ArrayList<Int?>() {
            init {
                add(1)
            }
```

```
    })
    fun add() {
        val last = list.last()
        list.add(last + 1)
    }
}
```

For the record, here is the equivalent in Java:

```
class A {
    List<Integer> list = Collections.synchronizedList(
        new ArrayList<Integer>() {{
            add(1);
        }}
    );

    void add() {
        Integer last = list.get(list.size() - 1);
        list.add(last + 1);
    }
}
```

There's a problem with both implementations. Can you spot it?

We could also have declared the list as:

```
var list: List<Int> = CopyOnWriteArrayList(lis
tOf(1))
```

which, in Java, is the equivalent of:

```
List<Integer> list = new CopyOnWriteArray
List<>(Arrays.asList(1));
```

CopyOnWriteArrayList is a thread-safe implementation of Array
List in which all mutative operations like add and set are implemented by making a fresh copy of the underlying array. Thread A
can safely iterate through the list. If in the meantime, thread B adds
an element to the list, a fresh copy will be created and only visible
from thread B. This in itself doesn't make the class thread-safe—it
is because add and set are guarded by a lock. This data structure is
useful when we are iterating over it more often than we are modi-
fying it, as copying the entire underlying array can be too costly.
Note that there is also a CopyOnWriteArraySet, which is simply a
Set implementation rather than a List implementation.

We've indeed fixed the concurrent access issue, although our class still doesn't conform to our invariant. In a test environment, we created two threads and started them. Each thread executes the add() method once, on the same instance of our class. The first time we ran our test, after the two threads finished their job, the resulting list was [1, 2, 3]. Curiously, we ran this same test multiple times, and the result was sometimes [1, 2, 2]. This is due to the exact same reason shown earlier: when a thread executes the first line inside add(), the other thread can execute the whole add() method before the first thread proceeds with the rest of its execution. See how pernicious a synchronization issue can be: it looks good, but our program is broken. And we can easily have it wrong, even on a trivial example.

A proper solution is:

```
class A {
    val list: MutableList<Int> = mutableListOf(1)

    @Synchronized
    fun add() {
        val last = list.last()
        list.add(last + 1)
    }
}
```

It may help to see the Java equivalent:

```
public class A {
    private List<Integer> list = new ArrayList<Integer>() {{
        add(1);
    }};

    synchronized void add() {
        Integer last = list.get(list.size() - 1);
        list.add(last + 1);
    }
}
```

As you can see, we actually didn't need to synchronize the list. Instead, the add() method should have been synchronized. Now when the add() method is first executed by a thread, the other one blocks when it tries to execute add(), until the first thread leaves the add() method. No two threads execute add() at the same time. The invariant is then honored.

This example demonstrates that a class can internally use thread-safe collections while not being thread-safe. A class or code is said to be thread-safe when its invariants are never violated. Those invariants, and how the class should be used according to their creators, define a policy that should be clearly expressed in the javadoc.

 This is Java's built-in mechanism to enforce mutual exclusion. A synchronized block is made of a lock and a block of code. In Java, every Object can be used as a lock. A synchronized method is a synchronized block whose lock is the instance of the class instance. When a thread enters a synchronized block, it acquires the lock. And when a thread leaves the block, it releases the lock.

Also note that the add method could have been declared as using a synchronized statement:

```
void add() {
    synchronized(this) {
        val last = list.last()
        list.add(last + 1)
    }
}
```

A thread cannot enter a synchronized block whose lock is already acquired by another thread. As a consequence, when a thread enters a synchronized method it prevents other threads from executing any synchronized method or any block of code guarded by this (also called *intrinsic* lock).

Thread Confinement

Another way to ensure thread safety is to ensure that only one thread owns the state. If the state isn't visible to other threads, there's simply no risk of having concurrency issues. For example, a public variable of a class (where usage is intended to be thread-confined to the main thread) is a potential source of bugs since a developer (unaware of this thread policy) could use the variable in another thread.

The immediate benefit of thread confinement is simplicity. For example, if we follow the convention that every class of type View should only be used from the main thread, then we can save ourselves from synchronizing our code all over the place. But this comes at a price. The correctness of the client code is now on the shoulders of the developer who uses our code. In Android, as we've seen in the previous chapter, manipulating views should only be done from the UI thread. This is a form of thread confinement—as long as you don't break the rules, you shouldn't have issues involving concurrent access to UI-related objects.

Another noteworthy form of thread confinement is ThreadLocal. A ThreadLocal instance can be seen as a provider to some object. This provider ensures that the given instance of the object is per-thread unique. In other words, each thread owns its own instance of the value. An example of usage is:

```
private val myConnection =
        object : ThreadLocal<Connection>() {
            override fun initialValue(): Connection? {
                return DriverManager.getConnection(connectionStr)
            }
        }
```

Often used in conjunction with JDBC connections, which aren't thread-safe, ThreadLocal ensures that each thread will use its own JDBC connection.

Thread Contention

Synchronization between threads is hard because a lot of problems can happen. We just saw potential thread-safety issues. There is another hazard that can affect performance: *thread contention*, which we encourage all programmers to familiarize themselves with. Consider this example:

```
class WorkerPool {
    private val workLock = Any() // In Java, we would have used `new
Object()`

    fun work() {
        synchronized(workLock) {
            try {
                Thread.sleep(1000) // simulate CPU-intensive task
            } catch (e: Exception) {
                e.printStackTrace()
            }
        }
    }

    // other methods which may use the intrinsic lock
}
```

So, we have a WorkerPool, which controls the work done by worker threads in such a way that only one worker at a time can do the real work inside the work method. This is the kind of situation you may encounter when the actual work involves the use of non-thread-safe objects and the developer decided to solve this using this locking policy. A dedicated lock was created for the work method, instead of synchronizing on this, because other methods can now be called by workers without mutual exclusion. This is also the reason why the lock is named after the related method.

If several worker threads are started and call this work method, they will contend for the same lock. Eventually, depending on the interleaving of the threads, a worker is blocked because another one acquired the lock. This isn't a problem if the time spent waiting for the lock is significantly less than the rest of the execution time. If this isn't the case, then we have a thread contention. Threads spend most of their time waiting for each other. Then the operating system may preemptively stall some threads so that other threads in the wait state can resume their execution, which makes the situation even worse because context switches between threads aren't free. It can result in a performance impact when they occur frequently.

As a developer, you should always avoid thread contention as it can rapidly degrade throughput and have consequences beyond the affected threads, since the rate of context switches is likely to increase, which in itself impacts performance overall.

One of the most effective ways to avoid such a situation is to avoid blocking calls, which we explain in the next section.

Blocking Call Versus Nonblocking Call

So far, we know that a thread can be blocked when attempting to obtain a lock held by another thread. The function that led the thread to be blocked is then a *blocking call*. Even if the lock might be acquired immediately, the fact that the call may potentially block makes it a `blocking call`. But this is just a particular case. There are actually two other ways of blocking a thread. The first one is by running CPU-intensive computations—this is also called a *CPU-bound* task. The second one is by waiting for a hardware response. For example, it happens when a network request causes the calling thread to wait for the response from a remote server—we then talk about an IO-bound task.[2]

Everything else that makes the call return quickly is considered *nonblocking*.

When you're about to make a blocking call, you should avoid doing it from the main thread (also called the UI thread, on Android).[3] This is because this thread runs the event loop that processes touch events, and all UI-related tasks like animations. If the main thread gets blocked repeatedly and for durations exceeding a few milliseconds,

---

2. IO operations aren't necessarily blocking. Nonblocking IO exists, though it's much more complicated to reason about. Android Link is helpful enough to warn you when you perform an HTTP request on the main thread, but other IO tasks—like reading a file or querying a database—do not do this. This may even be a deliberate and accepted practice if done under extremely thoughtful and careful supervision; while possible, this should be a rare exception to the standard.

3. Even for worker threads, executing a long-running task like working with 8-megapixel images, those blocking calls possibly block task packets the UI is waiting on.

the responsiveness is impacted and this is the cause of Android's *application not responding* (ANR) errors.

Nonblocking calls is one building block of a responsive app. You need now to recognize patterns which leverage this technique. Work queues is one of them, and we'll encounter various forms of them throughout this book.

 Most often, the terms *synchronous* and *asynchronous* are respectively used as synonyms for *blocking* and *nonblocking*. While they are conceptually close concepts, the usage of, for instance, asynchronous instead of nonblocking depends on the context. Asynchronous calls usually involve the idea of a callback, while this is not necessarily the case for nonblocking.

Work Queues

Communication between threads and, in particular, work submission from one thread to another is widely used in Android. It's an implementation of the *producer-consumer* design pattern. Applied to threads, the producer is in this context a thread which generates data that needs to be further processed by a consumer thread. Instead of having the producer directly interacting with the consumer through shared mutable state, a queue is used in between to enqueue the work generated by the producer. It decouples the producer from the consumer—but this isn't the only benefit, as we'll see. Often, the Queue works in a FIFO (first in, first out) manner.[4]

Semantically it can help to think of a Queue like a queue of moviegoers. As the first viewer arrives, they are put at the front of the queue. Each additional viewer is added behind the last. When the doors open and viewers are allowed to enter, the first person in line is let in first, then the next, and so on, until the entire Queue is empty.

The producer puts an object at the head of the queue, and the consumer pops an object at the tail of the queue. The put method might be a blocking call, but if it can be proven that most of the time it effectively doesn't block (and when it does, it's for a short time), then we have a very efficient way to offload work from the producer to the consumer in a nonblocking way (from the standpoint of the producer), as shown in Figure 5-1.

In practice, enqueued objects are often Runnable instances submitted by a background thread and processed by the main thread. Also, this isn't limited to one producer and one consumer. Multiple producers can submit work to the queue,

---

4. Although not all work queues use this data structure arrangement. Some of them are more sophisticated, like Android's MessageQueue.

concurrently with multiple consumers taking work out of the queue. This implies that the queue must be thread-safe.[5]

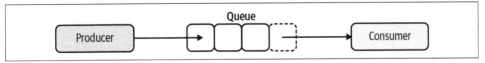

Figure 5-1. Producer-consumer.

 Don't confuse a `Queue` with a `Stack`, which uses LIFO (last in, first out) instead of FIFO.

Semantically, let's imagine a `Stack` as a stack of pancakes. When the kitchen makes more pancakes, they go on the top of the stack. When the diner eats pancakes, they also take them from the top of the stack.

Back Pressure

Imagine now that our producer is much faster than our consumer. The work objects then accumulate in the queue. If the queue happens to be unbounded, we risk exhausting memory resources and potentially an unrecoverable exception: the application may crash. While not only is this experience jarring and unpleasant for the user, but in an unhandled error like this, you're almost assuredly going to lose whatever stateful information was present. Unless you've taken great care to be aware of—and react to—this circumstance, you may experience a sudden termination without an opportunity to perform any cleanup you might do normally. In Android, when a Bitmap instance is no longer being used, the recycle method can be used to mark each underlying memory allocation as unreachable and eligible for garbage collection. In an untidy system exit, you might not have an opportunity to do that and may risk leaking that data.

In this case, a wise choice is to use a bounded queue. But what should happen when the queue is full and a producer attempts to put an object?

We'll circle back to it with coroutines, but since we're only talking about threads for now, the answer is: it should block the producer thread until the consumer takes at least one object out of the queue. Although this blocking should be part of the design and anticipate whatever circumstance or logic branch might deliver the user to this point in the program. While blocking a thread seems harmful, a blocked producer allows the consumer to catch up and free up enough space into the queue so that the producer is released.

---

5. Even with one producer and one consumer, the queue must be thread-safe.

This mechanism is known as *back pressure*—the ability of a data consumer that can't keep up with incoming data to slow down the data producer. It's a very powerful way to design robust systems. Example 5-1 shows a implementation of back pressure.

Example 5-1. Back pressure example

```
fun main() {
    val workQueue = LinkedBlockingQueue<Int>(5)   // queue of size 5

    val producer = thread {
        while (true) {
            /* Inserts one element at the tail of the queue,
             * waiting if necessary for space to become available. */
            workQueue.put(1)
            println("Producer added a new element to the queue")
        }
    }

    val consumer = thread {
        while (true) {
            // We have a slow consumer - it sleeps at each iteration
            Thread.sleep(1000)
            workQueue.take()
            println("Consumer took an element out of the queue")
        }
    }
}
```

Since Java 7, a family of queues for this purpose is BlockingQueue—it's an interface, and implementations range from a single-ended queue with LinkedBlockingQueue to a double-ended queue with LinkedBlockingDequeue (other implementations exist). The output of Example 5-1 is:

```
Producer added a new element to the queue
Producer added a new element to the queue
Producer added a new element to the queue
Producer added a new element to the queue
Producer added a new element to the queue
Consumer took an element out of the queue
Producer added a new element to the queue
Consumer took an element out of the queue
Producer added a new element to the queue
...
```

You can see that the producer quickly filled the queue with five elements. Then, on the sixth attempt to add a new element, it's blocked because the queue is full. One second later, the consumer takes an element out of the queue, releasing the producer which can now add a new element. At this point, the queue is full. The producer tries to add new elements but is blocked again. Again, one second later, the consumer takes one element—and so on.

It's important to note that the insertion of an element into a `BlockingQueue` isn't necessarily blocking. If you use the `put` method, then it blocks when the queue is full. Since `put` *might* block, we say that this is a blocking call. However, there's another method available to add a new element: `offer`, which attempts to immediately add the new element and returns a Boolean—whether or not the operation succeeded. Since the `offer` method does not block the underlying thread and only returns false when the queue is full, we say that `offer` is nonblocking.

Had we used `offer` instead of `put` in Example 5-1, the producer would never be blocked, and the output would be filled with `Producer added a new element to the queue`. There would be no back pressure at all—don't do this!

The `offer` method can be useful in situations where losing work is affordable, or if blocking the producer thread isn't suitable. The same reasoning applies when taking an object out of the queue, with `take` and `poll`, which are respectively blocking and nonblocking.

Conversely, if the consumer is faster than the producer, then the queue eventually becomes empty. In the case of a `BlockingQueue`, using the `take` method on a consumer site will block until the producer adds new elements in the queue. So in this case, the consumer is slowed down to match the rate of the producer.

Summary

- A class or code is said to be thread-safe when its invariants are never violated. So, thread safety always refers to a policy that should be clearly defined in the class javadoc.

- A class can use internally thread-safe data structures while not being thread-safe.

- Avoid or reduce thread contention as much as possible. Thread contention is often the consequence of a poor locking strategy. An efficient way to reduce this risk is to do nonblocking calls whenever possible.

- Work queues is a pattern you will often encounter in Android and other platforms like backend services. It simplifies how a producer (like UI thread) offloads tasks to consumers (your background threads). Consumers process the tasks whenever they can. When the task completes, a consumer can use another work queue to send back to the original producer the result of its work.

- A bounded `BlockingQueue` blocks a `put` operation when it's full. So a too-fast producer eventually gets blocked, which gives consumers the opportunity to catch up. This is an implementation of back pressure, which has one major downside: the thread of the producer might get blocked. Is it possible to have back pressure without blocking the producer thread? Yes—we'll see that in Chapter 9.

CHAPTER 6

Handling Concurrency Using Callbacks

The idiomatic way of handling concurrency in Kotlin is by using *coroutines*. However, for some time this has been done in Java using threads and callbacks. So why do we need coroutines?

To answer this question, we will revisit a typical Kotlin implementation on Android and discuss the pitfalls of using threads. Knowing the weak points of the traditional approach is the key to understanding the motivation behind the design of coroutines.

In Android applications, long-running tasks shouldn't be done on the UI thread, as you've seen in the previous chapter. If you block the main thread—the UI thread— your app might not have the resources it needs to draw the screen or update it appropriately. In fact, lint will complain if you attempt to do an obvious IO call (e.g., make an HTTP connection) while on the UI thread.

An Android application runs smoothly when the main thread completes all its tasks in less than frame time, which is 16 ms on most devices. This is a rather short amount of time, and all blocking calls, like network requests (blocking IO), should be performed on a background thread.[1]

When you delegate a task to another thread, you typically call a function which starts the asynchronous job. In some cases this is "fire-and-forget," but you're usually waiting for a result—and you need to act on it. This is done by providing a function which will be called once the job finishes. This function is called a *callback*. A callback often accepts arguments, so the background thread commonly calls the callback with the result of the job. Doing computation that calls an arbitrary or injected function when complete is known as the *callback pattern*.

---

1. Nonblocking IO using `java.nio.channels.SocketChannel` can be done on the UI thread without blocking it. However, most of the time when dealing with IO, you will be using blocking APIs like `java.io.InputStream`.

Using callbacks is quite efficient, though it has some limitations and drawbacks. To illustrate this, we'll implement a simple yet realistic example in Kotlin. Coroutines address all issues with callbacks, but before jumping right into coroutines, it's important to understand which problem they aim to solve.

Example-of-Purchase Feature

Suppose you're working on a paid feature of an Android application. After a user registers, you check the list of purchases this user has already made, then act on it. To get the list of purchases, let's use an object called `BillingClient`. Note that we're not talking about the actual `BillingClient` provided by the Android framework, `com.android.billingclient.api.BillingClient`. We're using our own, much simpler version of the basic concept, as shown in the following code:

```
interface BillingClient {
    fun interface BillingCallback {
        fun onInitDone(provider: PurchasesProvider?)
    }

    /* Implementations should be nonblocking */
    fun init(callback: BillingCallback)
}
```

A typical task flow would be:

1. Initialize a connection to the `BillingClient`. Wait for it to be ready—your callback provides a `PurchasesProvider`, or null in case of error. For now, we won't handle errors.

2. Use the returned `PurchasesProvider` to asynchronously fetch the user's list of purchases. Your program will wait for the response, which will contain the list of purchases and perhaps some additional metadata.

3. React to this new information; you might show a list of purchases with UI to provide even more details, or request status, cancel an item in an order, etc.

For further references, we'll call the preceding flow our *logic*.

As you can see, this is just an interface with a single method, taking a `BillingCall back` as input. The `BillingCallback` is declared inside the `BillingClient` interface because this callback is only used inside `BillingClient`. When an interface is declared inside a class or interface, it tells you about the relationship between the class and the interface: the author intended that the class shouldn't depend on another entity to provide the interface. This avoids the risk of breaking the compatibility between the class and the interface. The two are coupled, and if you ship a

BillingClient, you also ship a BillingCallback. Notice that we're using Kotlin 1.4's new fun interface instead of a classic interface. This will allow for a concise syntax when we'll provide implementations. Also, the documentation of the init method says that implementations should be nonblocking. If you haven't read the previous chapter, it means that whatever thread calls this method, it isn't blocked waiting for the method to return.

Similarly, our PurchasesProvider is shown in the following code:

```
interface PurchasesProvider {
    fun interface PurchaseFetchCallback {
        fun onPurchaseFetchDone(purchases: List<String>)
    }

    fun fetchPurchases(user: String, callback: PurchaseFetchCallback)
}
```

For now, let's assume that we provide those abstractions and their implementations. Even though a real application would use framework-provided classes, the important part of this example is the business logic, not the implementations of BillingClient and PurchasesProvider.

As an Android developer, we hope that you're familiar with the core concepts of Android Jetpack's ViewModel, but don't worry if this isn't the case, because the details of ViewModel operation aren't the focus of this discussion. Even without ViewModel, you've probably got some version of MVC or MVP or MVVM, all of which largely follow the same pattern. The view does presentation work, the model does logical work, and the controller or view-model is the glue that connects them and serves as the network that allows the two to communicate. The important part is the implementation of the *logic* inside the view-model. Everything else is context or framework code—but still important nevertheless. Figure 6-1 shows the target architecture.

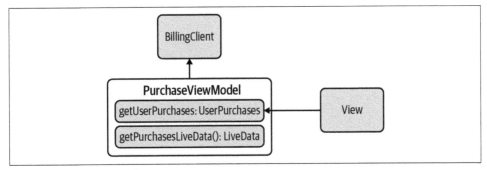

Figure 6-1. MVVM architecture.

Suppose now that you've structured your application following the *single-activity* architecture.[2] The view should be a fragment that displays the purchases of the current user. The lifecycle of the fragment should be taken into account in the design. At any moment, the device could be rotated, and the fragment re-created. The user could go back, and the fragment could be put into the back stack, if not destroyed.

This is where LiveData, a lifecycle-aware component, comes into play. Every time the fragment is created, it requests an instance of PurchaseViewModel. We will explain in more detail how it works later.

Creating the App

In this section, we'll show you a typical implementation inside an Android application. If you're already familiar with this, you might jump directly to the next section, where we discuss the implementation of the *logic*.

View-Model

So the business logic is implemented inside a ViewModel (see Example 6-1). The view-model requires a BillingClient instance to be constructor-injected[3] by some other component, as you'll see shortly. BillingClient is a dependency of the ViewModel, and PurchaseProvider is a dependency of BillingClient.

The view that interacts with this ViewModel triggers the getUserPurchases method (which we haven't implemented yet) in the getter of the purchasesLiveData property. You may have noticed that the type of the purchasesLiveData property is LiveData while the private backing property, _purchases, is a MutableLiveData. This is because the ViewModel should be the sole component to change the value of the Live Data. So the exposed type to clients of this ViewModel is only LiveData, as shown in Example 6-1.

---

2. A single activity and multiple fragments.

3. Developing to interfaces, and not to actual implementations, improves the testability and portability of your code. Inside a test environment, you're able to swap the actual implementations of the dependencies with custom-mocked ones. By portability, let's assume you have an interface called AnalyticsManager that provides some methods that you'll implement to notify your analytics service. Considering that a robust analytics SaaS with dashboards and heavy data visualization and authorization is a heavy lift by itself, most app developers are going to leverage a third-party library to handle that part of their flow. If, for example, you change from one provider to another, as long as you've *composed* your interactions to match the AnalyticsManager interface, your client code never gets touched, or changes, or potentially introduces a new bug; all that's updated is the business logic of the AnalyticsManager implementation.

Example 6-1. PurchasesViewModel

```kotlin
class PurchasesViewModel internal constructor(
    private val billingClient: BillingClient,
    private val user: String
) : ViewModel() {
    private var _purchases = MutableLiveData<UserPurchases>()

    private fun getUserPurchases(user: String) {
        // TODO: implement
    }

    val purchasesLiveData: LiveData<UserPurchases>
        get() {
            getUserPurchases(user)
            return _purchases
        }

    interface BillingClient { /* removed for brevity*/ }

    interface PurchasesProvider { /* removed for brevity*/ }
}
```

We're almost done—now all we're missing is the view.

View

In our architecture, the view is a `Fragment`. As you can see in the following code, the view depends on the view-model. This shows how we can use the view-model from inside the view:

```kotlin
class PurchasesFragment : Fragment() {
    override fun onCreate(savedInstanceState: Bundle?) {
        super.onCreate(savedInstanceState)

        /* Create a ViewModel the first time this Fragment is created.
         * Re-created Fragment receives the same ViewModel instance after
         * device rotation. */
        val factory: ViewModelProvider.Factory = PurchaseViewModelFactory()

❶      val model by viewModels<PurchasesViewModel> { factory }

❷      model.purchasesLiveData.observe(this) { (_, purchases) ->

❸          // update UI
            println(purchases)
        }
```

```
        }
    }
```

Every time the fragment is created, it subscribes to updates of UserPurchases by following three steps:

❶ Create a factory for the ViewModel (remember, the ViewModel has dependencies, and it's certainly not the responsibility of the Fragment to supply them). Strictly speaking, this factory shouldn't be created inside the fragment, as the factory is now tightly coupled with your fragment—a PurchasesFragment always uses a PurchaseViewModelFactory. In a test environment, where you should test the view independently, this would be a problem. So this factory should be injected inside the Fragment through either a dependency injection framework or manual injection. For the sake of simplicity, we've decided to create it here inside the fragment. For the record, ViewModel factory is shown in Example 6-2.

❷ An instance of PurchasesViewModel is obtained from the viewModels function. This is the recommended way to get a ViewModel instance.

❸ Finally, a LiveData instance is retrieved from the ViewModel, and is *observed* by an Observable instance using the method of the same name ("observe"). In this example, the observer is only a lambda function which prints the list of purchases into the console. In a production application you would typically trigger an update of all the related views inside the fragment.

A ViewModel also has its own lifecycle, which depends on whether the ViewModel is bound to a fragment or an activity. In this example, it is bound to a fragment. You can tell that by the use of by viewModels<..>. If instead we had used by activityViewModels<..>, the view-model would have been bound to the activity.

When bound to the fragment, the ViewModel survives device rotations but is destroyed when it isn't used anymore (e.g., when all fragments that were bound to it are destroyed, except for device rotation). If the ViewModel had been bound to the activity, it would outlive the activity on device rotation but would be destroyed in every other scenario where the activity is destroyed.

 As a ViewModel is retained through configuration change, which destroys and re-creates the containing activity, it should never reference a view, Lifecycle instance, or any class instance that may hold a reference to the activity context. It can, however, reference the Application context.

If you look at the actual code of the `BillingClient`, you can see that creating a `BillingClient.Builder` requires that you supply a context. It can be an activity context, because internally the builder calls `context.getApplicationContext()` and this is the only context reference kept by the `BillingClient`. An `ApplicationContext` remains the same during the whole `Application` lifetime. Therefore, you won't create a memory leak by referencing the `ApplicationContext` somewhere in your app. This is the reason why it is safe to reference `BillingClient` inside a `ViewModel`.

As shown in Example 6-2, the dependencies of the `ViewModel` are created inside `PurchaseViewModelFactory`.

Example 6-2. PurchaseViewModelFactory

```
class PurchaseViewModelFactory : ViewModelProvider.Factory {
    private val provider: PurchasesProvider = PurchasesProviderImpl()
    private val billingClient: BillingClient = BillingClientImpl(provider)
    private val user = "user" // Get in from registration service

    override fun <T : ViewModel?> create(modelClass: Class<T>): T {
        if (modelClass.isAssignableFrom(PurchasesViewModel::class.java)) {
            return PurchasesViewModel(billingClient, user) as T
        }
        throw IllegalArgumentException("Unknown ViewModel class")
    }
}
```

`BillingClientImpl` is the real implementation of the previously shown `BillingClient` interface (see Example 6-3 and Example 6-4).

Example 6-3. BillingClientImpl

```
class BillingClientImpl(private val purchasesProvider: PurchasesProvider) :
BillingClient {
    private val executor =
        Executors.newSingleThreadExecutor()

    override fun init(callback: BillingCallback) {
        /* perform asynchronous work here */
        executor.submit {
            try {
                Thread.sleep(1000)
                callback.onInitDone(purchasesProvider)
            } catch (e: InterruptedException) {
                e.printStackTrace()
            }
        }
    }
```

```
        }
    }
```

Example 6-4. PurchasesProviderImpl

```
class PurchasesProviderImpl : PurchasesProvider {
    private val executor =
        Executors.newSingleThreadExecutor()

    override fun fetchPurchases(
        user: String,
        callback: PurchaseFetchCallback
    ) {
        /* perform asynchronous work */
        executor.submit {
            try {
                // Simulate blocking IO
                Thread.sleep(1000)
                callback.onPurchaseFetchDone(
                    listOf("Purchase1", "Purchase2")
                )
            } catch (e: InterruptedException) {
                e.printStackTrace()
            }
        }
    }
}
```

To conform to the application design we established, the init and fetchPurchases methods should be nonblocking. This can be achieved with a background thread. For efficiency reasons (see the upcoming section), you may not want to create a new thread every time you connect to the BillingClient. Instead you can use a thread pool, which can be created using ThreadPoolExecutor instances directly, or many common configurations are available via the factory methods of java.util.concurrent.Executors. Using Executors.newSingleThreadExecutor(), you have a single dedicated thread at your disposal which can be reused for each asynchronous call. You might think that PurchasesProviderImpl and BillingClientImpl should share the same thread pool. It's up to you—though for brevity we didn't do it here. For a production app, you may have multiple ThreadPoolExecutors that service different parts of your app.

If you look at how callbacks are used in those implementations, you can see that they're called right after Thread.sleep() (which simulates a blocking IO call). Unless explicitly posted to the main thread (generally through an instance of the Handler class, or through a LiveData instance's postValue method), callbacks are invoked within the context of the background thread. This is critical, and it's very important to be aware of how to communicate between thread contexts, as you'll see in the next section.

 Be aware of which thread runs the provided callback, as it depends on the implementation. Sometimes the callback is asynchronously run on the calling thread, whereas it can be synchronously executed on the background thread.

Implement the Logic

Now that all the necessary components are set in place, the *logic* can be implemented. The steps are shown in Example 6-5.

Example 6-5. Logic

```
private fun getUserPurchases(user: String) {
    billingClient.init { provider ->                    ❶
        // this is called from a background thread
        provider?.fetchPurchases(user) { purchases ->   ❷
            _purchases.postValue(UserPurchases(user, purchases))
        }
    }
}
```

❶ Call `billingClient.init` and supply a callback which will be called whenever the client's initialization process finishes. If the client supplies a non-null `PurchasesProvider` instance, proceed with the next step.

❷ At this point you have the `PurchasesProvider` instance ready for use. Call `fetchPurchases`, providing the current user as the first parameter, and the callback that should be executed once the provider has done its job. Look carefully at the content of the callback:

```
_purchases.postValue(UserPurchases(user, purchases))
```

On a `MutableLiveData` instance, you use either the `setValue` or the `postValue` method. The difference between the two is that you're only allowed to use `setValue` if you're calling it from the main thread. When this isn't the case, using `postValue` adds the new value into a queue that the `MutableLiveData` will process on the next frame of the main thread. This is an implementation of the work queue pattern (see

"Work Queues" on page 110), and a thread-safe way to assign a new value to a `MutableLiveData`.

Discussion

So this is it. It works—or at least it fulfills the specifications. We invite you to step back a little and look at the big picture. What's the structure of `getUserPurchases`? It's made of a function call, which is provided another function, which itself calls a function, which is provided another function.... It's like Russian nesting dolls. It's already a little hard to follow, and adding exception handling can quickly turn it into "nesting hell" (see Figure 6-2). In order to keep our example logic simple and easy to follow, we've omitted corner cases where some API calls fail; for example, networking issues or authorization errors make some IO background work brittle and prone to failure, and production code should be able to handle this.

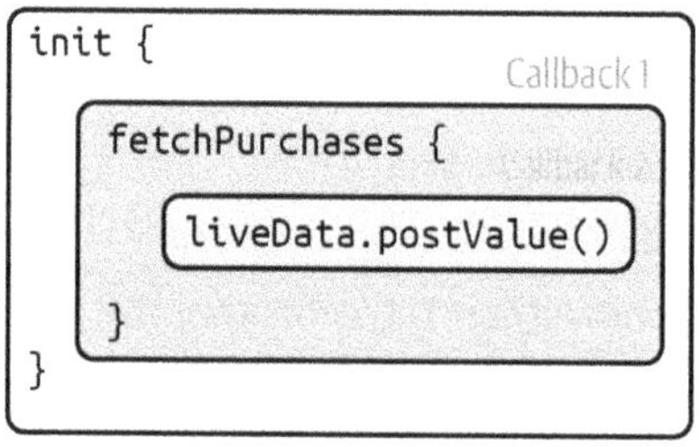

Figure 6-2. Callback usage.

The code that specifies what happens upon a response of the `BillingClient` (callback 2) is *included* in the code of the first callback. If you decide to inline all this code, like we did in Example 6-5, you have several levels of indentations, which rapidly grow as the problem to solve becomes more complex. On the other hand, if you decide to encapsulate the first callback into its own function, you will indeed reduce the indentation level of `getUserPurchases` and its apparent complexity. At the same time, you would increase the number of directions to follow to fully understand the business logic.

This is the first drawback of code using callbacks. It rapidly becomes complex, and may become hard to maintain if not administered with caution and thoughtful design. Some would consider that even with careful precautions this path is dangerous. As developers, we strive to create a system that we and our coworkers can handle.

Using `CompletableFuture` or another similar library like RxJava, you can rewrite `getUserPurchases` like this:

```
private void getUserPurchases(String user) {
    billingClient.initAsync()
    .thenCompose { provider ->
        fetchPurchasesAsync(provider, user)
    }
    .thenAccept { purchases ->
        this.purchases.postValue(...)
    }
}
```

It's a bit cleaner, with no nested indentations, and even handles exceptions properly. However, you can see that it relies on the combinators `thenCompose` and `thenAccept`, which operate on `CompletableFuture<T>`. While our simple example uses only two combinators, a lot of them exist, each one for a specific purpose. Some would consider the learning curve of another, unfamiliar pattern and API to be a weakness of this pattern.

Structured concurrency

Imagine now that some API calls are quite expensive computationally. For example, a user of your app navigates to a view which triggers some of those API calls, but as the content isn't loading instantly they lose patience and tap back, and start a new series of operations in another part of the app. In this situation, you don't want your expensive API calls to continue running, as they may put unnecessary load on your back-end servers, or even on the application itself. Further, what happens if a UI that should be updated when a callback fires no longer exists? A `NullPointerException` is probably your best case, and a memory leak your worst. Instead, let's cancel the procedure initialized inside the view-model. How would you do that? You would have to listen to a particular lifecycle event of the fragment lifecycle termination events: `onStop`, `onPause`, or `onDestroy`. In this specific case, you'd probably want to do that inside `onStop`, which would be fired just before resources are reclaimed. `onPause` would fire each time the application in the background in favor of an incoming call or when switching between apps, and `onDestroy` happens a little later than we need. When the `onStop` event fires, you should notify the view-model that it should stop any background processing. This requires a thread-safe way of interrupting threads. A volatile `isCancelled` Boolean would be checked inside the callbacks to decide whether they should proceed or not. So it's definitely possible, but cumbersome and fragile.

What if this cancellation was done automatically? Imagine that the background processing was tied to the lifecycle of the view-model. The moment that the view-model is destroyed, all background processing gets cancelled. It's not a fairy tale—it even has a name: *structured concurrency*.

Memory leaks

Automatically cancelling dangling background threads has another benefit: the less risk of a memory leak. A callback might hold a reference on a component which either has a lifecycle or is a child of a component that has one. If this component is eligible for garbage collection, while a reference of that component exists in some running thread, the memory can't be reclaimed, and you have a memory leak. Using LiveData like in the previous example is safe even if you don't cancel background tasks. Nevertheless, more generally speaking, it's never good to leave tasks running for nothing.

Cancellation isn't the only possible thing that can go wrong. There are other pitfalls to using threads as primitives for asynchronous computations (which we'll refer to as the *threading model*), and we'll cover them in the next section.

Limitations of the Threading Model

In an Android application, processes and tasks are always competing for memory. With only one main thread, or UI thread, the clever Android developer must find ways to manipulate and handle threading efficiently.

When using a single thread, asynchronous tasks offloaded to that thread execute serially—one task after another. If one of the tasks takes forever to execute, the remaining work cannot be processed until that task completes, as shown in Figure 6-3.

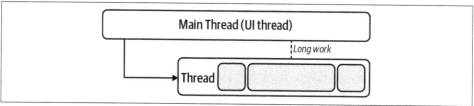

Figure 6-3. Tasks execute serially inside a thread.

In situations where a background task might take a long time to execute, you need more than one background thread. The ThreadPoolExecutor primitive lets you spin up a number of threads and toss onto it blocks of work to execute, as shown in Figure 6-4.

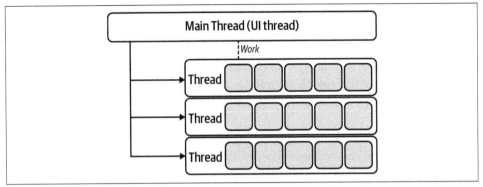

Figure 6-4. A `ThreadPoolExecutor` handles all the heavy lifting of spinning up the threads, load-balancing work across those threads, and even killing those threads.

However, having more threads isn't always a good thing. Here are some caveats:

- CPUs can only execute a certain number of threads in parallel.
- Threads themselves are expensive in terms of memory—each thread costs you at least 64 Kb of RAM.
- When a CPU core switches execution from one thread to another, a *thread context switch* happens.[4] Those switches aren't free. While it's not a problem when you have a few threads, the impact of thread context switches can be noticeable if you keep adding more threads. You could reach a point were your code is actually slower than if you were using fewer threads.

Summary

- You can implement asynchronous logic using callbacks. You might also want to check out some other related framework APIs like `Handler` and `HandlerThread`. Using callbacks can lead to complex nested function calls, or to situations where the flow of the logic is split in several classes and may become hard to follow. If this becomes problematic, one solution is to rely on `CompletableFutures`, or a similar API; the third-party framework RxJava has this kind of functionality, but requires learning yet another set of APIs that can quickly become coupled to your business logic and change the way you write your application code.
- Most often, asynchronous logic is about retrieving and manipulating data which is then rendered as view instances on-screen. To this purpose, Android Jetpack's

---

4. Thread switching involves saving and loading CPU registers and memory maps.

`ViewModel` offers lifecycle-aware components which help you produce more organized and maintainable code.

- When a component reaches the end of its lifecycle, chances are that some related background tasks should now be cancelled; otherwise, they just consume memory and increase the risk of memory leaks, or even an application crash. *Structured concurrency* is the ideal solution to this, which we'll cover in the next chapter.

- Using threads as concurrency primitives has its limitations. You need to make sure you are not creating too many of them because of their memory cost, and performance could suffer due to too many thread-context switches.

Coroutines are meant to address the limitations of the *threading model*. The next four chapters—which focus on coroutines, structured concurrency, channels, and flows—are the "peak" of the book and highlight how Kotlin gives Android developers a true advantage in gaining control over asynchronous computations.

CHAPTER 7

Coroutines Concepts

In the previous chapter, you learned of the pitfalls of the threading model. As an alternative to the threading model, the Kotlin language has a library called *kotlinx.coroutines* which aims at fixing the previously mentioned limitations. Coroutine-enabled primitives allow developers to write sequential, asynchronous code at a low cost. The design of coroutines comprises *suspending functions, structured concurrency,* and other specific considerations like *coroutine context* and *coroutine scope.* The subjects are closely related to one another. We'll cover each one of these considerations in a way that is incremental and digestible.

What Exactly Is a Coroutine?

The official Kotlin documentation qualifies coroutines as "lightweight threads" in an effort to leverage an existing and well-known paradigm. You may conceptualize coroutines as *blocks of code that can be dispatched to threads that are nonblocking.*

Coroutines are indeed *lightweight,* but it is important to note that *coroutines aren't threads* themselves. In fact, many coroutines can run on a single thread, although each has a lifecycle of its own. Rather, you'll see in this section that they really are just state machines, with each state corresponding to a block of code that some thread will eventually execute.

 You might be surprised to find that the concept of coroutines goes all the way back to the early 1960s with the creation of Cobol's compiler, which used the idea of suspending and launching functions in assembly language. Coroutines can also be spotted in the languages Go, Perl, and Python.

The coroutine library offers some facilities to manage those threads out of the box. However, you can configure the coroutine builder to manage your threads yourself if you need to.

Your First Coroutine

Throughout this section, we'll introduce a lot of new vocabulary and concepts from the kotlinx.coroutines package. To make this learning smooth, we chose to start with a simple coroutine usage, and explain how this works along the way.

The following example, as well as the others in this chapter, uses semantics declared in the kotlinx.coroutines package:

```kotlin
fun main() = runBlocking {
    val job: Job = launch {
        var i = 0
        while (true) {
            println("$i I'm working")
            i++
            delay(10)
        }
    }

    delay(30)
    job.cancel()
}
```

The method runBlocking runs a new coroutine and blocks the current thread until the coroutine work has completed. This coroutine builder is typically used in main functions and testing as it serves as a bridge to regular blocking code.

Inside the code block, we create a coroutine with the launch function. Since it creates a coroutine, it's a *coroutine builder*—you'll see later that other coroutine builders exist. The method launch returns a reference to a Job, which represents the lifecycle of the coroutine launched.

Inside the coroutine, there's a while-loop that executes indefinitely. Below the job coroutine, you may notice that the job is cancelled later on. To demonstrate what this means, we can run our program and the output is as follows:

```
0 I'm working
1 I'm working
2 I'm working
```

It appears that the coroutine ran like clockwork. In tandem, the code continues to execute in the main thread, giving us a total of three printed lines within a 30 ms window given to us by the delay call, as shown in Figure 7-1.

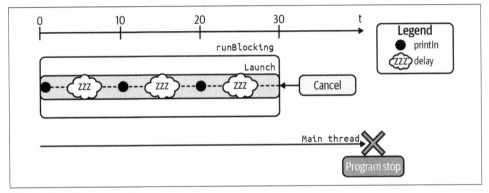

Figure 7-1. First coroutine.

The delay function looks suspiciously like Thread.sleep in its usage. The major difference is that delay is *nonblocking* while Thread.sleep(...) is *blocking*. To demonstrate what we mean, let's examine our code again, but replace the delay call in our coroutine with Thread.sleep:

```kotlin
fun main() = runBlocking {
    val job: Job = launch {
        while (true) {
            println("I'm working")
            Thread.sleep(10L)
        }
    }

    delay(30)
    job.cancel()
}
```

Observe what happens when we run the code again. We get the following output:

```
I'm working
I'm working
I'm working
I'm working
I'm working
I'm working
I'm working
I'm working
I'm working
I'm working
```

```
I'm working
.....
```

The output seems to run infinitely now. When the coroutine executes, the `Thread.sleep(10L)` call blocks the main thread until the coroutine started by `launch` completes. As the coroutine started with `launch` makes the main thread either sleep or print, the coroutine never completes, so execution never leaves the coroutine,[1] as shown in Figure 7-2.

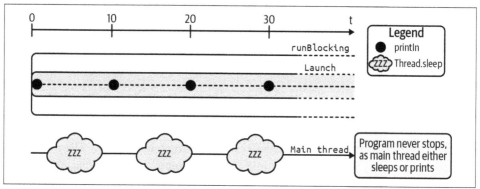

Figure 7-2. Never-ending program.

It's important to remember the following:

- The `launch` coroutine builder is "fire-and-forget" work—in other words, there is no result to return.
- Once called, it immediately returns a `Job` instance, and starts a new coroutine. A `Job` represents the coroutine itself, like a handle on its lifecycle. The coroutine can be cancelled by calling the `cancel` method on its `Job` instance.
- A coroutine that is started with `launch` will not return a result, but rather, a reference to the background job.

If, on the other hand, you need to get a result from an asynchronous computation, then you should use the `async` coroutine builder.

---

1. In this scenario, `job.cancel()` has no effect on the coroutine started by `launch`. We'll touch on that in the next chapter (a coroutine must be cooperative with cancellation to be cancellable).

The async Coroutine Builder

The `async` coroutine builder can be compared to Java's `Future/Promise` model to support asynchronous programming:

```
class WorkingClass() {
    public CompletableFuture<SomeOtherResult> doBothAsync() {
        somethingAsync().thenAcceptBoth(somethingElseAsync()) {
            one, two ->
            // combine results of both calls here
        };
    }
}
```

Instead of making a blocking call to get the data, an asynchronous function immediately returns a wrapper around the result. Depending on the library you use, this wrapper is called `Future`, `CompletableFuture`, `Promise`, etc. This wrapper is like a handle from which you can check if the result is available or not. If you wish, you can block a thread until the result is available with the `Future.get()` method.

Just like a `Future`, the `async` coroutine builder *returns a wrapper around a result*; and the type of this wrapper is `Deferred<T>` (the generic type is the type of the result), as shown in the following code:

```
fun main() = runBlocking {
    val slow: Deferred<Int> = async {
        var result = 0
        delay(1000)   // simulate some slow background work
        for (i in 1..10) {
            result += i
        }
        println("Call complete for slow: $result")
        result
    }

    val quick: Deferred<Int> = async {
        delay(100)   // simulate some quick background work
        println("Call complete for quick: 5")
        5
    }

    val result: Int = quick.await() + slow.await()
    println(result)
}
```

The data types `quick` and `slow` are a future result as an implementation of `Deferred<Int>`, otherwise known as a Job with a result. By calling the method `await` on each `Deferred<Int>` instance, the program waits for the result of each coroutine.

This time, we've launched two coroutines using the `async` coroutine builder. The code itself can give us a good guess at what might happen, but let's run it anyway to see the following output:

```
Call complete for quick: 5
Call complete for slow: 55
60
```

The preceding program delays the slow `async` job by 1,000 ms while the quick `async` job delays it by 100 ms—the `result` waits for both to complete before printing out the result.

It's important to remember the following:

- The `async` coroutine builder is intended for *parallel decomposition of work*—that is, you *explicitly* specify that some tasks will run concurrently.

- Once called, an `async` immediately returns a `Deferred` instance. `Deferred` is a specialized `Job`, with a few extra methods like `await`. It's a `Job` with a return value.

- Very similarly to `Futures` and `Promises`, you invoke the `await` method on the `Deferred` instance to get the returned value.[2]

You may have noticed by now that the examples provided with the coroutine builders `launch` and `async` are wrapped with a `runBlocking` call. We mentioned earlier that `runBlocking` runs a new coroutine and blocks the current thread until the coroutine work has completed. To better understand the role of `runBlocking`, we must first give a sneak preview on structured concurrency, a concept which will be explored in detail in the next chapter.

A Quick Detour About Structured Concurrency

Coroutines aren't just yet another fancy way to launch background tasks. The coroutines library is built around the structured concurrency paradigm. Before going further in your discovery of coroutines, you should understand what it is, and the problems the coroutine library aims to solve.

---

2. This suspends the calling coroutine until the value is retrieved, or an exception is thrown if the coroutine started with `async` is cancelled or failed with an exception. More on that later in this chapter.

Making development easier is a worthwhile goal. In the case of structured concurrency, it's almost a happy side effect of a response to a more general problem. Consider the simplest construct every developer is familiar with: a function.

Functions are predictable in the sense that they are executed from top to bottom. If we put aside the possibility that exceptions can be thrown from inside the function,[3] we know that prior to a function returning a value, execution order is serial: each statement executes prior to the next. What if inside the function, your program creates and starts another thread? It's perfectly legal, but now you have two flows of execution, as shown in Figure 7-3.

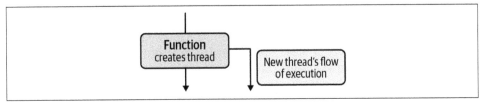

Figure 7-3. Two flows.

Calling this function doesn't only produce one result; it has the side effect of creating a parallel flow of execution. This can be problematic for the following reasons:

Exceptions aren't propagated
> If an exception is thrown inside the thread, and it isn't handled, then the JVM calls the thread's UncaughtExceptionHandler, which is a simple interface:

```
interface UncaughtExceptionHandler {
    fun uncaughtException(t: Thread, e: Throwable)
}
```

> You can provide a handler using the Thread.setUncaughtExceptionHandler method on your thread instance. By default, when you create a thread, it doesn't have a specific UncaughtExceptionHandler. When an exception isn't caught, *and* you haven't set a specific one, the default handler is invoked.

> In the Android framework, it's important to note that the default UncaughtException Handler will cause your app to crash by killing the app's native process. Android designers made this choice because it's generally better for an Android application to *fail-fast*, as the system shouldn't make decisions on behalf of the developer when it comes to unhandled exceptions. The stacktrace is then relevant to the real problem—while recovering from it might produce inconsistent

---

3. We assume that exceptions are handled and don't interfere with the execution flow.

behaviors and problems that are less transparent, because the root cause can be much earlier in the call stack.

In our example, there's nothing in place to inform our function if something bad happens in the background thread. Sometimes this is just fine because errors can be directly handled from the background thread, but you may have logic that is more complex and requires the calling code to monitor issues to react differently and specifically.

 There is a mechanism involved before the default handler is invoked. Every thread can belong to a `ThreadGroup` which can handle exceptions. Each thread group can also have a parent thread group. Within the Android framework, two groups are statically created: "system," and a child of the system group known as "main." The "main" group always delegates exception handling to the "system" group parent, which then delegates to `Thread.getDefaultUncaughtExceptionHandler()` if it isn't null. Otherwise, the "system" group prints the exception name and stacktrace to `System.err`.

Execution flow is hard to control

Since a thread can be created and started from anywhere, imagine that your background thread instantiates and starts three new threads to delegate some of its work, or performs tasks in reaction to computation performed in the parent thread's context, as shown in Figure 7-4.

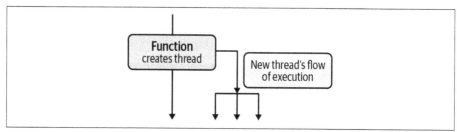

Figure 7-4. Multiple flows.

How do you make sure the function returns only when all background processing is done? This can be error-prone: you need to make sure that you wait for all child threads to finish their work.[4] When using a `Future`-based implementation

---

4. The `join()` method of a thread causes the calling thread to go into a waiting state. It remains in a waiting state until the original thread terminates.

(for example, `CompletableFutures`), even omitting a `Future.get` invocation might cause the flow of execution to terminate prematurely.

Later, and while the background thread and all of its children are still running, all this work might have to be cancelled (the user exited the UI, an error was thrown, etc.). In this case, there's no automatic mechanism to cancel the entire task hierarchy.

When working with threads, it's really easy to forget about a background task. *Structured concurrency is nothing but a concept meant to address this issue.*

In the next section, we'll detail this concept and explain how it relates to coroutines.

The Parent-Child Relationship in Structured Concurrency

Until now, we've spoken about threads, which were represented by arrows in the previous illustrations. Let's imagine a higher level of abstraction where some parent entity could create multiple children, as shown in Figure 7-5.

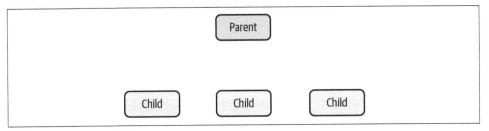

Figure 7-5. Parent-child.

Those children can run concurrently with each other as well as the parent. If the parent fails or is cancelled, then all its children are also cancelled.[5] Here is the first rule of structured concurrency:

Cancellation always propagates downward.

 How the failure of one child affects other children of the same level is a parameterization of the parent.

---

5. A failure of an entity corresponds to any abnormal event the entity cannot recover from. This is typically implemented using unhandled or thrown exceptions.

Just as a parent entity could fail or be cancelled, this can happen to any of the children. In the case of cancellation of one of the children, referencing the first rule, we know that the parent will not be cancelled (cancellation propagates downward, not upward). In case of failure, what happens next depends on the problem you're trying to solve. The failure of one child should or should not lead to the cancellation of the other children, as shown in Figure 7-6. Those two possibilities characterize the parent-child failure relationship, and is a parameterization of the parent.

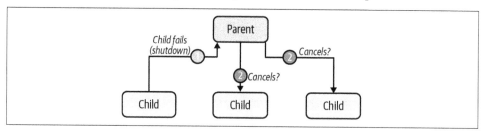

Figure 7-6. Cancellation policy.

The parent always waits for all its children to complete.

Other rules could be added around exception propagation, but they would be implementation specific, and it's time to introduce some concrete examples.

Structured concurrency is available in Kotlin coroutines with CoroutineScopes and CoroutineContexts. Both CoroutineScopes and CoroutineContexts play the role of the parent in previous illustrations, while Coroutines, on play the role of the children.

In the following section, we'll cover CoroutineScope and CoroutineContext in more detail.

CoroutineScope and CoroutineContext

We're about to dive into the details of the *kotlinx.coroutine* library. There will be *a lot* of new concepts in the upcoming section. While those concepts are important if you want to master coroutines, you don't have to understand everything right now to get started and be productive with coroutines. There will be a lot of examples following this section and in the next chapter, which will give you a good sense of how coroutines work. Therefore, you might find it easier to come back to this section after you've practiced a bit.

Now that you have an idea of what structured concurrency is, let's revisit the whole runBlocking thing again. Why not just call launch or async outside a runBlocking call?

The following code will not compile:

```
fun main() {
    launch {
        println("I'm working")        // will not compile
    }
}
```

The compiler reports: "Unresolved reference: launch." This is because coroutine builders are extension functions of CoroutineScope.

A CoroutineScope controls the lifecycle of a coroutine within a well-defined scope or lifecycle. It's an object that plays the role of the parent in structured concurrency—its purpose is to manage and monitor the coroutines you create inside it. You might be surprised to find that in the previous example with the async coroutine builder, a CoroutineScope had already been provided to launch a new coroutine. That CoroutineScope was provided by the runBlocking block. How? This is the simplified signature of runBlocking:

```
fun <T> runBlocking(
    // function arguments removed for brevity
    block: suspend CoroutineScope.() -> T): T { // impl
}
```

The last argument is a function with a receiver of type CoroutineScope. Consequently, when you supply a function for the block argument, there is a Coroutine Scope at your disposal which can invoke extension functions of CoroutineScope. As you can see in Figure 7-7, Android Studio is able to pick up the implicit type-referencing in Kotlin so that if you enable "type hints," you are able to see the type parameter.

```
  ▶  ⊟fun main() = runBlocking { this: CoroutineScope
            // my lambda
     ⊟}
```

Figure 7-7. Type hint in Android Studio.

Besides providing a CoroutineScope, what is the purpose of runBlocking? runBlocking blocks the current thread until its completion. It can be invoked from regular blocking code as a bridge to code containing suspending functions (we'll cover suspending functions later in this chapter).

To be able to create coroutines, we have to bridge our code to the "regular" function main in our code. However, the following sample won't compile, as we're trying to start a coroutine from regular code:

```kotlin
fun main() = launch {
    println("I'm a coroutine")
}
```

This is because the launch coroutine builder is actually an *extension function* of CoroutineScope:

```kotlin
fun CoroutineScope.launch(
    context: CoroutineContext = EmptyCoroutineContext,
    // other params removed for brevity,
    block: suspend CoroutineScope.() -> Unit
): Job { /* implementation */ }
```

Since regular code doesn't provide a CoroutineScope instance, you cannot directly invoke coroutine builders from there.

So what's this CoroutineContext? To answer this question, you need to understand the details of CoroutineScope.

If you look at the source code, a CoroutineScope is an interface:

```kotlin
interface CoroutineScope {
    val coroutineContext: CoroutineContext
}
```

In other words, a CoroutineScope is a container for a CoroutineContext.

The purpose of a CoroutineScope is to encapsulate concurrent tasks (coroutines and other scopes) by applying structured concurrency. Scopes and coroutines form a tree-like architecture with a scope at its root, as shown in Figure 7-8.

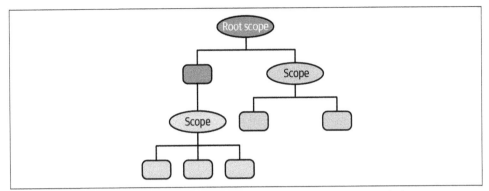

Figure 7-8. Tree-like relationship (coroutines are represented as rectangles).

A `CoroutineContext`, which we'll refer to as a *context* for future reference, is a broader concept. It's an immutable union set of context elements. For future reference, we'll use the term "element" to designate *context element*.

That's the theory. In practice, you'll most often use a special context element to control which thread, or which thread pool, will execute your coroutine(s). For example, imagine that you have to run CPU-heavy computations inside a `launch`, while not blocking the main thread. This is where the coroutine library is really handy because thread pools for most common usages are available out of the box. In the case of CPU-bound tasks, you don't have to define your own thread pool. All you have to do is use the special `Dispatchers.Default` context element like so:

```
fun main() = runBlocking<Unit> {
    launch(Dispatchers.Default) {
        println("I'm executing in ${Thread.currentThread().name}")
    }
}
```

The output is now:

```
I'm executing in DefaultDispatcher-worker-2 @coroutine#2
```

`Dispatchers.Main` is a context element. As you'll see later, different context elements can be combined using operators to tweak the behavior of coroutines even more.

As its name suggests, the purpose of a `Dispatcher` is to dispatch coroutines on a specific thread or thread pool. By default, there are four `Dispatchers` available out of the box—`Main`, `Default`, `IO`, and `Unconfined`:

`Dispatchers.Main`
> This uses the main thread, or the UI thread, of the platform you're using.

`Dispatchers.Default`
> This is meant for CPU-bound tasks, and is backed by a thread pool of four threads by default.

`Dispatchers.IO`
> This is meant for IO-bound tasks, and is backed by a thread pool of 64 threads by default.

`Dispatchers.Unconfined`
> This isn't something you should use or even need as you're learning coroutines. It's primarily used in the internals of the coroutines library.

By just changing the dispatcher, you can control which thread or thread pool your coroutine will be executed on. The context element `Dispatcher.Default` is a subclass of `CoroutineDispatcher`, but other context elements also exist.

By providing a dispatcher context, you can easily designate where logic flow executes. Thus, it is the developer's responsibility to supply the context to the coroutine builder.

In coroutine framework parlance, a coroutine always runs inside a context. *This* context is provided by a coroutine scope and is different from the context you supply. To avoid confusion, we'll call the context of the coroutine the *coroutine context*, and we'll call the context you supply to the coroutine builder the *supplied context*.

The difference is subtle—remember the `Job` object? A `Job` instance is a handle on the lifecycle of the coroutine—it's part of the coroutine context too. Every coroutine has a `Job` instance that represents it, and this job is part of the coroutine context.

It's time to unveil how those contexts are created. Look at Example 7-1, which differs slightly from the previous example.

Example 7-1. Dispatchers example

```
fun main() = runBlocking<Unit>(Dispatchers.Main) {
    launch(Dispatchers.Default) {
        val threadName = Thread.currentThread().name
        println("I'm executing in $threadName")
    }
}
```

This block of code creates two coroutines with their own respective Job instance: run Blocking starts the first coroutine, and the other one is started by launch.

The coroutine created by runBlocking has its own context. Since this is the root coroutine started inside the scope, we call this context the *scope context*. The scope context encompasses the coroutine context, as shown in Figure 7-9.

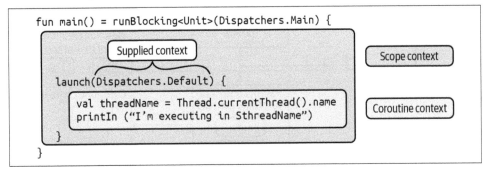

Figure 7-9. Contexts.

You've seen that launch is an extension function of CoroutineScope (which holds a context), and that it can receive a context as its first parameter. So there are two contexts at our disposal in this function, as shown in Example 7-1: one from the receiver type (the scope context), and the other one from the context parameter (the supplied context).

What does launch do in its implementation before calling our provided function? It merges the two contexts so that the elements from the context parameter take precedence over the other elements from the scope. From this merge operation we obtain the parent context. At this point, the Job of the coroutine isn't created yet.

At last, a new Job instance is created as a child of the Job from the parent context. This new Job is then added to the parent context, replacing the Job instance of the parent context to obtain the coroutine context.

These relationships and interactions are represented in Figure 7-10, in which a context is represented by a rectangle containing other context elements.

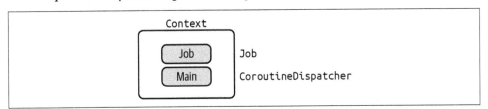

Figure 7-10. Representation of a Context.

Figure 7-10 represents a context that contains a `Job` instance, and a dispatcher which is `Dispatchers.Main`. With that representation in mind, Figure 7-11 shows how we would represent the context of Example 7-1.

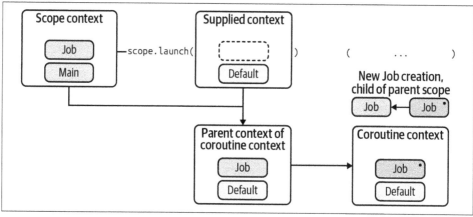

Figure 7-11. Context detail.

Everything you provide in the supplied context to the `launch` method takes precedence over the scope context. This results in a *parent context*, which inherits elements from the scope context which were not provided in the supplied context (a `Job`, in this case). Then a new `Job` instance is created (with a dot in the upper-right corner), as a child of the parent `Job` which is also, in this case, the `Job` of the scope context. The resulting coroutine context is made of elements from the parent context except for `Job` (which is a child `Job` of the `Job` in the parent context).

This *coroutine context* is the context in which the lambda we provide to `launch` will be executed.

Structured concurrency is possible because the `Job` in the coroutine context is a child of the `Job` from the parent context. If the scope is cancelled for any reason, every child coroutine started is then automatically cancelled.[6]

More importantly, the coroutine context inherits context elements from the scope context, which are not overridden by the context supplied as a parameter to `launch`; the `async` method behaves identically in this regard.

---

6. You may have noticed that nothing prevents you from passing a Job instance inside the "provided context." What happens then? Following the logic explained, this Job instance becomes the parent of the Job of the coroutine context (e.g., the newly created coroutine). So the scope is no longer the parent of the coroutine; the parent-child relationship is broken. This is the reason why doing this is strongly discouraged, except in specific scenarios which will be explained in the next chapter.

Suspending Functions

We've examined how to launch a coroutine with the coroutine builders launch and async, and touched on what it means for something to be blocking or nonblocking. At its core, Kotlin coroutines offer something different that will really reveal how powerful coroutines can be: *suspending functions.*

Imagine that you invoke two tasks serially. The first task completes before the second can proceed with its execution.

When task A executes, the underlying thread cannot proceed with executing other tasks—task A is then said to be a *blocking call.*

However, task A spending a reasonable amount of time waiting for a longer-running job (e.g., an HTTP request) ends up blocking the underlying thread, rendering the waiting task B useless.

So task B waits for task A to complete. The frugal developer may see this scenario as a waste of thread resources, since the thread could (and should) proceed with executing another task while task A is waiting for the result of its network call.

Using suspending functions, we can split tasks into chunks which can *suspend.* In the case of our example, task A can be suspended when it performs its remote call, leaving the underlying thread free to proceed with another task (or just a part of it). When task A gets the result of its remote call, it can be resumed at a later point in time, as shown in Figure 7-12.

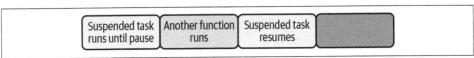

Figure 7-12. The time saved is represented at the end.

As you can see, the two tasks complete sooner than in the previous scenario. This interleaving of bits of tasks leaves the underlying thread always busy executing a task. Therefore, a suspending mechanism requires fewer threads to produce the same overall throughput, and this is quite important, when each thread has its own stack which costs a minimum of 64 Kb of memory. Typically, a thread occupies 1 MB of RAM.

Using a suspending mechanism, we can be more frugal by using more of the same resources.

Suspending Functions Under the Hood

So far, we've introduced a new concept: the fact that a task can *suspend*. A task can "pause" its execution without blocking the underlying thread. While this might sound like magic to you, it's important to understand that it all comes down to lower-level constructs, which we'll explain in this section.

A task, or more precisely, a coroutine, can suspend if it makes use of at least one *suspending function*. A suspending function is easily recognizable as it's declared with the suspend modifier.

When the Kotlin compiler encounters a suspending function, it compiles to a regular function with an additional parameter of type `Continuation<T>`, which is just an interface, as shown in Example 7-2:

Example 7-2. Interface `Continuation<T>`

```
public interface Continuation<in T> {
    /**
     * The context of the coroutine that corresponds to this continuation.
     */
    public val context: CoroutineContext

    /**
     * Resumes the execution of the corresponding coroutine passing a success-
ful
     * or failed [result] as the return value of the last suspension point.
     */
    public fun resumeWith(result: Result<T>)
}
```

Assuming that you define this suspending function as follows:

```
suspend fun backgroundWork(): Int {
    // some background work on another thread, which returns an Int
}
```

At compile time, this function is transformed into a regular function (without the suspend modifier), with an additional `Continuation` argument:

```
fun backgroundWork(callback: Continuation<Int>): Int {
    // some background work on another thread, which returns an Int
}
```

Suspending functions are compiled to regular functions taking an additional `Continuation` object argument. This is an implementation of *Continuation Passing Style* (CPS), a style of programming where control flow is passed on in the form of a `Continuation` object.

This `Continuation` object holds all the code that should be executed in the body of the `backgroundWork` function.

What does the Kotlin compiler actually generate for this `Continuation` object?

For efficiency reasons, the Kotlin compiler generates a state machine.[7] A state-machine implementation is all about allocating as few objects as possible, because coroutines being lightweight, thousands of them might be running.

Inside this state machine, each state corresponds to a *suspension point* inside the body of the suspending function. Let's look at an example. Imagine that in an Android project, we use the presenter layer to execute some long-running processes surrounding IO and graphics processing, where the following code block has two suspension points with the self-managed coroutine launched from the `viewModelScope`:[8]

```
suspend fun renderImage() {
    val path: String = getPath()
    val image = fetchImage(path)     // first suspension point (fetchImage
is a suspending function)
    val clipped = clipImage(image)   // second suspension point (clipImage
is a suspending function)
    postProcess(clipped)
}

/** Here is an example of usage of the [renderImage] suspending function */
fun onStart() {
    viewModelScope.launch(Dispatchers.IO) {
        renderImage()
    }
}
```

The compiler generates an anonymous class which implements the `Continuation` interface. To give you a sense of what is actually generated, we'll provide pseudocode of what is generated for the `renderImage` suspending function. The class has a `state`

---

7. Actually, when a suspending function only invokes a single suspending function as a tail call, a state machine isn't required.

8. `viewModelScope` is coming from the AndroidX implementation of `ViewModel`. A `viewModelScope` is scoped to the `ViewModel` lifetime. More on that in the next chapter.

field holding the current state of the state machine. It also has fields for each variable that are shared between states:

```
object : Continuation<Unit> {
    // state
    private var state = 0

    // fields
    private var path: String? = null
    private var image: Image? = null

    fun resumeWith(result: Any) {
        when (state) {
            0 -> {
                path = getPath()
                state = 1
                // Pass this state machine as Continuation.
                val firstResult = fetchImage(path, this)
                if (firstResult == COROUTINE_SUSPENDED) return
                // If we didn't get COROUTINE_SUSPENDED, we received an
                // actual Image instance, execution shall proceed to
                // the next state.
                resumeWith(firstResult)
            }
            1 -> {
                image = result as Image
                state = 2
                val secondResult = clipImage(image, this)
                if (secondResult == COROUTINE_SUSPENDED) return
                    resumeWith(secondResult)
            }
            2 -> {
                val clipped = result as Image
                postProcess(clipped)
            }
            else -> throw IllegalStateException()
        }
    }
}
```

This state machine is initialized with `state = 0`. Consequently, when the coroutine started with `launch` invokes the `renderImage` suspending function, the execution "jumps" to the first case (`0`). We retrieve a path, set the next state to 1, then invoke `fetchImage`—which is the first suspending function in the body of `renderImage`.

At this stage, there are two possible scenarios:

1. `fetchImage` requires some time to return an `Image` instance, and immediately returns the `COROUTINE_SUSPENDED` value. By returning this specific value, `fetch Image` basically says: "I need more time to return an actual value, so give me your state-machine object, and I'll use it when I have a result." When `fetchImage` finally has an `Image` instance, it invokes `stateMachine.resumeWith(image)`. Since at this point `state` equals 1, the execution "jumps" to the second case of the `when` statement.

2. `fetchImage` immediately returns an `Image` instance. In this case, execution proceeds with the next state (via `resumeWith(image)`).

The rest of the execution follows the same pattern, until the code of the last state invokes the `postProcess` function.

This explanation is not the exact state of the state machine generated in the bytecode, but rather, pseudocode of its representative logic to convey the main idea. For everyday use, it's less important to know the implementation details of the actual finite state machine generated in the Kotlin bytecode than it is to understand what happens under the hood.

Conceptually, when you invoke a suspending function, a callback (`Continuation`) is created along with generated structures so that the rest of the code after the suspending function will be called only when the suspending function returns. With less time spent on boilerplate code, you can focus on business logic and high-level concepts.

So far, we've analyzed how the Kotlin compiler restructures our code under the hood, in such a way that we don't have to write callbacks on our own. Of course, you don't have to be fully aware of finite state-machine code generation to use suspending functions. However, the concept is important to grasp! For this purpose, nothing is better than practicing!

Using Coroutines and Suspending Functions: A Practical Example

Imagine that in an Android application you wish to load a user's profile with an id. When navigating to the profile, it might make sense to fetch the user's data based on the id in a method named fetchAndLoadProfile.

You can use coroutines for that, using what you learned in the previous section. For now, assume that somewhere in your app (typically a controller in MVC architecture, or a ViewModel in MVVM) you have a CoroutineScope which has the Dispatchers.Main dispatcher in its CoroutineContext. In this case, we say that this scope dispatches coroutines on the main thread, which is identical to default behavior. In the next chapters we will give you detailed explanations and examples of coroutine scopes, and how you can access and create them yourself if you need to.

The fact that scope defaults to the main thread isn't limiting in any way, since you can create coroutines with any CoroutineDispatcher you want inside this scope. This implementation of fetchAndLoadProfile illustrates this:

```
fun fetchAndLoadProfile(id: String) {
    scope.launch {                                          ❶
        val profileDeferred = async(Dispatchers.Default) {  ❷
            fetchProfile(id)
        }
        val profile = profileDeferred.await()              ❸
        loadProfile(profile)                               ❹
    }
}
```

This is done in four steps:

❶ Start with a launch. You want the fetchAndLoadProfile to return immediately so that you can proceed serially on the main thread. Since the scope defaults to the main thread, a launch without additional context inherits the scope's context, so it runs on the main thread.

❷ Using async and Dispatchers.Default, you call fetchProfile, which is a blocking call. As a reminder, using Dispatchers.Default results in having fetch Profile executed on a thread pool. You immediately get a Deferred<Profile>, which you name profileDeferred. At this point, ongoing background work is being done on one of the threads of the thread pool. This is the signature of fetchProfile: fun fetchProfile(id: String): Profile { // impl }. It's a blocking call which might perform a database query on a remote server.

❸ You cannot use `profileDeferred` right away to load the profile—you need to wait for the result of the background query. You do this by using `profileDeferred.await()`, which will generate and return a `Profile` instance.

❹ Finally, you can invoke `loadProfile` using the obtained profile. As the outer launch inherits its context from the parent scope, `loadProfile` is invoked on the main thread. We're assuming that this is expected, as most UI-related operations have to be done on the main thread.

Whenever you invoke `fetchAndLoadProfile`, background processing is done off the UI thread to retrieve a profile. As soon as the profile is available, the UI is updated. You can invoke `fetchAndLoadProfile` from whatever thread you want—it won't change the fact that `loadProfile` is eventually called on the UI thread.

Not bad, but we can do better.

Notice how this code reads from top to bottom, without indirection or callbacks. You could argue that the "profileDeferred" naming and the `await` calls feel clunky. This could be even more apparent when you fetch a profile, wait for it, then load it. This is where suspending functions come into play.

Suspending functions are at the heart of the coroutine framework.

 Conceptually, a suspending function is a function which may not return immediately. If it doesn't return right away, it suspends the coroutine that called this suspending function while computation occurs. This inner computation *should not block* the calling thread. Later, the coroutine is resumed when the inner computation completes.

A suspending function can only be called from inside a coroutine or from another suspending function.

By "suspend the coroutine," we mean that the coroutine execution is stopped. Here is an example:

```
suspend fun backgroundWork(): Int {
    // some background work on another thread, which returns an Int
}
```

First off, a suspending function isn't a regular function; it has its own `suspend` keyword. It can have a return type, but notice that in this case it doesn't return a `Deferred<Int>`—only bare `Int`.

Second, it can only be invoked from a coroutine, or another suspending function.

Back to our previous example: fetching and waiting for a profile was done with an async block. Conceptually, this is exactly the purpose of a suspending function. We'll borrow the same name as the blocking `fetchProfile` function and rewrite it like this:

```
suspend fun fetchProfile(id: String): Profile {
    // for now, we're not showing the implementation
}
```

The two major differences with the original `async` block are the `suspend` modifier and the return type.

This allows you to simplify `fetchAndLoadProfile`:

```
fun fetchAndLoadProfile(id: String) {
    scope.launch {
        val profile = fetchProfile(id)    // suspends
        loadProfile(profile)
    }
}
```

Now that `fetchProfile` is a suspending function, the coroutine started by `launch` is suspended when invoking `fetchProfile`. Suspended means that the execution of the coroutine is stopped, and that the next line does not execute. It will remain suspended until the profile is retrieved, at which point the coroutine started by `launch` resumes. The next line (`loadProfile`) is then executed.

Notice how this reads like procedural code. Imagine how you would implement complex, asynchronous logic where each step requires a result from the previous one. You would call suspending functions like this, one after another, in a classic procedural style. Code that is easy to understand is more maintainable. This is one of the most immediately helpful aspects of suspending functions.

As a bonus, IntelliJ IDEA and Android Studio help you in spotting suspending calls in one glimpse. In Figure 7-13, you can see a symbol in the margin indicating a suspending call.

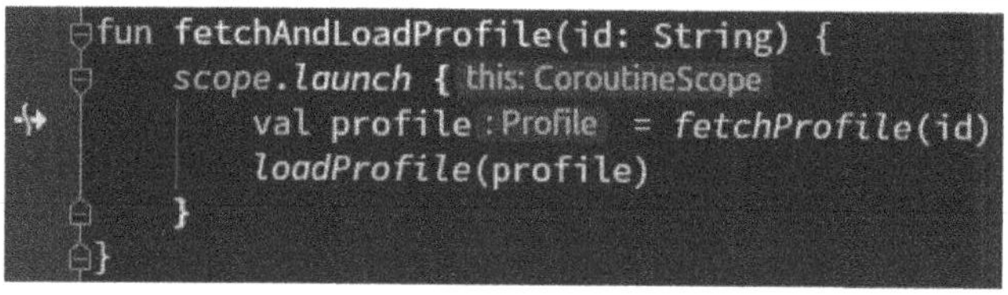

Figure 7-13. Suspending call.

When you see this symbol in the margin, you know that a coroutine can temporarily suspend at this line.

Don't Be Mistaken About the suspend Modifier

However impressive it looks, adding the `suspend` modifier to a regular function doesn't magically turn it into a nonblocking function. There's more to it. Here is an example with the suspending `fetchProfile` function:

```
suspend fun fetchProfile(id: String) = withContext(Dispatchers.Default) {
    // same implementation as the original fetchProfile, which returns a Pro
file instance
}
```

`fetchProfile(...)` uses the `withContext` function from the coroutines framework, which accepts a `CoroutineContext` as parameter. In this case, we provide `Dispatchers.Default` as the context. Almost every single time you use `withContext`, you'll only provide a `Dispatcher`.

The thread that will execute the body of `withContext` is determined by the provided `Dispatcher`. For example, using `Dispatchers.Default`, it would be one of the threads of the thread pool dedicated for CPU-bound tasks. In the case of `Dispatchers.Main`, it would be the main thread.

Why and how does `fetchProfile` suspend? This is an implementation detail of `withContext` and of the coroutine framework in general.

The most important concept to remember is simple: a coroutine calling a suspending function *might* suspend its execution. In coroutine parlance, we say that it reaches a suspension point.

Why did we say that it *might* suspend? Imagine that inside your implementation of `fetchProfile`, you check whether you have the associated profile in the cache. If you have the data in the cache, you may immediately return it. Then there's no need to suspend the execution of the outer coroutine.[9]

There are several ways to create a suspending function. Using `withContext` is only one of them, although probably the most common.

---

9. We'll show you how to do this in Chapter 8.

Summary

- Coroutines are always launched from a CoroutineScope. In structured concurrency parlance, the CoroutineScope is the parent, and coroutines themselves are children of that scope. A CoroutineScope can be a child of an existing Coroutine Scope. See the next chapter on how to get a CoroutineScope or make one.

- A CoroutineScope can be seen as a root coroutine. In fact, anything that has a Job can technically be considered a coroutine. The only difference is the intended usage. A scope is meant to encompass its child coroutines. As you've seen in the beginning of this chapter, a cancellation of a scope results in the cancellation of all of its child coroutines.

- launch is a coroutine builder which returns a Job instance. It is meant for "fire-and-forget."

- async is a coroutine builder which can return values, very much like Promise and Future. It returns an instance of Deferred<T>, which is a specialized Job.

- A Job is a handle on the lifecycle of a coroutine.

- The context of a newly created coroutine started with launch or async, the coroutine context, inherits from the scope context and from the context passed in as a parameter (the supplied context)—the latter taking precedence over the former. One context element is always freshly created: the Job of the coroutine. For example:

```
launch(Dispatchers.Main) {
    async {
        // inherits the context of the parent, so is dispatched on
        // the main thread
    }
}
```

- A suspending function denotes a function which might not return immediately. Using withContext and the appropriate Dispatcher, any blocking function can be turned into a nonblocking suspending function.

- A coroutine is typically made of several calls to suspending functions. Every time a suspending function is invoked, a suspension point is reached. The execution of the coroutine is stopped at each of those suspension points, until it is resumed.[10]

---

10. The coroutine mechanism resumes a coroutine when the suspending function which caused it to suspend exits.

A final word on this chapter: *scope* and *context* are new notions and are just parts of the coroutine machinery. Other topics like *exception handling* and *cooperative cancellation* will be covered in the next chapter.

CHAPTER 8

Structured Concurrency with Coroutines

In the previous chapter, we introduced a new asynchronous programming paradigm—coroutines. When using coroutines, it's important to know how to use suspending functions appropriately; we'll cover that topic in this chapter. As most programs have to deal with exception handling and cancellation, we'll also cover these topics—and you'll see that, in this regard, coroutines have their own set of rules you should be aware of.

The first section of this chapter covers the idiomatic usage of suspending functions. We'll take the example of a hiking app to compare two implementations: one based on threads and the other one based on suspending functions and coroutines. You'll see how this comparison highlights the power of coroutines in some situations.

As is common for most mobile apps, the hiking example requires a *cancellation mechanism*. We'll cover all you need to know about cancellation with coroutines. In order to prepare for most situations, we'll then cover *parallel decomposition* and *supervison*. Using these concepts, you'll be able to implement complex concurrent logic if you need to.

Finally, this chapter ends with an explanation of exception handling with coroutines.

Suspending Functions

Imagine that you're developing an application to help users plot, plan, track, draw, and share information about hiking. Your users should be able to navigate to any of the hikes they've already completed or that are in progress. Before going out for a given hike, some basic statistics are useful, like:

- Total distance
- The length of the last hike in both time and distance

- The current weather along the trail they chose
- Favorite hikes

Such an application would require various interactions between the client and server(s) for meteorological data and user information. How might we choose to store data for such an application?

We may choose to store this data locally for later use, or on remote servers (which is referred to as *persistence strategies*). Longer-running tasks, especially networking or IO tasks, can take shape with background jobs like reading from a database, a local file, or a protobuf; or querying a remote server. At its core, reading data from a host device will always be faster than reading the same data from the network.

So, the retrieved data may come at variable rates, depending on the nature of the query. Our worker logic must be resilient and flexible enough to support and survive this situation, and tough enough to handle circumstances beyond our control or even awareness.

Set the Scene

You need to build out a feature that allows users to retrieve their favorite hikes along with the current weather for each of those hikes.

We've already gone ahead and provided some library code of the application described in the beginning of the chapter. The following is a set of classes and functions already made available to you:

```
data class Hike(
    val name: String,
    val miles: Float,
    val ascentInFeet: Int)

class Weather // Implementation removed for brevity

data class HikeData(val hike: Hike, val weather: Weather?)
```

Weather isn't a Kotlin data class, because we need a name for a type for the weather attribute for HikeData (if we had declared Weather as a data class without providing attributes, the code wouldn't compile).

A Hike, in this example, is only:

1. A name
2. A total number of miles
3. The total ascent in feet

A HikeData pairs a Hike object with a *nullable* Weather instance (if we couldn't get the weather data for some reason).

We are also provided with the methods to fetch the list of a Hike given a user id along with weather data for a hike:

```
fun fetchHikesForUser(userId: String): List<Hike> {
    // implementation removed for brevity
}

fun fetchWeather(hike: Hike): Weather {
    // implementation removed for brevity
}
```

Those two functions might be long-running operations—like querying a database or an API. In order to avoid blocking the UI thread while fetching the list of hikes or the current weather, we'll leverage suspending functions.

We believe that the best way to understand how to use suspending functions is to compare the following:

- A "traditional" approach using threads and Handler
- An implementation using suspending functions with coroutines

First we'll show you how the traditional approach has its limitations in some situations, and that it's not easy to overcome them. Then we'll show you how using suspending functions and coroutines changes the way we implement asynchronous logic and how we can solve all the problems we had with the traditional approach.

Let's start with the thread-based implementation.

Traditional Approach Using java.util.concurrent.ExecutorService

fetchHikesForUser and fetchWeather functions should be invoked from a background thread. In Android, that might be done in any number of ways. Java has the traditional Thread library of course, and the Executors framework. The Android standard library has the (now legacy) AsyncTask, HandlerThread, as well as the ThreadPoolExecutor class.

Among all those possibilities, we want to take the best implementation in terms of expressiveness, readability, and control. For those reasons, we decided to leverage the Executors framework.

Inside a ViewModel, suppose you use one of the factory methods for ExecutorSer vice from the Executors class to get back a ThreadPoolExecutor for performing asynchronous work using the traditional thread-based model.

In the following, we've chosen a *work-stealing* pool. Compared to a simple-thread pool with a blocking queue, a work-stealing pool can reduce contention while keeping a targeted number of threads active. The idea behind this is that enough work queues are maintained so that an overwhelmed worker[1] might have one of its tasks "stolen" by another worker which is less loaded:

```
class HikesViewModel : ViewModel() {
    private val ioThreadPool: ExecutorService =
        Executors.newWorkStealingPool(10)

    fun fetchHikesAsync(userId: String) {
        ioThreadPool.submit {
            val hikes = fetchHikesForUser(userId)
            onHikesFetched(hikes)
        }
    }

    private fun onHikesFetched(hikes: List<Hike>) {
        // Continue with the rest of the view-model logic
        // Beware, this code is executed from a background thread
    }
}
```

When performing IO operations, having 10 threads is reasonable, even on Android devices. In the case of Executors.newWorkStealingPool, the actual number of threads grows and shrinks dynamically, depending on the load. Do note, however,

---

1. When performing CPU-bound tasks, a worker is bound to a CPU core.

that a work-stealing pool makes no guarantees about the order in which submitted tasks are executed.

 We could also have leveraged the Android primitive `ThreadPoolEx ecutor` class. More specifically, we could have created our thread pool this way:

```
private val ioThreadPool: ExecutorService =
    ThreadPoolExecutor(
        4,   // Initial pool size
        10,  // Maximum pool size
        1L,
        TimeUnit.SECONDS,
        LinkedBlockingQueue()
    )
```

The usage is then exactly the same. Even if there are subtle differences with the work-stealing pool we initially created, what's important to notice here is how you can submit tasks to the thread pool.

Using a thread pool just for `fetchHikesForUser` could be overkill—especially if you don't invoke `fetchHikesForUser` for different users concurrently. Consider the rest of the implementation that uses an `ExecutorService` for more sophisticated concurrent work, as shown in the following code:

```
class HikesViewModel : ViewModel() {
    // other attributes
    private val hikeDataList = mutableListOf<HikeData>()
    private val hikeLiveData = MutableLiveData<List<HikeData>>()

    fun fetchHikesAsync(userId: String) { // content hidden }

    private fun onHikesFetched(hikes: List<Hike>) {
        hikes.forEach { hike ->
            ioThreadPool.submit {
                val weather = fetchWeather(hike)              ❶
                val hikeData = HikeData(hike, weather)        ❷
                hikeDataList.add(hikeData)                    ❸
                hikeLiveData.postValue(hikeDataList)          ❹
            }
        }
    }
}
```

For each Hike, a new task is submitted. This new task:

❶ Fetches weather information

❷ Stores Hike and Weather objects inside a HikeData container

❸ Adds the HikeData instance to an internal list

❹ Notifies the view that the HikeData list has changed, which will pass the newly updated state of that list data

We explicitly left a common mistake in the preceding code. Can you spot it? Although it runs fine as is, imagine that we add a public method to add a new hike:

```
fun addHike(hike: Hike) {
    hikeDataList.add(HikeData(hike, null))
    // then fetch Weather and notify view using hikeLiveData
}
```

In step 3 in the onHikesFetched method, we added a new element to hikeDataList from one of the background threads of ioThreadPool. What could go wrong with such a harmless method?

You could try to invoke addHike from the main thread while hikeDataList is being modified by a background thread.

Nothing enforces the thread from which the public addHike is going to be called. In Kotlin on the JVM, a mutable list is backed by an ArrayList. However, an ArrayList isn't *thread-safe*. Actually, this isn't the only mistake we've made. hikeDataList isn't correctly published—there's no guarantee that in step 4 the background thread sees an updated value for hikeDataList. There is no *happens before*[2] enforcement here from the Java memory model—the background thread might not see an up-to-date state of hikeDataList, even if the main thread put a new element in the list beforehand.

Consequently, the iterator within the onHikesFetched chain will throw a Concurrent ModificationException when it realizes the collection has been "magically" modified. Populating hikeDataList from a background thread isn't safe in this case (see Figure 8-1).

---

2. See *Java Concurrency in Practice* (Addison-Wesley), Brian Goetz et al., 16.2.2.

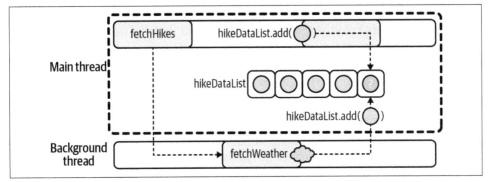

Figure 8-1. addHike adds to the existing hikeDataList that is already being modified in the background thread.

Falling into this pattern, even when safe, increases the likelihood that habit overtakes sensibility and that during the same day or week or month, this mistake repeats in a less safe circumstance. Consider other team members with edit access to the same codebase and you can see that we quickly lose control.

Thread safety matters anytime multiple threads are attempting to access the same resource at the same time, and it's hard to get right. This is why *defaulting to the main thread*[3] is considered a good practice.

So how would you do this? Are you able to get the background thread to tell the main thread "add this element to this list whenever you can, then notify the view with the updated list of HikeData"? For this purpose, you can use the handy HandlerThread and Handler classes.

A Reminder About HandlerThread

A HandlerThread is a thread to which a "message loop" is attached. It's an implementation of the producer-consumer design pattern, where the HandlerThread is the consumer. A Handler sits between the actual message queue and other threads that can send new messages. Internally, the loop that consumes the message queue is created using the Looper class (also called "looper"). A HandlerThread completes when you invoke its quit or quickSafely method. Paraphrasing Android's documentation, the quit method causes the handler thread's looper to terminate without processing any more messages in the message queue. The quitSafely method causes the handler thread's looper to terminate as soon as all remaining messages in the message queue, that are already due to be delivered, have been handled.

---

3. We mentioned this in Chapter 5. In this case, it means that we add a new element to hikeDataList from the main thread.

Be really careful about remembering to stop a HandlerThread. For example, imagine you start a HandlerThread within the lifecycle of an activity (say, in an onCreate method of a fragment). If you rotate the device, the activity is destroyed and then re-created. A new HandlerThread instance is then created and started while the old one is still running, leading to a serious memory leak (see Figure 8-2)!

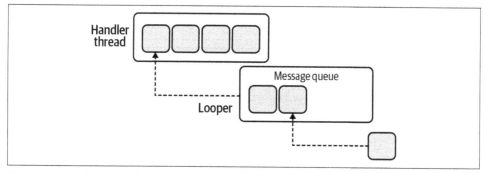

Figure 8-2. A HandlerThread consumes tasks coming from the MessageQueue.

On Android, the main thread is a HandlerThread. Because creating a Handler to post messages to the main thread is very common, a static method on the Looper class exists to get the reference on the main thread's Looper instance. Using a Handler, you can post a Runnable to be executed on the thread that the Looper instance associated with the Handler is attached to. The Java signature is:

```
public final boolean post(@NonNull Runnable r) { ... }
```

Since a Runnable only has one abstract method, run, it can be nice and syntactically sweetened in Kotlin using a lambda, as shown in the following code:

```
// Direct translation in Kotlin (though not idiomatic)
handler.post(object: Runnable {
    override fun run() {
        // content of run
    }
}
)

// ..which can be nicely simplified into:
handler.post {
    // content of `run` method
}
```

In practice, you just create it like this:

```
val handler: Handler = Handler(Looper.getMainLooper())
```

Then you can can utilize the loop handler in the previous example, as shown in the following code:

```
class HikesViewModel : ViewModel() {
    private val ioThreadPool: ExecutorService = Executors.newWorkStealing
Pool(10)
    private val hikeDataList = mutableListOf<HikeData>()
    private val hikeLiveData = MutableLiveData<List<HikeData>>()
    private val handler: Handler = Handler(Looper.getMainLooper())

    private fun onHikesFetched(hikes: List<Hike>) {
        hikes.forEach { hike ->
            ioThreadPool.submit {
                val weather = fetchWeather(hike)
                val hikeData = HikeData(hike, weather)

                // Here we post a Runnable
                handler.post {
                    hikeDataList.add(hikeData)          ❶
                    hikeLiveData.value = hikeDataList    ❷
                }
            }
        }
    }

    // other methods removed for brevity
}
```

This time, we post a `Runnable` to the main thread, in which:

❶ A new `HideData` instance is added to `hikeDataList`.

❷ `hikeLiveData` is given the `hikeDataList` as an updated value. Notice that we can use the highly readable and intuitive assignment operator here: `hikeLiveData.value = ..`, which is nicer than `hikeLiveData.postValue(..)`. This is because the `Runnable` will be executed from the main thread—`postValue` is only useful when updating the value of a `LiveData` from a background thread.

Doing this, all accessors of `hikeDataList` are *thread-confined* to the main thread (see Figure 8-3), eliminating all possible concurrency hazards.

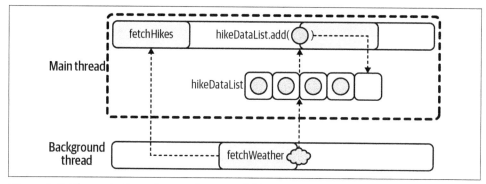

Figure 8-3. The main thread can only access hikeDataList.

That's it for the "traditional" approach. Other libraries like *RxJava/RxKotlin* and *Arrow* could have been used to perform essentially the same thing. The logic is made of several steps. You start the first one, giving it a callback containing the set of instructions to run when the background job is done. Each step is connected to the next by the code inside the callbacks. We've discussed it in Chapter 6, and we hope that we've illuminated some potential pitfalls and given you the tools to avoid them.

Interestingly, callback complexity doesn't seem to be an issue in this example—everything is done with two methods, a `Handler` and a `ExecutorService`. However, an insidious situation arises in the following scenario:

A user navigates to a list of hikes, then `fetchHikesAsync` is called on the `ViewModel`. The user just installed the application on a new device; thus the history isn't in cache, so the app has to access remote APIs to fetch fresh data from some remote service.

Let's assume that the wireless network is slow, but not so slow as to cause IO timeout errors. The view keeps showing that the list is updating, and the user might think that there is in fact a suppressed error, and retry the fetch (which might be available using some refresh UI like a `SwipeRefreshLayout`, an explicit refresh button, or even just using navigation to reenter the UI and presume a fetch will be called implicitly).

Unfortunately, nothing in our implementation anticipates this. When `fetchHikesAsync` is called, a workflow is launched and cannot be stopped. Imagining the worst case, every time a user navigates back and reenters in the hike list view, a new workflow is launched. This is clearly poor design.

A cancellation mechanism might be one possible solution. We might implement a cancellation mechanism by ensuring that every new call of `fetchHikesAsync` cancels any previous in-flight or pending call. Alternatively, you could discard new calls of `fetchHikesAsync` while a previous call is still running. Implementing that in this context requires thoughtfulness and deliberation.

A cancellation mechanism isn't as fire-and-forget as we might find in other flows, because you have to ensure that *every* background thread effectively stops their execution.

As you know from the previous chapter, coroutines and suspending functions can be a great fit here, and in similar circumstances. We chose this hiking app example because we have a great opportunity to use suspending functions.

Using Suspending Functions and Coroutines

As a reminder, we'll now implement the exact same logic; but this time we'll be using suspending functions and coroutines.

You declare a suspending function when the function may not return immediately. Therefore, any blocking function is eligible to be rewritten as a suspending function.

The `fetchHikesForUser` function is a good example because it blocks the calling thread until it returns a list of `Hike` instances. Therefore, it can be expressed as a suspending function, as shown in the following code:

```
suspend fun hikesForUser(userId: String): List<Hike> {
    return withContext(Dispatchers.IO) {
        fetchHikesForUser(userId)
    }
}
```

We had to pick another name for the suspending function. In this example, blocking calls are prefixed with "fetch" by convention.

Similarly, as shown in Example 8-1, you can declare the equivalent for `fetchWeather`.

Example 8-1. `fetchWeather` as suspending function

```
suspend fun weatherForHike(hike: Hike): Weather {
    return withContext(Dispatchers.IO) {
        fetchWeather(hike)
    }
}
```

Those suspending functions are wrappers around their blocking counterpart. When invoked from inside a coroutine, the `Dispatcher` supplied to the `withContext` function determines which thread pool the blocking call is executed on. Here, `Dispatchers.IO` is a perfect fit and is very similar to the work-stealing pool seen earlier.

Once you've wrapped blocking calls in suspending blocks like the suspending `weatherForHike` function, you're now ready to use those suspending functions inside coroutines—as you'll see shortly.

Actually, there's a convention with suspending functions to make everyone's life simpler: *a suspending function never blocks the calling thread*. In the case of `weatherForHike`, this is indeed the case, since regardless of which thread invokes `weatherForHike` from within a coroutine, the `withContext(Dispatchers.IO)` statement causes the execution to jump to another thread.[4]

Everything we've done using the callback pattern can now fit in a single public `update` method, which reads like procedural code. This is possible thanks to the suspending functions, as shown in Example 8-2.

Example 8-2. Using suspending functions in the view-model

```
class HikesViewModel : ViewModel() {
    private val hikeDataList = mutableListOf<HikeData>()
    private val hikeLiveData = MutableLiveData<List<HikeData>>()

    fun update() {
        viewModelScope.launch {                                    ❶
            /* Step 1: get the list of hikes */
            val hikes = hikesForUser("userId")                     ❷

            /* Step 2: for each hike, get the weather, wrap into a
             * container, update hikeDataList, then notify view
             * listeners by updating the corresponding LiveData */
            hikes.forEach { hike ->                                ❸
                launch {
                    val weather = weatherForHike(hike)             ❹
                    val hikeData = HikeData(hike, weather)
                    hikeDataList.add(hikeData)
                    hikeLiveData.value = hikeDataList
                }
            }
        }
    }
}
```

---

4. Unless the `Dispatchers.IO` suffers from thread starvation, which is highly unlikely.

We're going to provide the details of Example 8-2 step by step:

❶ When update is called, it immediately starts a coroutine, using the launch corou-tine builder. As you know, a coroutine is never launched out of the blue. As we've seen in Chapter 7, a coroutine must always be started within a CoroutineScope. Here, we're using viewModelScope.

Where does this scope come from? The Android Jetpack team from Google know that using Kotlin and coroutines requires a CoroutineScope. To ease your life, they maintain Android KTX (*https://oreil.ly/e3sqR*), which is a set of Kotlin extensions on the Android platform and other APIs. The goal is to use Kotlin idioms while still integrating nicely with the Android framework. They leverage extension functions, lambdas, parameter default values, and coroutines. Android KTX is made of several libraries. In this example, we used *lifecycle-viewmodel-ktx*. To use it in your app, you should add the following to your dependencies listed in your build.gradle (use a newer version if available): implementation "androidx.lifecycle:lifecycle-viewmodel-ktx:2.2.0".

❷ The line val hikes = hikesForUser("userId") is the first suspension point. The coroutine started by launch is stopped until hikesForUser returns.

❸ You've got your list of Hike instances. Now you can *concurrently* fetch the weather data for each of them. We can use a loop and start a new coroutine for each hike using launch.

❹ val weather = weatherForHike(hike) is another suspension point. Each of the coroutines started in the for loop will reach this suspension point.

Let's have a closer look at the coroutine started for each Hike instance in the following code:

```
launch {
    val weather = weatherForHike(hike)
    val hikeData = HikeData(hike, weather)
    hikeDataList.add(hikeData)
    hikeLiveData.value = hikeDataList
}
```

Since the parent scope (viewModelScope) defaults to the main thread, every single line inside the launch block is executed on the main thread, except the content of the suspending function weatherForHike, which uses Dispatchers.IO (see Example 8-1). The assignment of weather is done on the main thread. Therefore, the usages of hikeDataList are confined to the main thread—there are no thread-safety issues. As for hikeLiveData, you can use the setter of its value (and since we're in Kotlin, that means the assignment operator), instead of postValue, since we know we're calling this from the main thread.

 When using a coroutine scope, you should always be conscious of how it manages your coroutines, especially knowing what Dispatcher the scope uses. The following code shows how it's declared in the source code of the library:

```
val ViewModel.viewModelScope: CoroutineScope
  get() {
    val scope: CoroutineScope? = this.get
Tag(JOB_KEY)
    if (scope != null) {
      return scope
    }
    return setTagIfAbsent(
      JOB_KEY,
      CloseableCoroutineScope(
        SupervisorJob() + Dispatchers.Main.imme
diate))
  }
```

As you can see in this example, viewModelScope is declared as an extension property on the ViewModel class. Even if the ViewModel class has absolutely no notion of CoroutineScope, declaring it in this manner enables the syntax in our example. Then, an internal store is consulted to check whether a scope has already been created or not. If not, a new one is created using CloseableCoroutine Scope(..).[5] For instance, don't pay attention to SupervisorJob— we'll explain its role later when we discuss cancellation. What's particularly relevant here is Dispatchers.Main.immediate, a variation of Dispatcher.Main, which executes coroutines immediately when they are launched from the main thread. Consequently, this scope defaults to the main thread. This is a critical piece of information that you'll need to know moving forward from here.

---

5. It's just a subclass of the regular CoroutineScope, which invokes coroutineContext.cancel() inside its close() method.

Summary of Suspending Functions Versus Traditional Threading

Thanks to suspending functions, asynchronous logic can be written like procedural code. Since the Kotlin compiler generates all the necessary callbacks and boilerplate code under the hood, the code you write using a cancellation mechanism can be much more concise.[6] For example, a coroutine scope that uses `Dispatchers.Main` doesn't need `Handlers` or other communication primitives to pass data to and from a background thread to the main thread, as is still the case with purely multithreaded environments (without coroutines). Actually, all the problems we had in the thread-based approach are now nicely solved using coroutines—and that includes the cancellation mechanism.

Code using coroutines and suspending functions can also be more readable, as there can be far fewer implicit or indirect instructions (like nested calls, or SAM instances, as described in Chapter 6). Moreover, IntelliJ and Android Studio make those suspending calls stand out with a special icon in the margin.

In this section, we only scratched the surface of cancellation. The following section covers all you need to know about cancellation with coroutines.

Cancellation

Handling task cancellation is a critical part of an Android application. When a user navigates for the first time to the view displaying the list of hikes along with statistics and weather, a decent number of coroutines are started from the view-model. If for some reason the user decides to leave the view, then the tasks launched by the view-model are probably running for nothing. Unless of course the user later navigates back to the view, but it's dangerous to assume that. To avoid wasting resources, a good practice in this scenario is to cancel all ongoing tasks related to views no longer needed. This is a good example of cancellation you might implement yourself, as part of your application design. There's another kind of cancellation: the one that happens when something bad happens. So we'll distinguish the two types here:

Designed cancellation
> For example, a task that's cancelled after a user taps a "Cancel" button in a custom or arbitrary UI.

Failure cancellation
> For example, a cancellation that's caused by exceptions, either intentionally (thrown) or unexpectedly (unhandled).

---

6. Notice that the material on the suspending functions approach is relatively shorter (three and a half pages compared to seven pages for the traditional approach)—probably because suspending functions is an easier (and easier-to-explain) solution.

Keep those two types of cancellation in mind, as you'll see that the coroutine framework handles them differently.

Coroutine Lifecycle

To understand how cancellation works, you need to be aware that a coroutine has a lifecycle, which is shown in Figure 8-4.

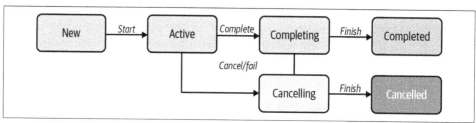

Figure 8-4. Coroutine lifecycle.

When a coroutine is created, for example, with the launch {..} function with no additional context or arguments, it's created in the Active state. That means it starts immediately when launch is called. This is also called *eagerly* started. In some situations, you might want to start a coroutine *lazily*, which means it won't do anything until you manually start it. To do this, launch and async can both take a named argument "start," of type CoroutineStart. The default value is CoroutineStart.DEFAULT (eager start), but you can use CoroutineStart.LAZY, as in the following code:

```
val job = scope.launch(start = CoroutineStart.LAZY) { ... }
// some work
job.start()
```

Don't forget to call job.start()! Because when started lazily, a coroutine needs to be explicitly started.[7] You don't have to do this by default, as a coroutine is created in the Active state.

When a coroutine is done with its work, it remains in the Completing state until all of its children reach the Completed state (see Chapter 7). Only then does it reach the Completed state. As usual, let's crack open the source code and take a look at the following:

---

7. When started lazily, a coroutine is in the New state. Only after invoking job.start() does the coroutine move to the Active state. Calling job.join() also starts the coroutine.

```
viewModelScope.launch {
    launch {
        fetchData()    // might take some time
    }
    launch {
        fetchOtherData()
    }
}
```

This `viewModelScope.launch` completes its work almost instantly: it only starts two child coroutines and does nothing else on its own. It quickly reaches the `Completing` state and moves to the `Completed` state only when the child coroutines complete.

Coroutine cancellation

While in `Active` or `Completing` state, if an exception is thrown or the logic calls `cancel()`, the coroutine transitions to `Cancelling` state. If required, this is when you perform necessary cleanup. The coroutine remains in this `Cancelling` state until the cleanup job is done with its work. Only then will the coroutine transition to the `Cancelled` state.

Job holds the state

Internally, all those states of the lifecycle are held by the `Job` of the coroutine. The `Job` doesn't have a property named "state" (whose values would range from "NEW" to "COMPLETED"). Instead, the state is represented by three Booleans (flags): `isActive`, `isCancelled`, and `isCompleted`. Each state is represented by a combination of those flags, as you can see in Table 8-1.

Table 8-1. Job states

State	isActive	isCompleted	isCancelled
New (optional initial state)	false	false	false
Active (default initial state)	true	false	false
Completing (transient state)	true	false	false
Cancelling (transient state)	false	false	true
Cancelled (final state)	false	true	true
Completed (final state)	false	true	false

As you can see, there is no way to distinguish the `Completing` state from the `Active` state using only those Booleans. Anyway, in most cases what you will really care about is the value of a particular flag, rather than the state itself. For example, if you check for `isActive`, you're actually checking for `Active` and `Completing` states at the same time. More on that in the next section.

Cancelling a Coroutine

Let's take a look at the following example, where we have a coroutine which simply prints on the console "job: I'm working.." twice per second. The parent coroutine waits a little before cancelling this coroutine:

```
val startTime = System.currentTimeMillis()
val job = launch(Dispatchers.Default) {
    var nextPrintTime = startTime
    while (true) {
        if (System.currentTimeMillis() >= nextPrintTime) {
            println("job: I'm working..")
            nextPrintTime += 500
        }
    }
}
delay(1200)
println("main: I'm going to cancel this job")
job.cancel()
println("main: Done")
```

You can see that the instance of Job returned by launch has a cancel() method. As its name suggests, it cancels the running coroutine. By the way, a Deferred instance—which is returned by the async coroutine builder—also has this cancel() method since a Deferred instance is a specialized Job.

Back to our example: you might expect this little piece of code to print "job: I'm working.." three times. Actually, the output is:

```
job: I'm working..
job: I'm working..
job: I'm working..
main: I'm going to cancel this job
main: Done
job: I'm working..
job: I'm working..
```

So the child coroutine is still running despite the cancellation from the parent. This is because the child coroutine isn't cooperative with cancellation. There are several ways to change that. The first one is by periodically checking for the cancellation status of the coroutine, using isActive, as shown in the following code:

```
val job = launch(Dispatchers.Default) {
    var nextPrintTime = startTime
    while (isActive) {
        if (System.currentTimeMillis() >= nextPrintTime) {
```

```
        println("job: I'm working..")
        nextPrintTime += 500
      }
    }
  }
```

You can call `isActive` this way because it's an extension property on `Coroutine Scope`, as shown in the following code:

```
/**
 * Returns true when the current Job is still active (has not
 * completed and was not cancelled yet).
 */
val CoroutineScope.isActive: Boolean (source)
```

Now that the code is cooperative with cancellation, the result is:

```
job: I'm working..
job: I'm working..
job: I'm working..
main: I'm going to cancel this job
main: Done
```

Using `isActive` is simply reading a Boolean value. Determining whether the job should be stopped, and both the setup and execution of that logic, is your r[.keep-together] esponsibility.

In lieu of `isActive`, `ensureActive` can be used. The difference between `isActive` and `ensureActive` is that the latter immediately throws a `CancellationException` if the job is no longer active.

So `ensureActive` is a drop-in replacement of the following code:

```
if (!isActive) {
    throw CancellationException()
}
```

Similarly to `Thread.yield()`, there is a third possibility: `yield()`, which is a suspending function. In addition to checking the cancellation status of the job, the underlying thread is released and is made available for other coroutines. This is especially useful when performing CPU-intensive computations inside a coroutine using `Dispatchers.Default` (or similar). Placing `yield()` at strategic places, you can avoid exhausting the thread pool. In other words, you probably don't want a coroutine to be too selfish, and keep a core busy with specific contextual responsibilities for an extended period of time, if those resources could be better served in another process. To be more cooperative, a greedy CPU-bound coroutine should yield() from time to time, giving other coroutines the opportunity to run.

Those ways of interrupting a coroutine are perfect when the cancellation is happening inside your code. What if you just delegated some work to a third-party library, like an HTTP client?

Cancelling a Task Delegated to a Third-Party Library

OkHttp is a widely deployed HTTP client on Android. If you're not familiar with this library, the following is a snippet taken from the official documentation, to perform an synchronous GET:

```
fun run() {
    val request = Request.Builder()
        .url("https://publicobject.com/helloworld.txt")
        .build()

    client.newCall(request).execute().use { response ->
        if (!response.isSuccessful)
            throw IOException("Unexpected code $response")

        for ((name, value) in response.headers) {
            println("$name: $value")
        }

        println(response.body?.string())
    }
}
```

This example is pretty straightforward. client.newCall(request) returns an instance of Call. You enqueue an instance of Callback while your code proceeds unfazed. Is this cancellable? Yes. A Call can be manually cancelled using call.cancel().

When using coroutines, the preceding example is the kind of code you might write inside a coroutine. It would be ideal if this cancellation was done automatically upon cancellation of the coroutine inside of which the HTTP request is done. Otherwise, the following shows what you would have to write:

```
if (!isActive) {
    call.cancel()
    return
}
```

The obvious caveat is that it pollutes your code—not to mention that you could forget to add this check, or have it at the wrong place. There must be a better solution to this.

Thankfully, the coroutine framework comes with functions specifically designed to turn a function that expects a callback into a suspending function. They come in several flavors including `suspendCancellableCoroutine`. The latter is designed to craft a suspending function which is *cooperative with cancellation*.

The following code shows how to create a suspending function as an extension function of `Call`, which is cancellable and suspends until you get the response of your HTTP request, or an exception occurs:

```
suspend fun Call.await() = suspendCancellableCoroutine<ResponseBody?> {
    continuation ->

    continuation.invokeOnCancellation {
        cancel()
    }

    enqueue(object : Callback {
        override fun onResponse(call: Call, response: Response) {
            continuation.resume(response.body)
        }

        override fun onFailure(call: Call, e: IOException) {
            continuation.resumeWithException(e)
        }
    })
}
```

If you've never seen code like this, it's natural to be afraid of its off-putting complexity. The great news is that this function is fully generic—it only needs to be written once. You can have it inside a "util" package of your project if you want, or in your parallelism package; or just remember the basics and use some version of it when performing conversions like that.

Before showing the benefits of such a utility method, we owe you a detailed explanation.

In Chapter 7, we explained how the Kotlin compiler generates a `Continuation` instance for each suspending function. The `suspendCancellableCoroutine` function gives you the opportunity to use this instance of `Continuation`. It accepts a lambda with `CancellableContinuation` as receiver, as shown in the following code:

```
public suspend inline fun <T> suspendCancellableCoroutine(
    crossinline block: (CancellableContinuation<T>) -> Unit
): T
```

A `CancellableContinuation` is a `Continuation` that is cancellable. We can register a callback that will be invoked upon cancellation, using `invokeOnCancellation { .. }`. In this case, all we want is to cancel the `Call`. Since we're inside an extension function of `Call`, we add the following code:

```
continuation.invokeOnCancellation {
    cancel()   // Call.cancel()
}
```

After we've specified what should happen upon cancellation of the suspending function, we perform the actual HTTP request by invoking `Call.enqueue()`, giving a `Callback` instance. A suspending function "resumes" or "stops suspending" when the corresponding `Continuation` is resumed, with either `resume` or `resumeWithException`.

When you get the result of your HTTP request, either `onResponse` or `onFailure` will be called on the `Callback` instance you provided. If `onResponse` is called, this is the "happy path." You got a response and you should now resume the continuation with a result of your choice. As shown in Figure 8-5, we chose the body of the HTTP response. Meanwhile, on the "sad path," `onFailure` is called, and `OkHttp API` gives you an instance of an `IOException`.

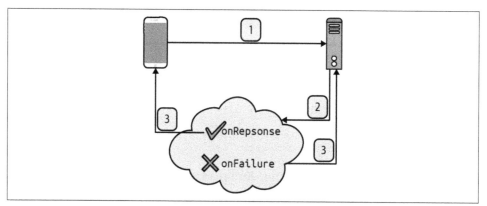

Figure 8-5. (1) First, a device will send an HTTP request to the server. (2) The type of the response being returned will determine what happens next. (3) If the request is a success, then onResponse is called. Otherwise, onFailure is executed.

It is important to resume the continuation with this exception, using `resumeWithException`. This way, the coroutine framework knows about the failure of this suspending function and will propagate this event all the way up the coroutine hierarchy.

Now, for the best part: a showcase of how to use it inside a coroutine, as shown in the following:

```
fun main() = runBlocking {
    val job = launch {                                      ❶
        val response = performHttpRequest()                 ❷
        println("Got response ${response?.string()}")
    }
    delay(200)                                              ❸
    job.cancelAndJoin()                                     ❹
    println("Done")
}

val okHttpClient = OkHttpClient()
val request = Request.Builder().url(
    "http://publicobject.com/helloworld.txt"
).build()

suspend fun performHttpRequest(): ResponseBody? {
    return withContext(Dispatchers.IO) {
        val call = okHttpClient.newCall(request)
        call.await()
    }
}
```

❶ We start off by launching a coroutine with `launch`.

❷ Inside the coroutine returned by `launch`, we invoke a suspending function `performHttpRequest`, which uses `Dispatchers.IO`. This suspending function creates a new `Call` instance and then invokes our suspending `await()` on it. At this point, an HTTP request is performed.

❸ Concurrently, and while step 2 is done on some thread of `Dispatchers.IO`, our main thread proceeds execution of the main method, and immediately encounters `delay(200)`. The coroutine running on the main thread is suspended for 200 ms.

❹ After 200 ms have passed, we invoke `job.cancelAndJoin()`, which is a convenience method for `job.cancel()`, then `job.join()`. Consequently, if the HTTP request takes longer than 200 ms, the coroutine started by `launch` is still in the `Active` state. The suspending `performHttpRequest` hasn't returned yet. Calling `job.cancel()` cancels the coroutine. Thanks to structured concurrency, the coroutine knows about all of its children. The cancellation is propagated all the way down the hierarchy. The `Continuation` of `performHttpRequest` gets cancelled, and so does the HTTP request. If the HTTP request takes less than 200 ms, `job.cancelAndJoin()` has no effect.

No matter how deep in the coroutine hierarchy the HTTP request is performed, if our predefined `Call.await()` is used, the cancellation of the `Call` is triggered if a parent coroutine is cancelled.

Coroutines That Are Cooperative with Cancellation

You've just seen the various techniques to make a coroutine cancellable. Actually, the coroutine framework has a convention: a well-behaved cancellable coroutine throws a `CancellationException` when it's cancelled. Why? Let's look at this suspending function in the following code:

```
suspend fun wasteCpu() = withContext(Dispatchers.Default) {
    var nextPrintTime = System.currentTimeMillis()
    while (isActive) {
        if (System.currentTimeMillis() >= nextPrintTime) {
            println("job: I'm working..")
            nextPrintTime += 500
        }
    }
}
```

It is indeed cancellable thanks to the `isActive` check. Imagine that you need to do some cleanup when this function is cancelled. You know when this function is cancelled when `isActive == false`, so you can add a cleanup block at the end, as shown in the following:

```
suspend fun wasteCpu() = withContext(Dispatchers.Default) {
    var nextPrintTime = System.currentTimeMillis()
    while (isActive) {
        if (System.currentTimeMillis() >= nextPrintTime) {
            println("job: I'm working..")
            nextPrintTime += 500
        }
    }

    // cleanup
    if (!isActive) { .. }
}
```

Sometimes you'll need to have the cleanup logic outside the cancelled function; for example, when this function comes from an external dependency. So you need to find a way to notify the call stack that this function is cancelled. Exceptions are perfect for this. This is why the coroutine framework follows this convention of throwing a `CancellationException`. Actually, *all* suspending functions from the *kotlinx.coroutines* package are cancellable and throw `CancellationException` when cancelled. `withContext` is one of them, so you could react to `wasteCpu` cancellation higher in the call stack, as shown in the following code:

```
fun main() = runBlocking {
    val job = launch {
        try {
            wasteCpu()
        } catch (e: CancellationException) {
            // handle cancellation
        }
    }
    delay(200)
    job.cancelAndJoin()
    println("Done")
}
```

If you run this code, you'll find that a `CancellationException` is caught. Even though we never explicitly threw a `CancellationException` from inside `wasteCpu()`, `withContext` did it for us.

By throwing `CancellationException` only in case of cancellation, the coroutine framework is able to differentiate a simple cancellation from a failure of a coroutine. In the latter case, an exception will be raised that isn't a subtype of `CancellationException`.

If you wish to investigate coroutine cancellation, you can *name* your coroutines and enable debugging of coroutines inside the IDE by adding the VM option `-Dkotlinx.coroutines.debug`. To name a coroutine, simply add a `CoroutineName` context element like so: `val job = launch(CoroutineName("wasteCpu")) {..}`. This way, when catching a `CancellationException`, the stacktrace is much more explicit and begins with the following line:

```
kotlinx.coroutines.JobCancellationException:
StandaloneCoroutine was cancelled; job="waste-
Cpu#2":StandaloneCoroutine{Cancelling}@53bd815b
```

In the previous example, if you swap `wasteCpu()` with `performHttpRequest()`—the suspending function we made earlier with `suspendCancellableCoroutine`—you will also find that a `CancellationException` is caught. So a suspending function made with `suspendCancellableCoroutine` also throws a `CancellationException` when cancelled.

delay Is Cancellable

Remember `delay()`? Its signature is shown in the following code:

```
public suspend fun delay(timeMillis: Long) {
    if (timeMillis <= 0) return // don't delay
    return suspendCancellableCoroutine sc@ { .. }
}
```

`suspendCancellableCoroutine` again! So this means that anywhere you use `delay`, you're giving a coroutine or suspending function the opportunity to cancel. Building on this, we could rewrite `wasteCpu()` as in the following:

```
private suspend fun wasteCpu() = withContext(Dispatchers.Default) {
    var nextPrintTime = System.currentTimeMillis()
    while (true) {               ❶
        delay(10)                ❷
        if (System.currentTimeMillis() >= nextPrintTime) {
            println("job: I'm working..")
            nextPrintTime += 500
        }
    }
}
```

Notice that:

❶ We removed the `isActive` check.

❷ Then we added a simple `delay`, with a small enough sleep time (so the behavior is similar to the previous implementation).

This new version of `wasCpu` turns out to be cancellable just like the original, and throws `CancellationException` when cancelled. This is because this suspending function spends most of its time in the `delay` function.

To summarize this section, you should strive to make your suspending functions cancellable. A suspending function can be made of several suspending functions. All of them should be cancellable. For example, if you need to perform a CPU-heavy computation, then you should use `yield()` or `ensureActive()` at strategic places. For example:

```
suspend fun compute() = withContext(Dispatch
ers.Default) {
    blockingCall()  // a regular blocking call,
hopefully not blocking too long
    yield()  // give the opportunity to cancel
    anotherBlockingCall()   // because why not
}
```

Handling Cancellation

In the previous section, you learned that it is possible to react to cancellation using a try/catch statement. However, imagine that inside the code handling the cancellation, you need to call some other suspending functions. You could be tempted to implement the strategy shown in the following code:

```
launch {
    try {
        suspendCall()
    } catch (e: CancellationException) {
        // handle cancellation
        anotherSuspendCall()
    }
}
```

Sadly, the preceding code doesn't compile. Why? Because *a cancelled coroutine isn't allowed to suspend*. This is another rule from the coroutine framework. The solution is to use `withContext(NonCancellable)`, as shown in the following code:

```
launch {
    try {
        suspendCall()
    } catch (e: CancellationException) {
        // handle cancellation
        withContext(NonCancellable) {
            anotherSuspendCall()
        }
    }
}
```

NonCancellable is specifically designed for withContext to make sure the supplied block of code won't be cancelled.[8]

Causes of Cancellation

As we've seen before, there are two kinds of cancellation: *by design* and *by failure*. Initially, we said that a failure is encountered when an exception is thrown. It was a bit of an overstatement. You've just seen that, when voluntarily cancelling a coroutine, a CancellationException is thrown. This is in fact what distinguishes the two kinds of cancellation.

When cancelling a coroutine Job.cancel (by design), the coroutine terminates without affecting its parent. If the parent also has other child coroutines, they also aren't affected by this cancellation. The following code illustrates this:

```
fun main() = runBlocking {
    val job = launch {
        val child1 = launch {
            delay(Long.MAX_VALUE)
        }
        val child2 = launch {
            child1.join()
            println("Child 1 is cancelled")

            delay(100)
            println("Child 2 is still alive!")
        }

        println("Cancelling child 1..")
        child1.cancel()
        child2.join()
        println("Parent is not cancelled")
    }
    job.join()
}
```

The output of this program is:

```
Cancelling child 1..
Child 1 is cancelled
Child 2 is still alive!
Parent is not cancelled
```

---

8. NonCancellable is actually a special implementation of Job which is always in Active state. So suspending functions that use ensureActive() under this context are never cancelled.

---

child1 delays forever while child2 waits for child1 to proceed. The parent quickly cancels child1, and we can see that child1 is indeed cancelled since child2 continues its execution. Finally, the output "Parent is not cancelled" is proof that the parent wasn't affected by this cancellation (nor was child2, by the way).

On the other hand, in the case of a failure (if an exception different from CancellationException was thrown), the default behavior is that the parent gets cancelled with that exception. If the parent also has other child coroutines, they are also cancelled. Let's try to illustrate this. Spoiler alert—don't do what we show in the following:

```
fun main() = runBlocking {
    val scope = CoroutineScope(coroutineContext + Job())    ❶

    val job = scope.launch {                                ❷
        launch {
            try {
                delay(Long.MAX_VALUE)                       ❸
            } finally {
                println("Child 1 was cancelled")
            }
        }

        launch {
            delay(1000)                                     ❹
            throw IOException()
        }
    }
    job.join()                                              ❺
}
```

What we're trying to create is a circumstance in which a child fails after some time, and we want to check that it causes the parent to fail. Then we need to confirm that all other child coroutines of that parent should be cancelled too, assuming that's the cancellation policy we passed.

At first glance, this code looks OK:

❶ We're creating the parent scope.

❷ We're starting a new coroutine inside this scope.

❸ The first child waits indefinitely. If this child gets cancelled, it should print "Child 1 was cancelled" since a CancellationException would have been thrown from the delay(Long.MAX_VALUE).

❹ Another child throws an IOException after a delay of 1 second.

❺ Wait for the coroutine started in step 2. If you don't do this, the execution of runBlocking terminates and the program stops.

Running this program, you indeed see "Child 1 was cancelled," though the program crashes right after with an uncaught IOException. Even if you surround job.join() with a try/catch block, you'll still get the crash.

What we're missing here is the origination of the exception. It was thrown from inside a launch, which propagates exceptions upward through the coroutine hierarchy until it reaches the parent scope. This behavior cannot be overridden. Once that scope sees the exception, it cancels itself and all its children, then propagates the exception to its parent, which is the scope of runBlocking.

It's important to realize that trying to catch the exception isn't going to change the fact that the root coroutine of runBlocking is going to be cancelled with that exception.

In some cases, you might consider this as an acceptable scenario: any unhandled exception leads to a program crash. However, in other scenarios you might prefer to prevent the failure of scope to propagate to the main coroutine. To this purpose, you need to register a CoroutineExceptionHandler (CEH):

```
fun main() = runBlocking {
    val ceh = CoroutineExceptionHandler { _, exception ->
        println("Caught original $exception")
    }
    val scope = CoroutineScope(coroutineContext + ceh + Job())

    val job = scope.launch {
        // same as in the previous code sample
    }
}
```

A CoroutineExceptionHandler is conceptually very similar to Thread.UncaughtExceptionHandler—except it's intended for coroutines. It's a Context element, which should be added to the context of a scope or a coroutine. The scope should create its own Job instance, as a CEH only takes effect when installed at the top of a coroutine hierarchy. In the preceding example, we added the CEH to the context of the scope. We could very well have added it to the context of the first launch, like so:

```
fun main() = runBlocking {
    val ceh = CoroutineExceptionHandler { _, exception ->
        println("Caught original $exception")
    }

    // The CEH can also be part of the scope
    val scope = CoroutineScope(coroutineContext + Job())

    val job = scope.launch(ceh) {
        // same as in the previous code sample
    }
}
```

Running this sample with the exception handler, the output of the program now is:

```
Child 1 was cancelled
Caught original java.io.IOException
```

The program no longer crashes. From inside the CEH implementation, you could retry the previously failed operations.

This example demonstrates that *by default*, the failure of a coroutine causes its parent to cancel itself along with all the other children of that parent. What if this behavior doesn't match your application design? Sometimes the failure of a coroutine is acceptable and doesn't require the cancellation of all other coroutines started inside the same scope. This is called *supervision* in the coroutine framework.

Supervision

Consider the real-world example of loading a fragment's layout. Each child View might require some background processing to be fully constructed. Assuming you're using a scope which defaults to the main thread, and child coroutines for the background tasks, the failure of one of those tasks shouldn't cause the failure of the parent scope. Otherwise, the whole fragment would become unresponsive to the user.

To implement this cancellation strategy, you can use SupervisorJob, which is a Job for which the failure or cancellation of a child doesn't affect other children; *nor* does it affect the scope itself. A SupervisorJob is typically used as a drop-in replacement for Job when building a CoroutineScope. The resulting scope is then called a "supervisor scope." Such a scope propagates cancellation downward only, as shown in the following code:

```
fun main() = runBlocking {
    val ceh = CoroutineExceptionHandler { _, e -> println("Handled $e") }
    val supervisor = SupervisorJob()
    val scope = CoroutineScope(coroutineContext + ceh + supervisor)
    with(scope) {
        val firstChild = launch {
            println("First child is failing")
            throw AssertionError("First child is cancelled")
        }

        val secondChild = launch {
            firstChild.join()

            delay(10) // playing nice with hypothetical cancellation
            println("First child is cancelled: ${firstChild.isCancelled},
but second one is still active")
        }

        // wait until the second child completes
        secondChild.join()
    }
}
```

The output of this sample is:

```
First child is failing
Handled java.lang.AssertionError: First child is cancelled
First child is cancelled: true, but second one is still active
```

Notice that we've installed a CEH in the context of the scope. Why? The first child throws an exception that is never caught. Even if a supervisor scope isn't affected by the failure of a child, it still propagates unhandled exceptions—which, as you know, might cause the program to crash. This is precisely the purpose of a CEH: to handle uncaught exceptions. Interestingly enough, the CEH could also have been installed into the context of the first launch, with the same result, as shown in the following:

```
fun main() = runBlocking {
    val ceh = CoroutineExceptionHandler { _, e -> println("Handled $e") }
    val supervisor = SupervisorJob()
    val scope = CoroutineScope(coroutineContext + supervisor)
    with(scope) {
        val firstChild = launch(ceh) {
            println("First child is failing")
            throw AssertionError("First child is cancelled")
        }

        val secondChild = launch {
```

```
            firstChild.join()

            delay(10)
            println("First child is cancelled: ${firstChild.isCancelled},
    but second one is still active")
        }

        // wait until the second child completes
        secondChild.join()
    }
}
```

A CEH is intended to be installed at the top of a coroutine hierarchy, as this is the place where uncaught exceptions can be handled.

In this example, the CEH is installed on a direct child of the coroutine scope. You can install it on a nested coroutine, as in the following:

```
val firstChild = launch {
    println("First child is failing")
    launch(ceh) {
        throw AssertionError("First child is cancelled")
    }
}
```

In this case, the CEH isn't accounted for, and the program might crash.

supervisorScope Builder

Similarly to coroutineScope builder—which inherits the current context and creates a new Job—supervisorScope creates a SupervisorJob. Just like coroutineScope, it waits for all children to complete. One crucial difference with coroutineScope is that it only propagates cancellation downward, and cancels all children only if it has failed itself. Another difference with coroutineScope is how exceptions are handled. We'll delve into that in the next section.

Parallel Decomposition

Imagine that a suspending function has to run multiple tasks in parallel before returning its result. Take, for example, the suspending function weatherForHike from our hiking app at the beginning of this chapter. Fetching the weather could involve multiple APIs, depending on the nature of the data. Wind data and temperature could be fetched separately, from separate data sources.

Assuming you have suspending functions `fetchWind` and `fetchTemperatures`, you could implement `weatherForHike` as follows:

```
private suspend fun weatherForHike(hike: Hike): Weather =
        withContext(Dispatchers.IO) {
    val deferredWind = async { fetchWind(hike) }
    val deferredTemp = async { fetchTemperatures(hike) }
    val wind = deferredWind.await()
    val temperatures = deferredTemp.await()
    Weather(wind, temperatures) // assuming Weather can be built that way
}
```

`async` can also be used in this example because `withContext` provides a `Coroutine Scope`—its last argument is a suspending lambda with `CoroutineScope` as the receiver. Without `withContext`, this sample wouldn't compile, because there wouldn't be any scope provided for `async`.

`withContext` is particularly useful when you need to change the dispatcher inside your suspending function. What if you don't need to change your dispatcher? The suspending `weatherForHike` could very well be called from a coroutine which is already dispatched to the IO dispatcher. Then, using `withContext(Dispatchers.IO)` would be redundant. In such situations, you could use `coroutineScope` instead of or in conjunction with `withContext`. It's a `CoroutineScope` builder, which you use as in the following:

```
private suspend fun weatherForHike(hike: Hike): Weather = coroutineScope {
    // Wind and temperature fetch are performed concurrently
    val deferredWind = async(Dispatchers.IO) {
        fetchWind(hike)
    }
    val deferredTemp = async(Dispatchers.IO) {
        fetchTemperatures(hike)
    }
    val wind = deferredWind.await()
    val temperatures = deferredTemp.await()
    Weather(wind, temperatures) // assuming Weather can be built that way
}
```

Here, `coroutineScope` replaces `withContext`. What does this `coroutineScope` do? First of all, have a look at its signature:

```
public suspend fun <R> coroutineScope(block: suspend CoroutineScope.() ->
R): R
```

From the official documentation, this function creates a CoroutineScope and calls the specified suspend block with this scope. The provided scope inherits its coroutineContext from the outer scope, but overrides the context's Job.

This function is designed for *parallel decomposition* of work. When any child coroutine in this scope fails, this scope fails and all the rest of the children are cancelled (for a different behavior, use supervisorScope). This function returns as soon as the given block and all its child coroutines are completed.

Automatic Cancellation

Applied to our example, if fetchWind fails, the scope provided by coroutineScope fails and fetchTemperatures is subsequently cancelled. If fetchTemperatures involves allocating heavy objects, you can see the benefit of the cancellation.

coroutineScope really shines when you need to *perform several tasks concurrently*.

Exception Handling

Exception handling is an important part of your application design. Sometimes you will just catch exceptions immediately after they're raised, while other times you'll let them bubble up the hierarchy until the dedicated component handles it. To that extent, the language construct try/catch is probably what you've used so far. However, in the coroutine framework, there's a catch (pun intended). We could have started this chapter with it, but we needed to introduce you to *supervision* and CoroutineExceptionHandler first.

Unhandled Versus Exposed Exceptions

When it comes to exception propagation, uncaught exceptions can be treated by the coroutine machinery as on of the following:

Unhandled to the client code
    Unhandled exceptions can only be handled by a CoroutineExceptionHandler.

Exposed to the client code
    Exposed exceptions are the ones the client code can handle using try/catch.

In this matter, we can distinguish two categories of coroutine builders based on how they treat uncaught exceptions:

- Unhandled (launch is one of them)
- Exposed (async is one of them)

First of all, do note that we're talking about uncaught exceptions. If you catch an exception *before* it is handled by a coroutine builder, everything works as usual—you catch it, so the coroutine machinery isn't aware of it. The following shows an example with `launch` and `try`/`catch`:

```
scope.launch {
    try {
        regularFunctionWhichCanThrowException()
    } catch (e: Exception) {
        // handle exception
    }
}
```

This example works as you would expect, *if* `regularFunctionWhichCanThrowExcep tion` is, as its name suggests, a regular function which does not involve, directly or indirectly, other coroutine builders—in which case, special rules can apply (as we'll see later in this chapter).

The same idea applies to the `async` builder, as shown in the following:

```
fun main() = runBlocking {

    val itemCntDeferred = async {
        try {
            getItemCount()
        } catch (e: Exception) {
            // Something went wrong. Suppose you don't care and consider it
should return 0.
            0
        }
    }

    val count = itemCntDeferred.await()
    println("Item count: $count")
}

fun getItemCount(): Int {
    throw Exception()
    1
}
```

The output of this program is, as you can easily guess:

```
Item count: 0
```

Alternatively, instead of try/catch, you could use runCatching. It allows for a nicer syntax if you consider that the happy path is when no exception is thrown:

```
scope.launch {
    val result = runCatching {
        regularFunctionWhichCanThrowException()
    }

    if (result.isSuccess) {
        // no exception was thrown
    } else {
        // exception was thrown
    }
}
```

Under the hood, runCatching is nothing but a try/catch, returning a Result object, which offers some sugar methods like getOrNull() and exceptionOrNull(), as in the following:

```
/**
 * Calls the specified function [block] with `this` value as its receiver
 * and returns its encapsulated result if invocation was successful,
 * catching and encapsulating any thrown exception as a failure.
 */
public inline fun <T, R> T.runCatching(block: T.() -> R): Result<R> {
    return try {
        Result.success(block())
    } catch (e: Throwable) {
        Result.failure(e)
    }
}
```

Some extension functions are defined on the Result and available out of the box, like getOrDefault which returns the encapsulated value of the Result instance if Result.isSuccess is true or a provided default value otherwise.

Exposed Exceptions

As we stated before, you can catch *exposed* exceptions using built-in language support: try/catch. The following code shows where we have created our own scope inside of which two concurrent tasks, task1 and task2, are started in a supervisor Scope. task2 immediately fails:

```kotlin
fun main() = runBlocking {

    val scope = CoroutineScope(Job())

    val job = scope.launch {
        supervisorScope {
            val task1 = launch {
                // simulate a background task
                delay(1000)
                println("Done background task")
            }

            val task2 = async {
                // try to fetch some count, but it fails
                throw Exception()
                1
            }

            try {
                task2.await()
            } catch (e: Exception) {
                println("Caught exception $e")
            }
            task1.join()
        }
    }

    job.join()
    println("Program ends")
}
```

The output of this program is:

```
Caught exception java.lang.Exception
Done background task
Program ends
```

This example demonstrates that inside a supervisorScope, async *exposes* uncaught exceptions in the await call. If you don't surround the await call with a try/catch block, then the scope of supervisorScope fails and cancels task1, then *exposes* to its parent the exception that caused its failure. So this means that even when using a supervisorScope, unhandled exceptions in a scope lead to the cancellation of the entire coroutine hierarchy beneath that scope—and the exception is propagated up. By handling the exception the way we did in this example, task 2 fails while task 1 isn't affected.

Interestingly enough, if you don't invoke `task2.await()`, the program executes as if no exception was ever—thrown `task2` silently fails.

Now we'll use the exact same example, but with a `coroutineScope` instead of `supervisorScope`:

```
fun main() = runBlocking {

    val scope = CoroutineScope(Job())

    val job = scope.launch {
        coroutineScope {
            val task1 = launch {
                delay(1000)
                println("Done background task")
            }

            val task2 = async {
                throw Exception()
                1
            }

            try {
                task2.await()
            } catch (e: Exception) {
                println("Caught exception $e")
            }
            task1.join()
        }
    }

    job.join()
    println("Program ends")
}
```

The output of this program is:

```
Caught exception java.lang.Exception
```

Then the program crashes on Android due to `java.lang.Exception`—we'll explain this shortly.

From this you can learn that inside a `coroutineScope`, `async` *exposes* uncaught exceptions but also notifies its parent. If you don't call `task2.await()`, the program still crashes because `coroutineScope` fails and *exposes* to its parent the exception that caused its failure. Then, `scope.launch` treats this exception as *unhandled*.

Unhandled Exceptions

The coroutine framework treats unhandled exceptions in a specific way: it tries to use a CEH if the coroutine context has one. If not, it delegates to the *global handler*. This handler calls a customizable set of CEH *and* calls the standard mechanism of unhandled exceptions: `Thread.uncaughtExceptionHandler`. By default on Android, the previously mentioned set of handlers is only made of a single CEH which prints the stacktrace of the unhandled exception. However, it is possible to register a custom handler which will be called in addition to the one that prints the stacktrace. So you should remember that if you don't handle an exception, the `Thread.uncaughtExcep tionHandler` *will* be invoked.

The default `UncaughtExceptionHandler` on Android makes your application crash, while on the JVM,[9] the default handler prints the stacktrace to the console. Consequently, if you execute this program not on Android but on the JVM, the output is:[10]

```
Caught exception java.lang.Exception
(stacktrace of java.lang.Exception)
Program ends
```

Back to Android. How could you handle this exception? Since `coroutineScope` *exposes* exceptions, you could wrap `coroutineScope` inside a `try`/`catch` statement. Alternatively, if you don't handle it correctly, the preceding `coroutineScope`, `scope.launch`, treats this exception as unhandled. Then your last chance to handle this exception is to register a CEH. There are at least two reasons you would do that: first, to stop the exception's propagation and avoid a program crash; and second, to notify your crash analytics and rethrow the exception—potentially making the application crash. In any case, we're not advocating for silently catching exceptions. If you do want to use CEH, there are a couple of things you should know. A CEH only works when registered to:

- `launch` (not `async`) when `launch` is a root coroutine builder[11]
- A scope
- `supervisorScope`s direct child

---

9. By JVM, we mean on a desktop application, or on the server side.

10. "Program ends" is printed because the *unhandled* exception makes scope fail, not the scope from `runBlocking`.

11. A root coroutine builder is a scope's direct child. In the previous example, at the line `val job = scope.launch {..}`, `launch` is a root coroutine builder.

In our example, the CEH should be registered either on `scope.launch` or on the scope itself. The following code shows this on the root coroutine:

```kotlin
fun main() = runBlocking {

    val ceh = CoroutineExceptionHandler { _, t ->
        println("CEH handle $t")
    }

    val scope = CoroutineScope(Job())

    val job = scope.launch(ceh) {
        coroutineScope {
            val task1 = launch {
                delay(1000)
                println("Done background task")
            }

            val task2 = async {
                throw Exception()
                1
            }

            task1.join()
        }
    }

    job.join()
    println("Program ends")
}
```

The output of this program is:

```
Caught exception java.lang.Exception
CEH handle java.lang.Exception
Program ends
```

Here is the same example, this time with the CEH registered on the scope:

```kotlin
fun main() = runBlocking {

    val ceh = CoroutineExceptionHandler { _, t ->
        println("CEH handle $t")
    }

    val scope = CoroutineScope(Job() + ceh)

    val job = scope.launch {
```

```
        // same as previous example
    }
}
```

Finally, we illustrate the use of a CEH on a supervisorScope direct child:

```
fun main() = runBlocking {

    val ceh = CoroutineExceptionHandler { _, t ->
        println("CEH handle $t")
    }

    val scope = CoroutineScope(Job())

    val job = scope.launch {
        supervisorScope {
            val task1 = launch {
                // simulate a background task
                delay(1000)
                println("Done background task")
            }

            val task2 = launch(ceh) {
                // try to fetch some count, but it fails
                throw Exception()
            }

            task1.join()
            task2.join()
        }
    }

    job.join()
    println("Program ends")
}
```

Notice that the coroutine builder on which the CEH is registered is a launch. It wouldn't have been taken into account with an async, which *exposes* uncaught exceptions, which can be handled with try/catch.

Summary

- When a function might not return immediately, it's a good candidate to be implemented as a suspending function. However, the `suspend` modifier doesn't magically turn a blocking call into a nonblocking one. Use `withContext` along with the appropriate `Dispatcher`, and/or call other suspending functions.

- A coroutine can be deliberately cancelled using `Job.cancel()` for `launch`, or `Deferred.cancel()` for `async`. If you need to call some suspending functions inside your cleanup code, make sure you wrap your cleanup logic inside a `with Context(NonCancellable) { .. }` block. The cancelled coroutine will remain in the cancelling state until the cleanup exits. After the cleanup is done, the aforementioned coroutine goes to the cancelled state.

- A coroutine always waits for its children to complete before completing itself. So cancelling a coroutine also cancels all of its children.

- Your coroutines should be cooperative with cancellation. All suspending functions from the *kotlinx.coroutines* package are cancellable. This notably includes `withContext`. If you're implementing your own suspending function, make sure it is cancellable by checking `isActive` or calling `ensureActive()` or `yield()` at appropriate steps.

- There are two categories of coroutine scope: the scopes using `Job` and the ones using `SupervisorJob` (also called supervisor scopes). They differ in how cancellation is performed and in exception handling. If the failure of a child should also cancel other children, use a regular scope. Otherwise, use a supervisor scope.

- `launch` and `async` differ in how they treat uncaught exceptions. `async` *exposes* exceptions, which can be caught by wrapping the `await` call in a `try/catch`. On the other hand, `launch` treats uncaught exceptions as unhandled, which can be handled using a CEH.

- A CEH is optional. It should only be used when you really need to do something with unhandled exceptions. Unhandled exceptions typically should make your application crash. Or, at least, recovering from some exceptions might leave your application in an undetermined state. Nevertheless, if you decide to use a CEH, then it should be installed at the top of the coroutine hierarchy—typically into the topmost scope. It can also be installed on a `supervisorScope` direct child.

- If a coroutine fails because of an uncaught exception, it gets cancelled along with all of its children and the exceptions propagate up.

Closing Thoughts

You learned how to write your own suspending functions, and how to use them inside coroutines. Your coroutines live within scopes. In order to implement the desired cancellation policy, you know how to choose between coroutineScope and supervisorScope. The scopes you create are children of other scopes higher in the hierarchy. In Android, those "root" scopes are library-provided—you don't create them yourself. A good example is the viewModelScope available in any ViewModel instance.

Coroutines are a perfect fit for one-time or repetitive tasks. However, we often have to work with asynchronous streams of data. Channels and Flows are designed for that, and will be covered in the next two chapters.

CHAPTER 9

Channels

In the previous chapter, you learned how to create coroutines, cancel them, and deal with exceptions. So you know that if task B requires the result of task A, you can implement them as two suspending functions called sequentially. What if task A produces a stream of values? `async` and suspending functions don't fit this use case. This is what `Channels`[1] are meant for—making coroutines communicate. In this chapter you'll learn in detail what channels are and how to use them.

Using nothing but channels and coroutines, we can design complex asynchronous logic using *communicating sequential processes* (CSP). What is CSP? Kotlin was inspired by several existing programming languages, such as Java, C#, JavaScript, Scala, and Groovy. Notably, Go (the language) inspired coroutines with its "goroutines."

In computer science, CSP is a concurrent programming language which was first described by Tony Hoare in 1978. It has evolved ever since, and the term CSP is now essentially used to describe a programming style. If you're familiar with the Actor model, CSP is quite similar—although there are some differences. If you've never heard of CSP, don't worry—we'll briefly explain the *idea* behind it with practical examples. For now, you can think of CSP as a programming style.

As usual, we'll start with a bit of theory, then implement a real-life problem. In the end, we'll discuss the benefits and trade-offs of CSP, using coroutines.

---

1. We'll sometimes refer to `Channels` as channels in the rest of this chapter.

Channels Overview

Going back to our introductory example, imagine that one task asynchronously produces a list of three Item instances (the producer), and another task acts on each of those items (the consumer). Since the producer doesn't return immediately, you could implement it like the following getItems suspending function:

```
suspend fun getItems(): List<Item> {
    val items = mutableListOf<Item>()
    items.add(makeItem())
    items.add(makeItem())
    items.add(makeItem())
    return items
}

suspend fun makeItem(): Item {
    delay(10) // simulate some asynchronism
    return Item()
}
```

As for the consumer, which consumes each of those items, you could simply implement it like so:

```
fun consumeItems(items: List<Item>) {
    for (item in items) println("Do something with $item")
}
```

Putting it all together:

```
fun main() = runBlocking {
    val items = getItems()
    consumeItems(items)
}
```

As you would expect, "Do something with .." is printed three times. However, in this case, we're most interested in the order of execution. Let's take a closer look at what's really happening, as shown in Figure 9-1.

In Figure 9-1, item consumption only begins after all items have been produced. Producing items might take quite some time, and waiting for all of them to be produced isn't acceptable in some situations. Instead, we could act on each asynchronously produced item, as shown in Figure 9-2.

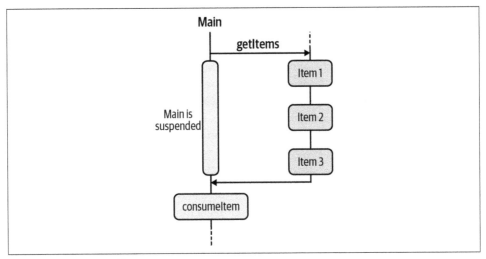

Figure 9-1. Process all at once.

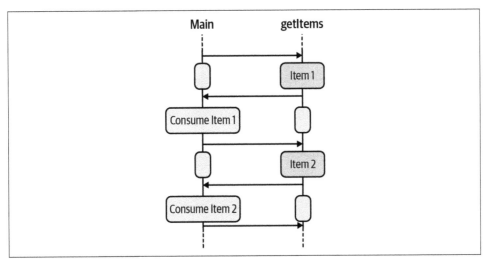

Figure 9-2. Process one after another.

To achieve this, we can't implement getItems as a suspending function like before. A coroutine should act as a producer of Item instances, and send them to the main coroutine. It's a typical producer-consumer problem.

In Chapter 5, we explained how BlockingQueues can be used to implement *work queues*—or, in this case, a data queue. As a reminder, a BlockingQueue has blocking methods put and take to respectively insert and take an object from the queue. When the queue is used as the only means of communication between two threads (a producer and a consumer), it offers the great benefit of avoiding a shared mutable state. Moreover, if the queue is bounded (has a size limit), a too-fast producer will eventually get blocked in a put call if consumers are too slow. This is known as back pressure: a blocked producer gives the consumers the opportunity to catch up, thus releasing the producer.

Using a BlockingQueue as a communication primitive between coroutines wouldn't be a great idea, since a coroutine shouldn't involve blocking calls. Instead, coroutines can suspend. A Channel can be seen just like that: a queue with suspending functions send and receive, as shown in Figure 9-3. A Channel also has nonsuspending counterparts: trySend and tryReceive. These two methods are also nonblocking. trySend tries to immediately add an element to the channel, and returns a wrapper class around the result. That wrapper class, ChannelResult<T>, also indicates the success or the failure of the operation. tryReceive tries to immediately retrieve an element from the channel, and returns a ChannelResult<T> instance.

Figure 9-3. Channel.

Like queues, Channels come in several flavors. We'll cover each of those Channel variants with basic examples.

Rendezvous Channel

"Rendezvous" is a French word that means "appointment" or "a date"—it depends on the context (we don't mean CoroutineContext here). A rendezvous channel does not have any buffer at all. An element is transferred from sender to receiver only when send and receive invocations meet in time (rendezvous), so send suspends until another coroutine invokes receive, and receive suspends until another coroutine invokes send.

As another way to put it, a rendezvous channel involves a back-and-forth communication between producers (coroutines calling send) and consumers (coroutines calling receive). There can't be two consecutive sends without a receive in the middle.

By default, when you create a channel using Channel<T>(), you get a rendezvous channel.

We can use a rendezvous channel to correctly implement our previous example:

```kotlin
fun main() = runBlocking {
    val channel = Channel<Item>()
    launch {                                    ❶
        channel.send(Item(1))                   ❸
        channel.send(Item(2))                   ❹
        println("Done sending")
    }

    println(channel.receive())                  ❷
    println(channel.receive())                  ❺

    println("Done!")
}

data class Item(val number: Int)
```

The output of this program is:

```
Item(number=1)
Item(number=2)
Done!
Done sending
```

In this example, the main coroutine starts a child coroutine with `launch`, at ❶, then reaches ❷ and suspends until some coroutine sends an `Item` instance in the channel. Shortly after, the child coroutine sends the first item at ❸, then reaches and suspends at the second send call at ❹ until some coroutine is ready to receive an item. Subsequently, the main coroutine (which is suspended at ❷) is resumed and receives the first item from the channel and prints it. Then the main coroutine reaches ❺ and immediately receives the second item since the child coroutine was already suspended in a send call. Immediately after, the child coroutine continues its execution (prints "Done sending").

Iterating over a Channel

A `Channel` can be iterated over, using a regular `for` loop. Note that since channels aren't regular collections,[2] you can't use `forEach` or other similar functions from the Kotlin Standard Library. Here, channel iteration is a specific language-level feature that can only be done using the `for`-loop syntax:

---

2. Specifically, `Channel` doesn't implement `Iterable`.

```
for (x in channel) {
    // do something with x every time some coroutine sends an element in
    // the channel
}
```

Implicitly, x is equal to `channel.receive()` at each iteration. Consequently, a coroutine iterating over a channel could do so indefinitely, unless it contains conditional logic to break the loop. Fortunately, there's a standard mechanism to break the loop: closing the channel. Here is an example:

```
fun main() = runBlocking {
    val channel = Channel<Item>()
    launch {
        channel.send(Item(1))
        channel.send(Item(2))
        println("Done sending")
        channel.close()
    }

    for (x in channel) {
        println(x)
    }
    println("Done!")
}
```

This program has similar output, with a small difference:

```
Item(number=1)
Item(number=2)
Done sending
Done!
```

This time, "Done sending" appears before "Done!" This is because the main coroutine only leaves the channel iteration when channel is closed. And that happens when the child coroutine is done sending all elements.

Internally, closing a channel sends a special token into the channel to indicate that no other elements will be sent. As items in the channel are consumed *serially* (one after another), all items sent to the rendezvous channel before the close special token are guaranteed to be sent to the receiver.

Beware—trying to call `receive` from an already-closed channel will throw a `ClosedReceiveChannelException`. However, trying to iterate on such a channel doesn't throw any exception:

```kotlin
fun main() = runBlocking {
    val channel = Channel<Int>()
    channel.close()

    for (x in channel) {
        println(x)
    }
    println("Done!")
}
```

The output is: Done!

Other flavors of Channel

In the previous example, the `Channel` appears to be created using a class constructor. If you look at the source code, you can see that it's actually a public function named with a capital C, to give the illusion that you're using a class constructor:

```kotlin
public fun <E> Channel(capacity: Int = RENDEZVOUS): Channel<E> =
    when (capacity) {
        RENDEZVOUS -> RendezvousChannel()
        UNLIMITED -> LinkedListChannel()
        CONFLATED -> ConflatedChannel()
        BUFFERED -> ArrayChannel(CHANNEL_DEFAULT_CAPACITY)
        else -> ArrayChannel(capacity)
    }
```

You can see that this `Channel` function has a `capacity` parameter that defaults to RENDEZVOUS. For the record, if you step into the RENDEZVOUS declaration, you can see that it's equal to 0. For each `capacity` value there is a corresponding channel implementation. There are four different flavors of channels: rendezvous, *unlimited*, *conflated*, and *buffered*. Don't pay too much attention to the concrete implementations (like RendezvousChannel()), because those classes are internal and may change in the future. On the other hand, the values RENDEZVOUS, UNLIMITED, CONFLATED, and BUFFERED are part of the public API.

We'll cover each of those channel types in the next sections.

Unlimited Channel

An *unlimited* channel has a buffer that is only limited by the amount of available memory. Senders to this channel never suspend, while receivers only suspend when the channel is empty. Coroutines exchanging data via an *unlimited* channel don't need to meet in time.

At this point, you might be thinking that such a channel should have concurrent modification issues when senders and receivers are executed from different threads. After all, coroutines are dispatched on threads, so a channel might very well be used from different threads. Let's check the Channel's robustness ourselves! In the following example, we send Ints from a coroutine dispatched on Dispatchers.Default while another coroutine reads the same channel from the main thread, and if the Channels aren't thread-safe, we will notice:

```
fun main() = runBlocking {
    val channel = Channel<Int>(UNLIMITED)
    val childJob = launch(Dispatchers.Default) {
        println("Child executing from ${Thread.currentThread().name}")
        var i = 0
        while (isActive) {
            channel.send(i++)
        }
        println("Child is done sending")
    }

    println("Parent executing from ${Thread.currentThread().name}")
    for (x in channel) {
        println(x)

        if (x == 1000_000) {
            childJob.cancel()
            break
        }
    }

    println("Done!")
}
```

The output of this program is:

```
Parent executing from main
Child executing from DefaultDispatcher-worker-2
0
1
..
1000000
Done!
Child is done sending
```

You can run this sample as much as you want, and it always completes without concurrent issues. That's because a Channel internally uses a lock-free algorithm.[3]

 Channels are thread-safe. Several threads can concurrently invoke send and receive methods in a thread-safe way.

Conflated Channel

This channel has a buffer of size 1, and only keeps the last sent element. To create a *conflated* channel, you invoke Channel<T>(Channel.CONFLATED). For example:

```
fun main() = runBlocking {
    val channel = Channel<String>(Channel.CONFLATED)

    val job = launch {
        channel.send("one")
        channel.send("two")
    }

    job.join()
    val elem = channel.receive()
    println("Last value was: $elem")
}
```

---

3. If you want to learn how such an algorithm works, we recommend that you read Section 15.4, "NonBlocking Algorithms," in *Java Concurrency in Practice*, by Brian Goetz et al. There is also this interesting YouTube video, Lock-Free Algorithms for Kotlin Coroutines (Part 1) (*https://oreil.ly/WDE1F*) from Roman Elizarov, lead designer of Kotlin coroutines.

The output of this program is:

```
Last value was: two
```

The first sent element is "one." When "two" is sent, it replaces "one" in the channel. We wait until the coroutine-sending elements complete, using job.join(). Then we read the value two from the channel.

Buffered Channel

A *buffered* channel is a Channel with a fixed capacity—an integer greater than 0. Senders to this channel don't suspend unless the buffer is full, and receivers from this channel don't suspend unless the buffer is empty. To create a buffered channel of Int with a buffer of size 2, you would invoke Channel<Int>(2). Here is an example of usage:

```
fun main() = runBlocking<Unit> {
    val channel = Channel<Int>(2)

    launch {
        for (i in 0..4) {
            println("Send $i")
            channel.send(i)
        }
    }

    launch {
        for (i in channel) {
            println("Received $i")
        }
    }
}
```

The output of this program is:

```
Send 0
Send 1
Send 2
Received 0
Received 1
Received 2
Send 3
Send 4
Received 3
Received 4
```

In this example, we've defined a Channel with a fixed capacity of 2. A coroutine attempts to send five integers, while another coroutine consumes elements from the channel. The sender coroutine manages to send 0 and 1 in one go, then attempts to send 3. The println("Send $i") is executed for the value 3 but the sender coroutine gets suspended in the send call. The same reasoning applies for the consumer coroutine: two elements are received consecutively with an additional print before suspending.

Channel Producers

Until now, you've seen that a Channel can be used for both sending *and* receiving elements. Sometimes you might want to be more explicit about how a channel should be used for either sending or receiving. When you're implementing a Channel that is meant to be read only by other coroutines, you can use the produce builder:

```
fun CoroutineScope.produceValues(): ReceiveChannel<String> = produce {
    send("one")
    send("two")
}
```

As you can see, produce returns a ReceiveChannel—which only has methods relevant to receiving operations (receive is among them). An instance of ReceiveChannel cannot be used to send elements.

 Also, we've defined produceValues() as an extension function of CoroutineScope. Calling produceValues will start a new coroutine that sends elements into a channel. There's a convention in Kotlin: every function that starts coroutines should be defined as an extension function of CoroutineScope. If you follow this convention, you can easily distinguish in your code which functions are starting new coroutines from suspending functions.

The main code that makes use of produceValues could be:

```
fun main() = runBlocking {
    val receiveChannel = produceValues()

    for (e in receiveChannel) {
        println(e)
    }
}
```

Conversely, a `SendChannel` only has methods relevant to sending operations. Actually, looking at the source code, a `Channel` is an interface deriving from both `ReceiveChannel` and `SendChannel`:

```
public interface Channel<E> : SendChannel<E>, ReceiveChannel<E> {
    // code removed for brevity
}
```

Here is how you can use a `SendChannel`:

```
fun CoroutineScope.collectImages(imagesOutput: SendChannel<Image>) {
    launch(Dispatchers.IO) {
        val image = readImage()
        imagesOutput.send(image)
    }
}
```

Communicating Sequential Processes

Enough of the theory, let's get started and see how channels can be used to implement a real-life problem. Imagine that your Android application has to display "shapes" in a canvas. Depending on the inputs of the user, your application has to display an arbitrary number of shapes. We're purposely using generic terms—a shape could be a point of interest on a map, an item in a game, anything that may require some background work like API calls, file reads, database queries, etc. In our example, the main thread, which already handles user input, will simulate requests for new shapes to be rendered. You can already foresee that it's a producer-consumer problem: the main thread makes requests, while some background task handles them and returns the results to the main thread.

Our implementation should:

- Be thread-safe
- Reduce the risk of overwhelming the device memory
- Have no thread contention (we won't use locks)

Model and Architecture

A `Shape` is made of a `Location` and some useful `ShapeData`:

```
data class Shape(val location: Location, val data: ShapeData)
data class Location(val x: Int, val y: Int)
class ShapeData
```

Given a `Location`, we need to fetch the corresponding `ShapeData` to build a `Shape`. So in this example, `Location`s are the input, and `Shape`s the output. For brevity, we'll use the words "location" for `Location` and "shape" for `Shape`.

In our implementation, we'll distinguish two main components:

view-model
> This holds most of the application logic related to shapes. As the user interacts with the UI, the view gives the view-model a list of locations.

`shapeCollector`
> This is responsible for fetching shapes given a list of locations.

Figure 9-4 illustrates the bidirectional relationship between the view-model and the shape collector.

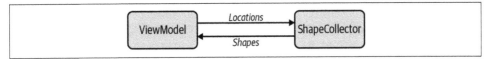

Figure 9-4. High-level architecture.

The `ShapeCollector` follows a simple process:

```
                    fetchData
    Location -------------------> ShapeData
```

As an additional prerequisite, our `ShapeCollector` should maintain an internal "registry" of locations being processed. Upon receiving a location to process, the `Shape Collector` shouldn't attempt to download it if it's already being processed.

A First Implementation

We can start with this first naïve implementation of the ShapeCollector, which is far from being complete, but you'll get the idea:

```
class ShapeCollector {
    private val locationsBeingProcessed = mutableListOf<Location>()

    fun processLocation(location: Location) {
        if (locationsBeingProcessed.add(location)) {
            // fetch data, then send back a Shape instance to
            // the view-model
        }
    }
}
```

If we were programming with threads, we would have several threads sharing an instance of ShapeCollector, executing processLocation concurrently. Using this approach, however, leads to sharing mutable states. In the previous snippet, loca tionsBeingProcessed is one example.

As you learned in Chapter 5, making mistakes using locks is surprisingly easy. Using coroutines, we don't have to share mutable state. How? Using coroutines and channels, we can *share by communicating* instead of *communicate by sharing*.

The key idea is to encapsulate mutable states inside coroutines. In the case of the list of Locations being processed, it can be done with:

```
launch {
    val locationsBeingProcessed = mutableListOf<Location>()      ❶

    for (location in locations) {                                ❷
        // same code from previous figure
    }
}
```

❶ In the preceding example, only the coroutine that started with launch can touch the mutable state, which is locationsBeingProcessed.

❷ However, we now have a problem. How do we provide the locations? We have to somehow provide this iterable to the coroutine. So we'll use a Channel, and use it as input of a function we'll declare. Since we're launching a coroutine inside a function, we declare this function as an extension function of CoroutineScope:

```
private fun CoroutineScope.collectShapes(
    locations: ReceiveChannel<Location>
) = launch {
    // code removed for brevity
}
```

As this coroutine will be receiving Locations from the view-model, we declare the Channel as a ReceiveChannel. By the way, you've seen in the previous section that a Channel can be iterated over, just like a list. So now, we can fetch the corresponding ShapeData for each Location instance received from the channel. As you'll want to do this in parallel, you might be tempted to write something like so:

```
private fun CoroutineScope.collectShapes(
    locations: ReceiveChannel<Location>
) = launch {
    val locationsBeingProcessed = mutableListOf<Location>()

    for (loc in locations) {
        if (!locationsBeingProcessed.contains(loc) {
            launch(Dispatchers.IO) {
                // fetch the corresponding `ShapeData`
            }
        }
    }
}
```

Beware, as there's a catch in this code. You see, for each received location, we start a new coroutine. Potentially, this code might start a lot of coroutines if the locations channel debits a lot of items. For this reason, this situation is also called *unlimited concurrency*. When we introduced coroutines, we said that they are lightweight. It's true, but the work they do might very well consume significant resources. In this case, launch(Dispatchers.IO) in itself has an insignificant overhead, while fetching the ShapeData could require a REST API call on a server with limited bandwidth.

So we'll have to find a way to limit concurrency—we don't want to start an unlimited number of coroutines. When facing this situation with threads, a common practice is to use a thread pool coupled with a work queue (see Chapter 5). Instead of a thread pool, we'll create a *coroutine pool*, which we'll name *worker pool*. Each coroutine from this worker pool will perform the actual fetch of ShapeData for a given location. To communicate with this worker pool, collectShapes should use an additional channel to which it can send locations to the worker pool, as shown in Figure 9-5.

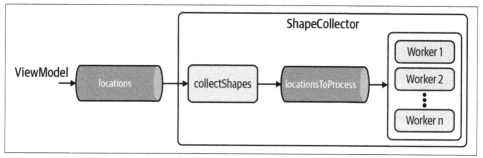

Figure 9-5. Limit concurrency.

 When you use `Channels`, *be careful not to have unlimited concurrency*. Imagine that you have to instantiate a lot of `Bitmap` instances. The underlying memory buffer which stores pixel data takes a nonnegligible amount of space in memory. When working with a lot of images, allocating a fresh instance of `Bitmap` every time you need to create an image causes significant pressure on the system (which has to allocate memory in RAM while the garbage collector cleans up all the previously created instances that aren't referenced anymore). A canonical solution to this problem is `Bitmap` pooling, which is only a particular case of the more general pattern of *object pooling*. Instead of creating a fresh instance of `Bitmap`, you can pick one from the pool (and reuse the underlying buffer when possible).

This is how you would modify `collectShapes` to take an additional channel parameter:

```
private fun CoroutineScope.collectShapes(
    locations: ReceiveChannel<Location>,
    locationsToProcess: SendChannel<Location>,
) = launch {
    val locationsBeingProcessed = mutableListOf<Location>()

    for (loc in locations) {
        if (!locationsBeingProcessed.contains(loc) {
            launch(Dispatchers.IO) {
                locationsToProcess.send(loc)
            }
        }
    }
}
```

Notice how `collectShapes` now sends a location to the `locationsToProcess` channel, only if the location isn't in the list of locations currently being processed.

As for the worker implementation, it simply reads from the channel we just created—except that from the worker perspective, it's a `ReceiveChannel`. Using the same pattern:

```
private fun CoroutineScope.worker(
        locationsToProcess: ReceiveChannel<Location>,
) = launch(Dispatchers.IO) {
        for (loc in locationsToProcess) {
            // fetch the ShapeData, see later
        }
}
```

For now, we are not focusing on how to fetch a `ShapeData`. The most important notion to understand here is the `for` loop. Thanks to the iteration on the `locationsToProcess` channel, each individual `worker` coroutine will receive its own location without interfering with the others. No matter how many workers we'll start, a location sent from `collectShapes` to the `locationsToProcess` channel will only be received by one worker. You'll see that each worker will be created with the same channel instance when we wire all those things up. In message-oriented software, this pattern, which implies delivery of a message to multiple destinations, is called *fan-out*.

Looking back at the missing implementation inside the `for` loop, this is what we'll do:

1. Fetch the `ShapeData` (which from now on we'll simply refer to as "data").

2. Create a `Shape` from the location and the data.

3. Send the shape to some channel, which other components in our application will use to get the shapes from `ShapeCollector`. Obviously, we haven't created such a channel yet.

4. Notify the `collectShapes` coroutine that the given location has been processed, by sending it back to its sender. Again, such a channel has to be created.

Do note that this isn't the only possible implementation. You could imagine other ways and adapt to your needs. After all, this is what this chapter is all about: to give you examples and inspiration for your next developments.

Back on our horse, Example 9-1 shows the final implementation of the worker coroutine.

Example 9-1. Worker coroutine

```
private fun CoroutineScope.worker(
    locationsToProcess: ReceiveChannel<Location>,
    locationsProcessed: SendChannel<Location>,
```

```
        shapesOutput: SendChannel<Shape>
) = launch(Dispatchers.IO) {
    for (loc in locationsToProcess) {
        try {
            val data = getShapeData(loc)
            val shape = Shape(loc, data)
            shapesOutput.send(shape)
        } finally {
            locationsProcessed.send(loc)
        }
    }
}
```

Just like the collectShapes was adapted earlier to take one channel as an argument, this time we're adding two more channels: locationsProcessed and shapesOutput.

Inside the for loop, we first get a ShapeData instance for a location. For the sake of this simple example, Example 9-2 shows our implementation.

Example 9-2. Getting shape data

```
private suspend fun getShapeData(
    location: Location
): ShapeData = withContext(Dispatchers.IO) {
    /* Simulate some remote API delay */
    delay(10)
    ShapeData()
}
```

Since the getShapeData method might not return immediately, we implement it as a suspend function. Imagining that the downstream code involves a remote API, we use Dispatchers.IO.

The collectShapes coroutine has to be adapted again, since it has to accept one more channel—the one from which the workers send back locations they're done processing. You're starting to get used to it—it'll be a ReceiveChannel from the collectShapes perspective. Now collectShapes accepts two ReceiveChannels and one SendChannel.

Let's try it:

```
private fun CoroutineScope.collectShapes(
    locations: ReceiveChannel<Location>,
    locationsToProcess: SendChannel<Location>,
    locationsProcessed: ReceiveChannel<Location>
): Job = launch {
    ...
    for (loc in locations) {
        // same implementation, hidden for brevity
    }
    // but.. how do we iterate over locationsProcessed?
}
```

Now we have a problem. How can you receive elements from multiple ReceiveChannels at the same time? If we add another for loop right below the locations channel iteration, it wouldn't work as intended as the first iteration only ends when the locations channel is closed.

For that purpose, you can use the select expression.

The select Expression

The select expression waits for the result of multiple suspending functions simultaneously, which are specified using *clauses* in the body of this select invocation. The caller is suspended until one of the clauses is either *selected* or *fails*.

In our case, it works like so:

```
select<Unit> {
    locations.onReceive { loc ->
        // do action 1
    }
    locationsProcessed.onReceive { loc ->
        // do action 2
    }
}
```

If the select expression could talk, it would say: "Whenever the locations channel receives an element, I'll do action 1. Or, if the locationsProcessed channel receives something, I'll do action 2. I can't do both actions at the same time. By the way, I'm returning Unit."

The "I can't do both actions at the same time" is important. You might wonder what would happen if action 1 takes half an hour—or worse, if it never completes. We'll describe a similar situation in "Deadlock in CSP" on page 227. However, the implementation that follows is guaranteed *never* to block for a long time in each action.

Since `select` is an expression, it returns a result. The result type is inferred by the return type of the lambdas we provide for each case of the `select`—pretty much like the when expression. In this particular example, we don't want any result, so the return type is Unit. As `select` returns after either the `locations` or `locationsPro cessed` channel receives an element, it doesn't iterate over channels like our previous for loop. Consequently, we have to wrap it inside a `while(true)`. The complete implementation of `collectShapes` is shown in Example 9-3.

Example 9-3. Collecting shapes

```
private fun CoroutineScope.collectShapes(
    locations: ReceiveChannel<Location>,
    locationsToProcess: SendChannel<Location>,
    locationsProcessed: ReceiveChannel<Location>
) = launch(Dispatchers.Default) {

    val locationsBeingProcessed = mutableListOf<Location>()

    while (true) {
        select<Unit> {
            locationsProcessed.onReceive {                    ❶
                locationsBeingProcessed.remove(it)
            }
            locations.onReceive {                             ❷
                if (!locationsBeingProcessed.any { loc ->
                    loc == it }) {
                    /* Add it to the list of locations being processed */
                    locationsBeingProcessed.add(it)

                    /* Now download the shape at location */
                    locationsToProcess.send(it)
                }
            }
        }
    }
}
```

❶ When the `locationsProcessed` channel receives a location, we know that this location has been processed by a worker. It should now be removed from the list of locations being processed.

❷ When the `locations` channel receives a location, we have to first check whether we've already been processing the same location or not. If not, we'll add the location to the `locationsBeingProcessed` list, and then send it to the `locationsToProcess` channel.

Putting It All Together

The final architecture of the `ShapeCollector` takes shape, as shown in Figure 9-6.

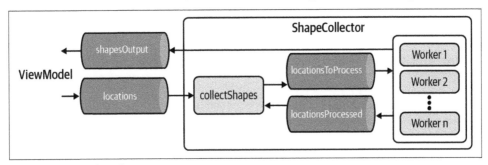

Figure 9-6. Final architecture.

Remember that all the channels we used to implement the `collectShapes` and `worker` methods have to be created somewhere. To respect encapsulation, a good place to do that is in a `start` method, as shown in Example 9-4.

Example 9-4. Shape collector

```
class ShapeCollector(private val workerCount: Int) {
    fun CoroutineScope.start(
        locations: ReceiveChannel<Location>,
        shapesOutput: SendChannel<Shape>
    ) {
        val locationsToProcess = Channel<Location>()
        val locationsProcessed = Channel<Location>(capacity = 1)

        repeat(workerCount) {
            worker(locationsToProcess, locationsProcessed, shapesOutput)
        }
        collectShapes(locations, locationsToProcess, locationsProcessed)
    }

    private fun CoroutineScope.collectShapes // already implemented

    private fun CoroutineScope.worker        // already implemented

    private suspend fun getShapeData         // already implemented
}
```

This start method is responsible for starting the whole shape collection machinery. The two channels that are exclusively used inside the ShapeCollector are created: locationsToProcess and locationsProcessed. We are not explicitly creating ReceiveChannel or SendChannel instances here. We're creating them as Channel instances because they'll further be used either as ReceiveChannel or SendChannel. Then the worker pool is created and started, by calling the worker method as many times as workerCount was set. It's achieved using the repeat function from the standard library.

Finally, we call collectShapes once. Overall, we started workerCount + 1 coroutines in this start method.

You might have noticed that locationsProcessed is created with a capacity of 1. This is intended, and is an important detail. We'll explain why in the next section.

Fan-Out and Fan-In

You just saw an example of multiple coroutines receiving from the same channel. Indeed, all worker coroutines receive from the same locationsToProcess channel. A Location instance sent to the locationsToProcess channel will be processed by only one worker, without any risk of concurrent issues. This particular interaction between coroutines is known as *fan-out*, as shown in Figure 9-7. From the standpoint of the coroutine started with the collectShapes function, locations are fanned-out to the worker pool.

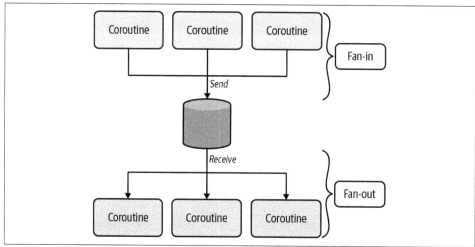

Figure 9-7. Fan-out and fan-in.

Fan-out is achieved by launching several coroutines which all iterate over the same instance of ReceiveChannel (see the worker implementation in Example 9-1). If one of the workers fails, the other ones will continue to receive from the channel—making the system resilient to some extent.

Inversely, when several coroutines send elements to the same SendChannel instance, we're talking about *fan-in*. Again, you've got a good example since all workers send Shape instances to shapesOutput.

Performance Test

Alright! Time to test the performance of our ShapeCollector. The following snippet has a main function, which calls the functions consumeShapes and sendLocations. Those functions start a coroutine that, respectively, consumes Shape instances from the ShapeCollector and sends Location instances. Overall, this code is close to what you'd write in a real view-model, as shown in Example 9-5.

Example 9-5. Shape collector

```
fun main() = runBlocking<Unit> {
    val shapes = Channel<Shape>()                    ❶
    val locations = Channel<Location>()

    with(ShapeCollector(4)) {                        ❷
        start(locations, shapes)
        consumeShapes(shapes)
    }

    sendLocations(locations)
}

var count = 0

fun CoroutineScope.consumeShapes(
    shapesInput: ReceiveChannel<Shape>
) = launch {
    for (shape in shapesInput) {
        // increment a counter of shapes
        count++                                      ❸
    }
}

fun CoroutineScope.sendLocations(
    locationsOutput: SendChannel<Location>
) = launch {
    withTimeoutOrNull(3000) {                        ❹
        while (true) {
            /* Simulate fetching some shape location */
            val location = Location(Random.nextInt(), Random.nextInt())
            locationsOutput.send(location)
        }
    }
```

```
    }
    println("Received $count shapes")
}
```

❶ We set up the channels according to the needs of the ShapeCollector—see
Figure 9-4.

❷ We create a ShapeCollector with four workers.

❸ The consumeShapes function only increments a counter. That counter is declared
globally—which is fine because the coroutine started with consumeShapes is the
only one to modify count.

❹ In the sendLocations functions, we set up a timeout of three seconds.
withTimeoutOrNull is a suspending function that suspends until the provided
time is out. Consequently, the coroutine started with sendLocations only prints
the received count after three seconds.

If you recall the implementation of getShapeData in Example 9-2, we added
delay(10) to simulate a suspending call of 10 ms long. Running four workers for
three seconds, we would ideally receive 3,000 / 10 × 4 = 1,200 shapes, if our implementation had zero overhead. On our test machine, we got 1,170 shapes—that's an
efficiency of 98%.

Playing a little bit with more workers (64), with delay(5) in each worker, we got
122,518 shapes in 10 seconds (the ideal number being 128,000)—that's an efficiency
of 96%.

Overall, the throughput of ShapeCollector is quite decent, event with a sendLoca
tions function that continuously sends Location instances without any pause
between two sends.

Back Pressure

What happens if our workers are too slow? This could very well happen if a remote
HTTP call takes time to respond, or a backend server is overwhelmed—we don't
know. To simulate this, we can dramatically increase the delay inside getShapeData
(see Example 9-2). Using delay(500), we got only 20 shapes in three seconds, with
four workers. The throughput decreased, but this isn't the interesting part. As always
with producer-consumer problems, issues can arise when consumers slow down—as
producers might accumulate data and the system may ultimately run out of memory.
You can add println() logs inside the producer coroutine and run the program
again:

```
fun CoroutineScope.sendLocations(locationsOutput: SendChannel<Location>) =
launch {
    withTimeoutOrNull(3000) {
        while (true) {
            /* Simulate fetching some shape location */
            val location = Location(Random.nextInt(), Random.nextInt())
            println("Sending a new location")
            locationsOutput.send(location)        // suspending call
        }
    }
    println("Received $count shapes")
}
```

Now, "Sending a new location" is printed only about 25 times in the console.

So the producer is being slowed down. How?

Because `locationsOutput.send(location)` is a suspending call. When workers are slow, the `collectShapes` function (see Example 9-3) of the `ShapeCollector` class quickly becomes suspended at the line `locationsToProcess.send(it)`. Indeed, `locationsToProcess` is a rendezvous channel. Consequently, when the coroutine started with `collectShapes` reaches that line, it's suspended until a worker is ready to receive the location from `locationsToProcess`. When the previously mentioned coroutine is suspended, it can no longer receive from the `locations` channel—which corresponds to `locationsOutput` in the previous example. This is the reason why the coroutine that started with `sendLocation` is in turn suspended. When workers finally do their job, `collectShapes` can resume, and so does the producer coroutine.

Similarities with the Actor Model

In CSP, you create coroutines that encapsulate mutable state. Instead of communicating by sharing their state, they share by communicating (using `Channels`). The coroutine started with the `collectShapes` function (see Example 9-3) uses three channels to communicate with other coroutines—one `SendChannel` and two `ReceiveChannels`, as shown in Figure 9-8.

In CSP parlance, `collectShapes` and its three channels is a *process*. A process is a computational entity that communicates with other actors using asynchronous message passing (channels). It can do only one thing at a time—reading, writing to channels, or processing.

In the Actor model, an *actor* is quite similar. One noticeable difference is that an actor only has one channel—called a mailbox. If an actor needs to be responsive and non-blocking, it must delegate its long-running processing to child actors. This similarity is the reason why CSP is sometimes referred to as an Actor model implementation.

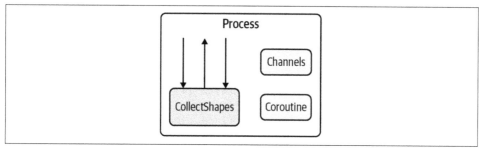

Figure 9-8. Process in CSP.

Execution Is Sequential Inside a Process

We've just seen that a *process* is made of a single coroutine and channels. The very nature of a coroutine is for it to be executed on some thread. So unless this coroutine starts other child coroutines (which run concurrently, and in some cases in parallel), all lines of that coroutine are executed sequentially. That includes receiving from channels, sending objects to other channels, and mutating some private state. Consequently, the actors implemented in this chapter could either receive from a channel or send to another channel, but not do both at the same time. Under load, this kind of actor can be efficient because it doesn't involve blocking calls, only suspending functions. When a coroutine is suspended, the overall efficiency isn't necessarily affected, because the thread executing the suspended coroutine can then execute another coroutine which has something to do. This way, threads can be used to their full potential, never contending to some lock.

Final Thoughts

This mechanism using CSP style has very little internal overhead. Thanks to `Chan nels` and coroutines, our implementation is lock-free. Therefore, there's *no thread contention*—the `ShapeCollector` is less likely to impact other threads of your application. Similarly, there's a chance that the `Dispatchers` we use in the `ShapeCollector` might also be used in other features in our application. By leveraging lock-free implementations, a coroutine suspended while receiving from a channel won't prevent the underlying thread from executing other coroutines. In other words, we can do more with the same resources.

Moreover, this architecture provides built-in back pressure. If some `ShapeData` instances suddenly take more time to fetch, producers of `ShapeLocation` instances will be slowed down so that locations don't accumulate—which reduces the risk of running out of memory. This back pressure comes for free—you didn't explicitly write code for such a feature.

The example given in this chapter is generic enough to be taken as is and adapted to fit your needs. In the event that you need to significantly deviate from our example, then we owe you a deeper explanation. For example, why did we set a capacity of 1 for the locationsProcessed channel in Example 9-4? The answer is admittedly nontrivial. If we had created a regular rendezvous channel, our ShapeCollector would have suffered from a *deadlock*—which brings us to the next section.

Deadlock in CSP

Deadlocks are most commonly encountered when working with threads. When thread A holds lock 1 and attempts to seize lock 2, while thread B holds lock 2 and attempts to seize lock 1, you have a deadlock. The two threads indefinitely wait for each other and neither progresses. Deadlocks can have disastrous consequences when they happen in critical components of an application. An efficient way to avoid such a situation is to ensure that a deadlock cannot happen under any imaginable circumstances. Even when conditions are highly unlikely to be met, you can trust Murphy's Law to strike some day.

However, deadlocks can also happen in CSP architecture. We can do a little experiment to illustrate this. Instead of setting a capacity of 1 to the channel locationsPro cessed in Example 9-4, let's use a channel with no buffer (a rendezvous channel) and run the performance test sample in Example 9-5. The result printed in the console is:

```
Received 4 shapes
```

For the record, we should have received 20 shapes. So, what's going on?

 Fair warning: the following explanation goes into every necessary detail, and is quite long. We encourage you to take the time to read it carefully until the end. It's the ultimate challenge to test your understanding of channels.

You might also skip it entirely and jump to "TL;DR" on page 229.

Let's have a closer look at the internals of our ShapeCollector class and follow each step as though we were a live debugger. Imagine that you've just started the performance test sample in Example 9-5, and the first Location instance is sent to the loca tions channel. That location goes through the collectShapes method with its select expression. At that moment, locationsProcessed has nothing to provide, so the select expression goes through the second case: locations.onReceive{..}. If you look at what's done inside this second case, you can see that a location is sent to the locationsToProcess channel—which is a receive channel for each worker. Consequently, the coroutine started by the collectShapes method (which we'll refer to as the collectShapes coroutine) is suspended at the locationsToProcess.send(it) invocation until a worker handshakes the locationsToProcess rendezvous channel. This happens fairly quickly, since at that time all workers are idle.

When a worker receives the first Location instance, the collectShapes coroutine is resumed and is able to receive other locations. As in our worker implementation, we've added some delay to simulate a background processing, you can consider workers slow compared to other coroutines—which are the collectShapes coroutine and the producer coroutine started with the sendLocations method in the test sample (which we'll refer to as the sendLocations coroutine). Therefore, another location is received by the collectShapes coroutine while the worker that which took the first location is still busy processing it. Similarly, a second worker quickly handles the second location, and a third location is received by the collectShapes coroutine, etc.

The execution continues until all four workers are busy, while a fifth location is received by the collectShapes coroutine. Following the same logic as before, the collectShapes coroutine is suspended until a worker is ready to take the Location instance. Unfortunately, all workers are busy. So the collectShapes coroutine isn't able to take incoming locations anymore. Since the collectShapes and sendLocations coroutines communicate through a rendezvous channel, the sendLocations coroutine is in turn suspended until collectShapes is ready to take more locations.

Time goes by until a worker makes itself available to receive the fifth location. Eventually, a worker (probably the first worker) is done processing its Location instance. Then it sends the result to the shapesOutput channel and it tries to send back the processed location to the collectShapes coroutine, using the locationsProcessed channel. Remember that this is our mechanism to notify the collectShapes coroutine when a location has been processed. However, the collectShapes coroutine is suspended at the locationsToProcess.send(it) invocation. So collectShapes can't receive from the locationsProcessed channel. There's no issue to this situation: this is a *deadlock*,[4] as shown in Figure 9-9.

Eventually, the first four locations processed by the workers are processed and four Shape instances are sent to the shapesOutput channel. The delay in each worker is only of 10 ms, so all workers have time to complete before the three-second timeout. Hence the result:

```
Received 4 shapes
```

---

4. While there's no lock or mutex involved here, the situation is very similar to a deadlock involving threads. This is why we use the same terminology.

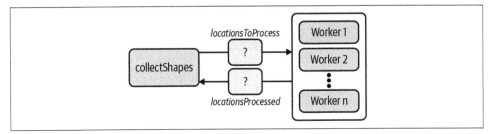

Figure 9-9. Deadlock in CSP.

If the locationsProcessed channel had a capacity of at least 1, the first available worker would have been able to send back its Location instance and then receive from the locationsToProcess channel—releasing the collectShapes coroutine. Subsequently, in the select expression of the collectShapes coroutine, the locationsToProcess channel is *always* checked before the locations channel. This ensures that when the collectShapes coroutine is eventually suspended at the locationsToProcess.send(it) invocation, the buffer of the locationsProcessed channel is guaranteed to be empty—so a worker can send a location without being suspended. If you're curious, try to revert the two cases locationsProcessed.onReceive {..} and locations.onReceive {..} while having a capacity of 1 for the locationsProcessed channel. The result will be: "Received 5 shapes."

TL;DR

Not only is the capacity of 1 for the locationsProcessed channel extremely important, the order in which channels are read in the select expression of the collectShapes coroutine also matters.[5] What should you remember from this? Deadlocks are possible in CSP. Even more important, understanding what caused the deadlock is an excellent exercise to test your understanding of how channels work.

If we look back at the structure of the ShapeCollector, we can represent the structure as a cyclic graph, as shown in Figure 9-10.

---

5. Actually, our implementation, which uses a capacity of 1 for locationsProcessed, isn't the only possible implementation that works without deadlocks. There's at least one solution that uses locationsProcessed as a rendezvous channel. We leave this as an exercise for the reader.

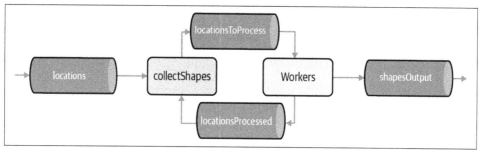

Figure 9-10. Cyclic graph.

This new representation emphasizes an important property of the structure: it's *cyclic*. Location instances travel back and forth between the collectShapes coroutine and workers.

Cycles in CSP are actually the cause of deadlocks. Without cycles, there's no possibility of deadlock. Sometimes, however, you'll have no choice but to have those cycles. In this case, we gave you the key ideas to reason about CSP, so you can find solutions by yourself.

Limitations of Channels

Up until now, we've held off on discussing the limitations of channels, so we'll describe some of those limitations now. Using notions from this chapter, creating a stream of Int values is typically done as shown in Example 9-6.

Example 9-6. Producing numbers

```
fun CoroutineScope.numbers(): ReceiveChannel<Int> = produce {
    send(1)
    send(2)
    // send other numbers
}
```

On the receiving side, you can consume those numbers like so:

```
fun main() = runBlocking {
    val channel = numbers()
    for (x in channel) {
        println(x)
    }
}
```

Pretty straightforward. Now, what if you need to apply a transformation for each of those numbers? Imagine that your transformation function was:

```
suspend fun transform(n: Int) = withContext(Dispatchers.Default) {
    delay(10) // simulate some heavy CPU computations
    n + 1
}
```

You could modify the `numbers` function like so:

```
fun CoroutineScope.numbers(): ReceiveChannel<Int> = produce {
    send(transform(1))
    send(transform(2))
}
```

It works, but it's not elegant. A much nicer solution would look like this:

```
fun main() = runBlocking {
    /* Warning - this doesn't compile */
    val channel = numbers().map {
        transform(it)
    }
    for (x in channel) {
        println(x)
    }
}
```

Actually, as of Kotlin 1.4, this code doesn't compile. In the early days of channels, we had "channel operators" such as `map`. However, those operators have been deprecated in Kotlin 1.3, and removed in Kotlin 1.4.

Why? Channels are communication primitives between coroutines. They are specifically designed to distribute values so that every value is received by only one receiver. It's not possible to use channels to broadcast values to multiple receivers. The designers of coroutines have created `Flows` specifically for asynchronous data streams on which we can use transformation operators; we'll see how in the next chapter.

So, channels are not a convenient solution to implement pipelines of data transformations.

Channels Are Hot

Let's have a look at the source code of the produce channel builder. Two lines are interesting, as shown in the following:

```
public fun <E> CoroutineScope.produce(                                    ❶
    context: CoroutineContext = EmptyCoroutineContext,
    capacity: Int = 0,
    @BuilderInference block: suspend ProducerScope<E>.() -> Unit
): ReceiveChannel<E> {
    val channel = Channel<E>(capacity)
    val newContext = newCoroutineContext(context)
    val coroutine = ProducerCoroutine(newContext, channel)
    coroutine.start(CoroutineStart.DEFAULT, coroutine, block)               ❷
    return coroutine
}
```

❶ produce is an extension function on CoroutineScope. Remember the convention? It indicates that this function starts a new coroutine.

❷ We can confirm that with the coroutine.start() invocation. Don't pay too much attention to how this coroutine is started—it's an internal implementation.

Consequently, when you invoke the produce channel builder, a new coroutine is started and immediately starts producing elements and sending them to the returned channel even if no coroutine is consuming those elements.

This is the reason why channels are said to be *hot*: a coroutine is actively running to produce or consume data. If you know RxJava, this is the same concept as hot observables: they emit values independently of individual subscriptions. Consider this simple stream:

```
fun CoroutineScope.numbers(): ReceiveChannel<Int> = produce {
    use(openConnectionToDatabase()) {
        send(1)
        send(2)
    }
}
```

Also, imagine that no other coroutines are consuming this stream. As this function returns a rendezvous channel, the started coroutine will suspend on the first send. So you might say: "OK, we're fine—no background processing is done until we provide a consumer to this stream." It's true, but if you forget to consume the stream, the database connection will remain open—notice that we used the use function from the standard library, which is the equivalent of the try-with-resources statement in Java.

While it might not be harmful as is, this piece of logic could be part of a retry loop, in which case a significant amount of resources would leak.

To sum up, channels are intercoroutine communication primitives. They work really well in a CSP-like architecture. However, we don't have handy operators such as `map` or `filter` to transform them. We can't broadcast values to multiple receivers. Moreover, their hot nature can cause memory leaks in some situations.

Flows have been created to address those channels' limitations. We'll cover flows in the next chapter.

Summary

- Channels are communication primitives that provide a way to transfer streams of values between coroutines.

- While channels are conceptually close to Java's `BlockingQueue`, the fundamental difference is that `send` and `receive` methods of a channel are suspending functions, not blocking calls.

- Using channels and coroutines, you can *share by communicating* instead of the traditional *communicate by sharing*. The goal is to avoid shared mutable-state and thread-safety issues.

- You can implement complex logic using CSP style, leveraging back pressure. This results in potentially excellent performance since the nonblocking nature of suspending functions reduces thread contention to its bare minimum.

- Beware that deadlock in CSP is possible, if your architecture has cycles (a coroutine sends objects to another coroutine, while also receiving objects from the same coroutine). You can fix those deadlocks by, for example, tweaking the order in which the `select` expression treats each cases, or by adjusting the capacity of some channels.

- Channels should be considered low-level primitives. Deadlocks in CSP are one example of misuse of channels. The next chapter will introduce *flows*—higher-level primitives that exchange streams of data between coroutines. It doesn't mean that you shouldn't use channels—there are still situations where channels are necessary (the `ShapeCollector` in this chapter is an example). However, you'll see that in many situations, flows are a better choice. In any case, it's important to know about channels because (as you'll see) flows sometimes use channels under the hood.

CHAPTER 10

Flows

Up to now, we've covered coroutines, suspending functions, and how to deal with streams using Channels. We've seen from the previous chapter that working with Channels implies starting coroutines to send and/or receive from those Channels. The aforementioned coroutines are then *hot* entities that are sometimes hard to debug, or can leak resources if they aren't cancelled when they should be.

Flows, like Channels, are meant to handle asynchronous streams of data, but at a higher level of abstraction and with better library tooling. Conceptually, Flows are similar to Sequences, except that each step of a Flow can be asynchronous. It is also easy to integrate flows in structured concurrency, to avoid leaking resources.

However, Flows[1] aren't meant to replace Channels. Channels are building blocks for flows. Channels are still appropriate in some architectures such as in CSP (see Chapter 9). Nevertheless, you'll see that flows suit most needs in asynchronous data processing.

In this chapter, we'll introduce you to cold and hot flows. You'll see how *cold* flows can be a better choice when you want to make sure never to leak any resources. On the other hand, *hot* flows serve a different purpose such as when you need a "publish-subscribe" relationship between entities in your app. For example, you can implement an event bus using hot flows.

The best way to understand flows is to see how they are used in real-life applications. So this chapter will also go through a series of typical use cases.

---

1. We'll refer to Flows as *flows* in the rest of this chapter.

An Introduction to Flows

Lets reimplement Example 9-6, using a Flow:

```
fun numbers(): Flow<Int> = flow {
    emit(1)
    emit(2)
    // emit other values
}
```

Several aspects are important to notice:

1. Instead of returning a Channel instance, we're returning a Flow instance.
2. Inside the flow, we use the emit suspending function instead of send.
3. The numbers function, which returns a Flow instance, isn't a suspending function. Invoking the numbers function doesn't start anything by itself—it just immediately returns a Flow instance.

To sum up, you define in the flow block the emission of values. When invoked, the numbers function quickly returns a Flow instance without running anything in the background.

On the consuming site:

```
fun main() = runBlocking {
    val flow = numbers()        ❶
    flow.collect {              ❷
        println(it)
    }
}
```

❶ We get an instance of Flow, using the numbers function.

❷ Once we get a flow, instead of looping over it (like we would with a channel), we use the collect function which, in flows parlance, is called a *terminal operator*. We'll extend on *flows operators* and terminal operators in "Operators" on page 239. For now, we can summarize the purpose of the collect terminal operator: it consumes the flow; foor example, iterate over the flow and execute the given lambda on each element of the flow.

That's it—you've seen the basic usage of a flow. As we mentioned earlier, we'll now take a more realistic example, so you'll see the real interest of Flows.

A More Realistic Example

Imagine that you need to get tokens from a remote database,[2] then query additional data for each of those tokens. You need to do that only once in a while, so you decide not to maintain an active connection to the database (which could be expensive). So you create a connection only when fetching the data, and close it when you're done.

Your implementation should first establish the connection to the database. Then you get a token using a suspending function getToken. This getToken function performs a request to the database and returns a token. Then you asynchronously get optional data associated with this token. In our example, this is done by invoking the suspending function getData, which takes a token as a parameter. Once you get the result of getData, you wrap both the token and the result in one TokenData class instance, defined as:

```
data class TokenData(val token: String, val opt: String? = null)
```

To sum up, you need to produce a stream of TokenData objects. This stream requires first establishing a database connection, then performing asynchronous queries for retrieving tokens and getting associated data. You choose how many tokens you need. After you've processed all the tokens, you disconnect and release underlying database connection resources. Figure 10-1 shows how to implement such a flow.

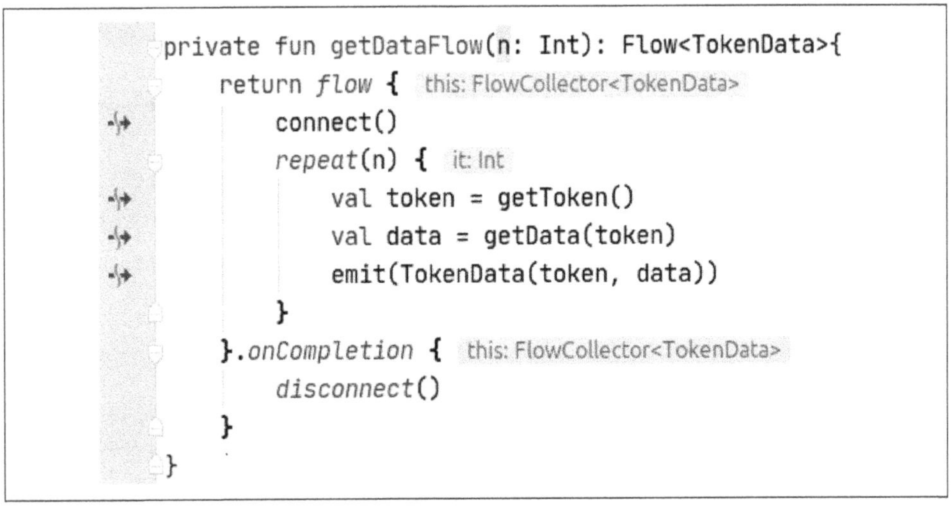

```
private fun getDataFlow(n: Int): Flow<TokenData>{
    return flow {    this: FlowCollector<TokenData>
        connect()
        repeat(n) {    it: Int
            val token = getToken()
            val data = getData(token)
            emit(TokenData(token, data))
        }
    }.onCompletion {    this: FlowCollector<TokenData>
        disconnect()
    }
}
```

Figure 10-1. Data flow.

---

2. A token is generally encrypted registration data which the client application stores in memory so that further database access doesn't require explicit authentication.

You can find the corresponding source code in GitHub (*https://oreil.ly/dU4uZ*).

 In this chapter, we sometimes use images instead of code blocks because the screenshots from our IDE show suspension points (in the margin) and type hints, which are really helpful.

Several aspects of this implementation are particularly important to notice:

- Creating a connection to the database and closing it on completion is completely transparent to the client code that consumes the flow. Client code only sees a flow of TokenData.

- All operations inside the flow are sequential. For example, once we get the first token (say, "token1"), the flow invokes getData("token1") and suspends until it gets the result (say, "data1"). Then the flow emits the first TokenData("token1," "data1"). Only after that does the execution proceed with "token2," etc.

- Invoking the getDataFlow function does nothing on its own. It simply returns a flow. The code inside the flow executes only when a coroutine collects the flow, as shown in Example 10-1.

Example 10-1. Collecting a flow

```
fun main() = runBlocking<Unit> {
    val flow = getDataFlow(3) // Nothing runs at initialization

    // A coroutine collects the flow
    launch {
        flow.collect { data ->
            println(data)
        }
    }
}
```

- If the coroutine that collects the flow gets cancelled or reaches the end of the flow, the code inside the onCompletion block executes. This guarantees that we properly release the connection to the database.

As we already mentioned, collect is a terminal operator that consumes all elements of the flow. In this example, collect invokes a function on each collected element of the flow (e.g., println(data) is invoked three times). We'll cover other terminal operators in "Examples of Cold Flow Usage" on page 240.

Until now, you've seen examples of flows that don't run any code until a coroutine collects them. In flows parlance, they are cold flows.

Operators

If you need to perform transformations on a flow, much like you would do on collections, the coroutines library provides functions such as `map`, `filter`, `debounce`, `buffer`, `onCompletion`, etc. Those functions are called *flow operators* or *intermediate operators*, because they operate on a flow and return another flow. A regular operator shouldn't be confused with a terminal operator, as you'll see later.

In the following, we have an example usage of the `map` operator:

```
fun main() = runBlocking<Unit> {
    val numbers: Flow<Int> = // implementation hidden for brevity

    val newFlow: Flow<String> = numbers().map {
        transform(it)
    }
}

suspend fun transform(i :Int): String = withContext(Dispatchers.Default) {
    delay(10) // simulate real work
    "${i + 1}"
}
```

The interesting bit here is that `map` turns a `Flow<Int>` into a `Flow<String>`. The type of the resulting flow is determined by the return type of the lambda passed to the operator.

 The `map` flow operator is conceptually really close to the `map` extension function on collections. There's a noticeable difference, though: the lambda passed to the `map` flow operator can be a suspending function.

We'll cover most of the common operators in a series of use cases in the next section.

Terminal Operators

A terminal operator can be easily distinguished from other regular operators since it's a suspending function that starts the collection of the flow. You've previously seen `collect`.

Other terminal operators are available, like `toList`, `collectLatest`, `first`, etc. Here is a brief description of those terminal operators:

- `toList` collects the given flow and returns a `List` containing all collected elements.

- `collectLatest` collects the given flow with a provided action. The difference from `collect` is that when the original flow emits a new value, the action block for the previous value is cancelled.

- `first` returns the first element emitted by the flow and then cancels the flow's collection. It throws a `NoSuchElementException` if the flow was empty. There's also a variant, `firstOrNull`, which returns `null` if the flow was empty.

Examples of Cold Flow Usage

As it turns out, picking one single example making use of all possible operators isn't the best path to follow. Instead, we'll provide different use cases, which will illustrate the usage of several flow operators.

Use Case #1: Interface with a Callback-Based API

Suppose that you're developing a chat application. Your users can send messages to one another. A message has a date, a reference to the author of the message, and content as plain text.

Here is a `Message`:

```
data class Message(
    val user: String,
    val date: LocalDateTime,
    val content: String
)
```

Unsurprisingly, we'll represent the stream of messages as a flow of the `Message` instance. Every time a user posts a message into the app, the flow will transmit that message. For now, assume that you can invoke a function `getMessageFlow`, which returns an instance of `Flow<Message>`. With the Kotlin Flows library, you are able to create your own custom flows. However, it makes the most sense to start by exploring how the flow API can be used in common use cases:

```
fun getMessageFlow(): Flow<Message> {
    // we'll implement it later
}
```

Now, suppose that you want to translate all messages from a given user in a different language, on the fly. Moreover, you'd like to perform the translation on a background thread.

To do that, you start by getting the flow of messages, by invoking getMessageFlow(). Then you apply operators to the original flow, as shown in the following:

```
fun getMessagesFromUser(user: String, language: String): Flow<Message> {
    return getMessageFlow()
        .filter { it.user == user }          ❶
        .map { it.translate(language) }      ❷
        .flowOn(Dispatchers.Default)         ❸
}
```

❶ The first operator, filter, operates on the original flow and returns another flow of messages which all originate from the same user passed as a parameter.

❷ The second operator, map, operates on the flow returned by filter and returns a flow of translated messages. From the filter operator standpoint, the original flow (returned by getMessageFlow()) is the *upstream flow*, while the *downstream flow* is represented by all operators happening *after* filter. The same reasoning applies for all intermediate operators—they have their own relative upstream and downstream flow, as illustrated in Figure 10-2.

❸ Finally, the flowOn operator changes the context of the flow it is operating on. It changes the coroutine context of the upstream flow, while not affecting the downstream flow. Consequently, steps 1 and 2 are done using the dispatcher Dispatchers.Default.

In other words, the upstream flow's operators (which are filter and map) are now encapsulated: their execution context will always be Dispatchers.Default. It doesn't matter in which context the resulting flow will be collected; the previously mentioned operators will be executed using Dispatchers.Default.

This is a very important property of flows, called *context preservation*. Imagine that you're collecting the flow on the UI thread of your application—typically, you would do that using the viewModelScope of a ViewModel. It would be embarrassing if the context of execution of one of the flow's operators leaked downstream and affected the thread in which the flow was ultimately collected. Thankfully, this will never happen. For example, if you collect a flow on the UI thread, all values are emitted by a coroutine that uses Dispatchers.Main. All the necessary context switches are automatically managed for you.

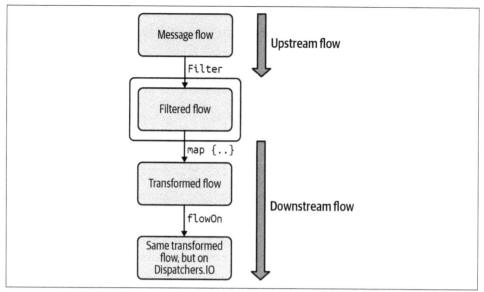

Figure 10-2. Upstream and downstream flows.

Under the hood, flowOn starts a new coroutine when it detects that the context is about to change. This new coroutine interacts with the rest of the flow through a channel that is internally managed.

In flow parlance, an intermediate operator like map operates on the upstream flow and returns another flow. From the map operator standpoint, the returned flow is the downstream flow.

The map operator accepts a suspending function as a transformation block. So if you wanted to only perform message translation using Dispatchers.Default (and not message filtering), you could remove the flowOn operator and declare the translate function like so:

```
private suspend fun Message.translate(
    language: String
): Message = withContext(Dispatchers.Default) {
    // this is a dummy implementation
    copy(content = "translated content")
}
```

See how easy it is to offload parts of data transformation to other threads, while still having a big picture of the data flow?

As you can see, the Flow API allows for a declarative way to express data transformation. When you invoke getMessagesFromUser("Amanda," "en-us"), nothing is actually running. All those transformations involve intermediate operators, which will be triggered when the flow will be collected.

On the consuming site, if you need to act on each received message, you can use the collect function like so:

```
fun main() = runBlocking {
    getMessagesFromUser("Amanda", "en-us").collect {
        println("Received message from ${it.user}: ${it.content}")
    }
}
```

Now that we've shown how to transform the flow and consume it, we can provide an implementation for the flow itself: the getMessageFlow function. The signature of this function is to return a flow of Messages. In that particular situation, we can reasonably assume that the message machinery is actually a service that runs in its own thread. We'll name this service MessageFactory.

Like most services of that kind, the message factory has a *publish/subscribe* mechanism—we can register or unregister observers for new incoming messages, as shown in the following:

```
abstract class MessageFactory : Thread() {
    /* The internal list of observers must be thread-safe */
    private val observers = Collections.synchronizedList(
        mutableListOf<MessageObserver>())
    private var isActive = true

    override fun run() = runBlocking {
        while(isActive) {
            val message = fetchMessage()
            for (observer in observers) {
                observer.onMessage(message)
            }
            delay(1000)
        }
    }

    abstract fun fetchMessage(): Message

    fun registerObserver(observer: MessageObserver) {
        observers.add(observer)
    }

    fun unregisterObserver(observer: MessageObserver) {
        observers.removeAll { it == observer }
```

```
        }

        fun cancel() {
            isActive = false
            observers.forEach {
                it.onCancelled()
            }
            observers.clear()
        }

        interface MessageObserver {
            fun onMessage(msg: Message)
            fun onCancelled()
            fun onError(cause: Throwable)
        }
    }
```

This implementation polls for new messages every second and notifies observers. Now the question is: how do we turn a hot[3] entity such as this `MessageFactory` into a flow? `MessageFactory` is also said to be *callback-based*, because it holds references to `MessageObserver` instances and calls methods on those instances when new messages are retrieved. To bridge the flow world with the "callback" world, you can use the `callbackFlow` flow builder. Example 10-2 shows how you can use it.

Example 10-2. Making a flow from a callback-based API

```
fun getMessageFlow(factory: MessageFactory) = callbackFlow<Message> {
    val observer = object : MessageFactory.MessageObserver {
        override fun onMessage(msg: Message) {
            trySend(msg)
        }

        override fun onCancelled() {
            channel.close()
        }

        override fun onError(cause: Throwable) {
            cancel(CancellationException("Message factory error", cause))
        }
    }

    factory.registerObserver(observer)
    awaitClose {
        factory.unregisterObserver(observer)
```

---

3. As opposed to cold, a hot entity lives on its own until explicitly stopped.

```
        }
    }
```

The `callbackFlow` builder creates a cold flow which doesn't perform anything until you invoke a terminal operator. Let's break it down. First off, it's a parameterized function which returns a `Flow` of the given type. It's always done in three steps:

```
callbackFlow {
    /*
    1. Instantiate the "callback." In this case, it's an observer.
    2. Register that callback using the available api.
    3. Listen for close event using `awaitClose`, and provide a
       relevant action to take in this case. Most probably,
       you'll have to unregister the callback.
    */
}
```

It's worth having a look at the signature of `callbackFlow`:

```
public inline fun <T> callbackFlow(
    @BuilderInference noinline block: suspend ProducerScope<T>.() -> Unit
): Flow<T>
```

Don't be impressed by this. One key piece of information is that `callbackFlow` takes a suspending function with `ProducerScope` receiver as the argument. This means that inside the curly braces of the block following `callbackFlow`, you have a `Producer Scope` instance as an implicit `this`.

Here is the signature of `ProducerScope`:

```
public interface ProducerScope<in E> : CoroutineScope, SendChannel<E>
```

So a `ProducerScope` is a `SendChannel`. And that's what you should remember: `call backFlow` provides you with an instance of `SendChannel`, which you can use inside your implementation. You send the object instances you get from your callback to this channel. This is what we do in step 1 of Example 10-2.

Use Case #2: Concurrently Transform a Stream of Values

Sometimes you have to apply a transformation on a collection or stream of objects, to get a new collection of transformed objects. When those transformations should be done asynchronously, things start getting a bit complicated. Not with flows!

Imagine that you have a list of Location instances. Each location can be resolved to a Content instance, using the transform function:

```
suspend fun transform(loc: Location): Content = withContext(Dispatchers.IO)
{
    // Actual implementation doesn't matter
}
```

So you are receiving Location instances, and you have to transform them on the fly using the transform function. However, processing one Location instance might take quite some time. So you don't want that processing of a location to delay the transformation of the next incoming locations. In other words, transformations should be done *in parallel*, as shown in Figure 10-3.

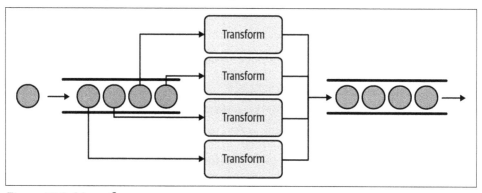

Figure 10-3. Merge flows.

In the preceding schema, we've limited the concurrency to four; in other words, at most, four locations can be transformed simultaneously at a given point in time.

Figure 10-4 shows how you would implement this behavior using flows.

```
18 ▶    fun main() = runBlocking { this: CoroutineScope
19          // Defining the Flow of Content - nothing is executing yet
20          val contentFlow : Flow<Content> = locationsFlow.map { loc : Location ->
21              flow { this: FlowCollector<Content>
22                  emit(transform(loc))
23              }
24          }.flattenMerge( concurrency: 4)
25
26          // We now collect the entire flow using the toList terminal operator
27          val contents : List<Content> = contentFlow.toList()
28      }
```

Figure 10-4. Implementing merging flows.

You can find the corresponding source code in GitHub (*https://oreil.ly/LhW77*).

To understand what's going on here, you should realize that locations.map{..} returns a flow of a flow (e.g., the type is Flow<Flow<Content>>). Indeed, inside the map{..} operator, a new flow is created upon emission of a location by the upstream flow (which is locationsFlow). Each of those created flows is of type Flow<Content> and individually performs location transformation.

The last statement, flattenMerge, merges all those created flows inside a new resulting Flow<Content> (which we assign to contentFlow). Also, flattenMerge has a "concurrency" parameter. Indeed, it would probably be inappropriate to concurrently create and collect a flow every time we receive a location. With a concurrency level of 4, we ensure that no more than four flows will be collected at a given point in time. This is handy in the case of CPU-bound tasks, when you know that your CPU won't be able to transform more than four locations *in parallel* (assuming the CPU has four cores). In other words, flattenMerge's concurrency level refers to how many operations/transformations will be done in parallel *at most* at a given point in time.

Thanks to the suspending nature of flows, you get *back pressure* for free. New locations are collected from locationsFlow only when the machinery is available to process them. A similar mechanism could be implemented without flows or coroutines, using a thread pool and a blocking queue. However, that would require considerably more lines of code.

As of this writing, the flattenMerge operator is marked as @Flow Preview in the source code, which means that this declaration is in a preview state and can be changed in a backward-incompatible manner with a best-effort migration.

We hope that by the time we finish writing this book, the flow-merging API will be stabilized. Otherwise, a similar operator might replace flattenMerge.

What Happens in Case of Error?

If one of the transform functions raises an exception, the entire flow will be cancelled, and the exception will be propagated downstream. While this good default behavior, you might want to handle some exceptions right inside the flow itself.

We'll show how to do that in "Error Handling" on page 251.

Final Thoughts

- Do you realize that we've just created a worker pool that concurrently transforms an incoming stream of objects, using only five lines of code?

- You're guaranteed that the flow machinery is thread-safe. No more headaches figuring out the proper synchronization strategy to pass object references from a thread pool to a collecting thread.

- You can easily tweak the concurrency level, which, in this case, means the maximum number of parallel transformations.

Use Case #3: Create a Custom Operator

Even if a lot of flow operators are available out of the box, sometimes you'll have to make your own. Thankfully, flows are composable, and it's not that difficult to implement custom reactive logic.

For example, by the time we write those lines, there's no Flows operator equivalent of the Project Reactor's bufferTimeout (*https://oreil.ly/udGs0*).

So, what is `bufferTimeout` supposed to do? Imagine that you have an upstream flow of elements, but you want to process those elements by batches and at a fixed maximum rate. The flow returned by `bufferTimeout` should buffer elements and emit a list (batch) of elements when either:

- The buffer is full.
- A predefined maximum amount of time has elapsed (timeout).

Before going through the implementation, let's talk about the key idea. The flow returned by `bufferTimeout` should internally consume the upstream flow and buffer elements. When the buffer is full, or a timeout has elapsed, the flow should emit the content of the buffer (a list). You can imagine that internally we'll start a coroutine that receives two types of events:

- "An element has just been received from the upstream flow. Should we just add it to the buffer or also send the whole buffer?"
- "Timeout! Send the content of the buffer right now."

In Chapter 9 (CSP section), we've discussed a similar situation. The `select` expression is perfect for dealing with multiple events coming from several channels.

Now we're going to implement our `bufferTimeout` flow operator:

```
/**
 * Buffers the upstream flow producing lists of elements when:
 * * A number of [maxSize] elements have been emitted
 * * A timeout of [maxDelayMillis] has expired
 *
 * Consequently, the produced lists of elements have a maximum size of [maxSize].
 */
fun <T> Flow<T>.bufferTimeout(maxSize: Int, maxDelayMillis: Long): Flow<List<T>> = flow {
    require(value: maxSize > 0) { "maxSize should be greater than 0" }
    require(value: maxDelayMillis > 0) { "maxDelayMillis should be greater than 0" }

    coroutineScope { this: CoroutineScope
        val channel : ReceiveChannel<T> = produceIn(scope: this)
        val ticker : ReceiveChannel<Unit> = ticker(maxDelayMillis)
        val buffer : MutableList<T> = mutableListOf<T>()

        suspend fun emitBuffer() {
            if (buffer.isNotEmpty()) {
                emit(buffer.toList())
                buffer.clear()
            }
        }

        try {
            whileSelect { this: SelectBuilder<Boolean>
                channel.onReceive { value : T ->
                    buffer.add(value)
                    if (buffer.size >= maxSize) emitBuffer()
                    true  ^onReceive
                }
                ticker.onReceive {
                    emitBuffer()
                    true  ^onReceive
                }
            }
        } catch (e: ClosedReceiveChannelException) {
            emitBuffer()
        } finally {
            channel.cancel()
            ticker.cancel()
        }
    }
}
```

You can find the corresponding source code in GitHub (*https://oreil.ly/JxkZj*).

Here is the explanation:

- First of all, the signature of the operator tells us a lot. It's declared as an extension function of `Flow<T>`, so you can use it like this: `upstreamFlow.bufferTimeout(10, 100)`. As for the return type, it's `Flow<List<T>>`. Remember that you want to process elements by batches, so the flow returned by `bufferTimeout` should return elements as `List<T>`.

- Line 17: we're using a `flow{}` builder. As a reminder, the builder provides you an instance of `FlowCollector`, and the block of code is an extension function with `FlowCollector` as the receiver type. In other words, you can invoke `emit` from inside the block of code.

- Line 21: we're using `coroutineScope{}` because we'll start new coroutines, which is only possible within a `CoroutineScope`.

- Line 22: from our coroutine standpoint,[4] received elements should come from a `ReceiveChannel`. So another inner coroutine should be started to consume the upstream flow and send them over a channel. This is exactly the purpose of the `produceIn` flow operator.

- Line 23: we need to generate "timeout" events. A library function already exists exactly for that purpose: `ticker`. It creates a channel that produces the first item after the given initial delay, and subsequent items with the given delay between them. As specified in the documentation, `ticker` starts a new coroutine *eagerly*, and we're fully responsible for cancelling it.

- Line 34: we're using `whileSelect`, which really is just syntax sugar for looping in a `select` expression while clauses return `true`. Inside the `whileSelect{}` block you can see the logic of adding an element to the buffer only if it's not full, and emitting the whole buffer otherwise.

- Line 46: when the upstream flow collection completes, the coroutine started with `produceIn` will still attempt to read from that flow, and a `ClosedReceiveChannelException` will be raised. So we catch that exception, and we know that we should emit the content of the buffer.

- Lines 48 and 49: channels are hot entities—they should be cancelled when they're not supposed to be used anymore. As for the `ticker`, it should be cancelled too.

---

4. The coroutine started with `coroutineScope{}`.

Usage

Figure 10-5 shows an example of how `bufferTimeout` can be used.

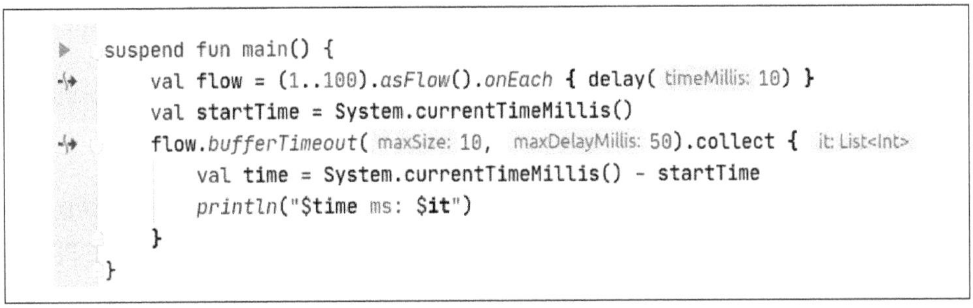

```
suspend fun main() {
    val flow = (1..100).asFlow().onEach { delay( timeMillis: 10) }
    val startTime = System.currentTimeMillis()
    flow.bufferTimeout( maxSize: 10,   maxDelayMillis: 50).collect {   it: List<Int>
        val time = System.currentTimeMillis() - startTime
        println("$time ms: $it")
    }
}
```

Figure 10-5. bufferTimeout usage.

You can find the corresponding source code in GitHub (*https://oreil.ly/Y2xVe*).

The output is:

```
139 ms: [1, 2, 3, 4]
172 ms: [5, 6, 7, 8]
223 ms: [9, 10, 11, 12, 13]
272 ms: [14, 15, 16, 17]
322 ms: [18, 19, 20, 21, 22]
...
1022 ms: [86, 87, 88, 89, 90]
1072 ms: [91, 92, 93, 94, 95]
1117 ms: [96, 97, 98, 99, 100]
```

As you can see, the upstream flow is emitting numbers from 1 to 100, with a delay of 10 ms between each emission. We set a timeout of 50 ms, and each emitted list can contain at most five numbers.

Error Handling

Error handling is fundamental in reactive programming. If you're familiar with RxJava, you probably handle exceptions using the `onError` callback of the `subscribe` method:

```
// RxJava sample
someObservable().subscribe(
    { value -> /* Do something useful */ },
    { error -> println("Error: $error") }
)
```

Using flows, you can handle errors using a combination of techniques, involving:

- The classic try/catch block.
- The catch operator—we'll cover this new operator right after we discuss the try/catch block.

The try/catch Block

If we define a dummy upstream flow made of only three Ints, and purposely throw an exception inside the collect{} block, we can catch the exception by wrapping the whole chain in a try/catch block:

```
val upstream : Flow<Int> = flowOf( ...elements: 1, 2, 3)

fun main() : Unit = runBlocking {   this: CoroutineScope
    try {
        upstream.collect { value : Int ->
            if (value > 2) {
                throw RuntimeException()
            }
            println("Received $value")
        }
    } catch (e: Throwable) {
        println("Caught $e")
    }
}
```

You can find the corresponding source code in GitHub (*https://oreil.ly/qcOKV*).

The output is:

```
Received 1
Received 2
Caught java.lang.RuntimeException
```

It is important to note that try/catch also works when the exception is raised from inside the upstream flow. For example, we get the exact same result if we change the definition of the upstream flow to:

```
val upstream : Flow<Int>  = flowOf( ...elements: 1, 2, 3)
    .onEach { value : Int ->
        if (value > 2) throw RuntimeException()
    }

fun main() = runBlocking { this: CoroutineScope
    try {
        upstream.collect { value : Int ->
            println("Received $value")
        }
    } catch (e: Throwable) {
        println("Caught $e")
    }
}
```

You can find the corresponding source code in GitHub (*https://oreil.ly/lrrGt*).

However, if you try to intercept an exception in the flow itself, you're likely to get unexpected results. Here is an example:

```
// Warning: DON'T DO THIS, this flow swallows downstream exceptions
val upstream: Flow<Int> = flow {
    for (i in 1..3) {
        try {
            emit(i)
        } catch (e: Throwable) {
            println("Intercept downstream exception $e")
        }
    }
}

fun main() = runBlocking {
    try {
        upstream.collect { value ->
            println("Received $value")
            check(value <= 2) {
                "Collected $value while we expect values below 2"
            }
        }
    } catch (e: Throwable) {
        println("Caught $e")
    }
}
```

In this example, we're using the `flow` builder to define `upstream`, and we wrapped the `emit` invocation inside a `try/catch` statement. Even if it seems useless because `emit` isn't throwing exceptions, it could make sense with nontrivial emission logic nevertheless. At the consuming site, in the `main` function, we collect that flow and we check that we don't get values strictly greater than 2. Otherwise, the `catch` block should print `Caught java.lang.IllegalStateException Collected x` while we expect values below 2.

We expect the following output:

```
Received 1
Received 2
Caught java.lang.IllegalStateException: Collected 3 while we expect values
below 2
```

However, this is what we actually get:

```
Received 1
Received 2
Received 3
Intercept downstream exception java.lang.IllegalStateException: Collected 3
while we expect values below 2
```

Despite the exception raised by `check(value <= 2) {..}`, that exception gets caught not by the `try/catch` statement of the `main` function, but by the `try/catch` statement of the flow.

 A try/catch statement inside a flow builder might catch *downstream* exceptions—which includes exceptions raised during the collection of the flow.

Separation of Concern Is Important

A flow implementation shouldn't have a side effect on the code that collects that flow. Likewise, the code that collects a flow shouldn't be aware of the implementation details of the upstream flow. A flow should always be *transparent to exceptions*: it should propagate exceptions coming from a collector. In other words, a flow should never swallow downstream exceptions.

Throughout this book, we'll refer to *exception transparency* to designate a flow that is *transparent to exceptions*.

Exception Transparency Violation

The previous example was an example of exception transparency violation. Trying to emit values from inside a try/catch block is another violation. Here is an example (again, don't do this!):

```
val violatesExceptionTransparency: Flow<Int> = flow {
    for (i in 1..3) {
        try {
            emit(i)
        } catch (e: Throwable) {
            emit(-1)
        }
    }
}

fun main() = runBlocking {
    try {
        violatesExceptionTransparency.collect { value ->
            check(value <= 2) { "Collected $value" }
        }
    } catch (e: Throwable) {
        println("Caught $e")
    }
}
```

The output is:

```
Caught java.lang.IllegalStateException: Flow exception transparency is
violated:
Previous 'emit' call has thrown exception java.lang.IllegalStateException:
Collected 3, but then emission attempt of value '-1' has been detected.
Emissions from 'catch' blocks are prohibited in order to avoid unspecified
behaviour, 'Flow.catch' operator can be used instead.
For a more detailed explanation, please refer to Flow documentation.
```

The try/catch block should *only* be used to surround the collector, to handle exceptions raised from the collector itself, or (possibly, although it's not ideal) to handle exceptions raised from the flow.

To handle exceptions inside the flow, you should use the catch operator.

The catch Operator

The `catch` operator allows for a declarative style of catching exceptions, as shown in Figure 10-6. It catches all upstream exceptions. By all exceptions, we mean that it even catches `Throwables`. Since it only catches upstream exceptions, the `catch` operator doesn't have the exception issue of the `try/catch` block.

```kotlin
val upstream : Flow<Int> = flowOf( ...elements: 1, 2, 3)

val encapsulateError : Flow<Int> = upstream
    .onEach { it: Int
        if (it > 2) throw RuntimeException()
    }
    .catch { e : Throwable ->
        println("Caught $e")
    }

fun main() = runBlocking { this: CoroutineScope
    encapsulateError.collect { it: Int
        println("Received $it")
    }
}
```

Figure 10-6. Declarative style.

You can find the corresponding source code in GitHub (*https://oreil.ly/QcUeq*).

The output is:

```
Received 1
Received 2
Caught java.lang.RuntimeException
```

The flow raises a `RuntimeException` if it's passed a value greater than 2. Right after, in the `catch` operator, we print in the console. However, the collector never get the value 3. So the `catch` operator automatically cancels the flow.

Exception transparency

From inside this operator, you can only catch *upstream exceptions*. When we say upstream, we mean relative to the `catch` operator. To show what we mean, we'll pick an example where the collector throws an exception before the flow internally throws another exception. The collector should be able to catch the raised exception (the exception shouldn't be caught by the flow):

```
val upstream : Flow<Int> = flowOf( ...elements: 1, 3, -1)

val encapsulateError : Flow<Int> = upstream
    .onEach { it: Int
        if (it < 0) throw NumberFormatException("Values should be greater than 0")
    }
    .catch { e : Throwable ->
        println("Caught $e")
    }

fun main() = runBlocking { this: CoroutineScope
    try {
        encapsulateError.collect { it: Int
            if (it > 2) throw RuntimeException()
            println("Received $it")
        }
    } catch (e: RuntimeException) {
        println("Collector stopped collecting the flow")
    }
}
```

You can find the corresponding source code in GitHub (*https://oreil.ly/0U5h1*).

In this example, the collector throws a RuntimeException if it collects a value greater than 2. The collection logic is wrapped in a try/catch statement because we don't want our program to crash and log the exception. The flow internally raises a Number formatException if the value is negative. The catch operator acts as a safeguard (logs the exception and cancels the flow).

The output is:

```
Received 0
Collector stopped collecting the flow
```

Note that the flow didn't intercept the exception raised inside the collector, because it was caught in the catch clause of the try/catch. The flow never got to raise a NumberformatException, because the collector prematurely cancelled the collection.

Another example

In "Use Case #2: Concurrently Transform a Stream of Values" on page 245, we held off on talking about error handling. Suppose the transform function might raise exceptions, among which is NumberFormatException. You can selectively handle Num berFormatException using the catch operator:

```
fun main() = runBlocking {
    // Defining the Flow of Content - nothing is executing yet
    val contentFlow = locationsFlow.map { loc ->
        flow {
            emit(transform(loc))
        }.catch { cause: Throwable ->
            if (cause is NumberFormatException) {        ❶
                println("Handling $cause")
            } else {
                throw cause                              ❷
            }
        }
    }.flattenMerge(4)

    // We now collect the entire flow using the toList terminal operator
    val contents = contentFlow.toList()
}
```

❶ As the catch operator catches Throwables, we need to check the type of the error. If the error is a NumberFormatException, then we handle it inside the if statement. You can add other checks there for different error types.

❷ Otherwise, you don't know the error's type. In most cases, it's preferable not to swallow the error and rethrow.

You can use emit from inside catch

Sometimes it will make sense to emit a particular value when you catch an exception from inside the flow:

```
val upstream : Flow<Int> = flowOf( ...elements: 1, 3, -1)

val encapsulateError : Flow<Int> = upstream
    .onEach { it: Int
        if (it < 0) throw NumberFormatException("Values should be greater than 0")
    }
    .catch { e : Throwable ->
        emit( value: 0)
    }

fun main() = runBlocking { this: CoroutineScope
    encapsulateError.collect { it: Int
        println("Received $it")
    }
}
```

You can find the corresponding source code in GitHub (*https://oreil.ly/vknEm*).

The output is:

```
Received 1
Received 3
Received 0
```

Emitting values from inside catch is especially useful to *materialize exceptions*.

Materialize Your Exceptions

Materializing exceptions[5] is the process of catching exceptions and emitting special values or objects that represent those exceptions. The goal is to avoid throwing exceptions from inside the flow, because code execution then goes to whatever place that collects that flow. It doesn't matter whether collection code handles exceptions thrown by the flow or not. If the flow throws exceptions, the collection code needs to be aware of those exceptions and catch them in order to avoid undefined behavior. Consequently, the flow has a *side effect on the collection code*, and this is a violation of the exception transparency principle.

 The collection code shouldn't be aware of implementation details of the flow. For example, if the flow is a Flow<Number>, you should only expect to get Number values (or subtypes)—not exceptions.

Let's take another example. Imagine you're fetching images, given their URLs. You have an incoming flow of URLs:

```
// We don't use realistic URLs, for brevity
val urlFlow = flowOf("url-1", "url-2", "url-retry")
```

You also have this function already available:

```
suspend fun fetchImage(url: String): Image {
    // Simulate some remote call
    delay(10)

    // Simulate an exception thrown by the server or API
    if (url.contains("retry")) {
```

---

5. *Materialize* comes from the Rx operator of the same name. See the Rx documentation (*https://oreil.ly/SEiRP*) for more insight.

```
        throw IOException("Server returned HTTP response code 503")
    }

    return Image(url)
}

data class Image(val url: String)
```

This `fetchImage` function may throw IOExceptions. In order to craft a "flow of images" using the `urlFlow` and the `fetchImage` function, you should materialize IOExceptions. Regarding the `fetchImage` function, it either succeeds or fails—you either get an `Image` instance, or an exception is thrown. You can represent these outcomes by a `Result` type, with `Success` and `Error` subclasses:[6]

```
sealed class Result
data class Success(val image: Image) : Result()
data class Error(val url: String) : Result()
```

In the case of a success, we wrap the actual result—the `Image` instance. In the case of failure, we felt it was appropriate to wrap the URL for which image retrieval failed. However, you're free to wrap all data that might be useful for the collection code, such as the exception itself.

Now you can encapsulate `fetchImage` usage, by creating a `fetchResult` function which returns `Result` instances:

```
suspend fun fetchResult(url: String): Result {
    println("Fetching $url..")
    return try {
        val image = fetchImage(url)
        Success(image)
    } catch (e: IOException) {
        Error(url)
    }
}
```

Finally, you can implement a `resultFlow` and collect it safely:

```
fun main() = runBlocking {
    val urlFlow = flowOf("url-1", "url-2", "url-retry")

    val resultFlow = urlFlow
```

---

6. These subclasses are an algebraic data type.

```
        .map { url -> fetchResult(url) }

    val results = resultFlow.toList()
    println("Results: $results")
}
```

The output is:

```
Fetching url-1..
Fetching url-2..
Fetching url-retry..
Results: [Success(image=Image(url=url-1)), Success(image=Image(url=url-2)),
Error(url=url-retry)]
```

A bonus

Imagine that you'd like to automatically retry fetching an image in the event of an error. You can implement a custom flow operator that retries an `action` while the `predicate` returns true:

```
fun <T, R : Any> Flow<T>.mapWithRetry(
    action: suspend (T) -> R,
    predicate: suspend (R, attempt: Int) -> Boolean
) = map { data ->
    var attempt = 0L
    var shallRetry: Boolean
    var lastValue: R? = null
    do {
        val tr = action(data)
        shallRetry = predicate(tr, ++attempt)
        if (!shallRetry) lastValue = tr
    } while (shallRetry)
    return@map lastValue
}
```

If you'd like to retry, three times (at most) before returning an error, you can use this operator like so:

```
fun main() = runBlocking {
    val urlFlow = flowOf("url-1", "url-2", "url-retry")

    val resultFlowWithRetry = urlFlow
        .mapWithRetry(
            { url -> fetchResult(url) },
            { value, attempt -> value is Error && attempt < 3L }
        )
```

```
    val results = resultFlowWithRetry.toList()
    println("Results: $results")
}
```

The output is:

```
Fetching url-1..
Fetching url-2..
Fetching url-retry..
Fetching url-retry..
Fetching url-retry..
Results: [Success(image=Image(url=url-1)), Success(image=Image(url=url-2)),
Error(url=url-retry)]
```

Hot Flows with SharedFlow

Previous implementations of flow were *cold*: nothing runs until you start collecting the flow. This is made possible because for each emitted value, only one collector would get the value. Therefore, there's no need to run anything until the collector is ready to collect the values.

However, what if you need to *share* emitted values among several collectors? For example, say an event like a file download completes in your app. You might want to directly notify various components, such as some view-models, repositories, or even some views. Your file downloader might not have to be aware of the existence of other parts of your app. A good separation of concerns starts with a loose coupling of classes, and the *event bus* is one architecture pattern that helps in this situation.

The principle is simple: the downloader emits an event (an instance of a class, optionally holding some state) by giving it to the event bus, and all subscribers subsequently receive that event. A SharedFlow can act just like that, as shown in Figure 10-7.

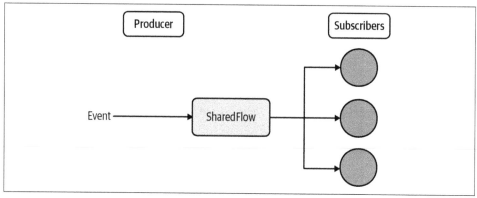

Figure 10-7. SharedFlow.

A SharedFlow broadcasts events to all its subscribers. Actually, SharedFlow really is a toolbox that can be used in many situations—not just to implement an event bus. Before giving examples of usage, we'll show how to create a SharedFlow and how you can tune it.

Create a SharedFlow

In its simplest usage, you invoke MutableSharedFlow() with no parameter. As its name suggests, you can *mutate* its state, by sending values to it. A common pattern when creating a SharedFlow is to create a private mutable version and a public non-mutable one using asSharedFlow(), as shown in the following:

```
private val _sharedFlow = MutableSharedFlow<Data>()
val sharedFlow: SharedFlow<Data> = _sharedFlow.asSharedFlow()
```

This pattern is useful when you ensure that subscribers will only be able to *read* the flow (e.g., not send values). You might be surprised to find that MutableSharedFlow is not a class. It's actually a function that accepts parameters, which we'll cover later in this chapter. For now, we're only showing the default no-arg version of MutableSharedFlow.

Register a Subscriber

A subscriber registers when it starts collecting the SharedFlow—preferably the public nonmutable version:

```
scope.launch {
    sharedFlow.collect { data ->
        println(data)
    }
}
```

A subscriber can only live in a scope, because the collect terminal operator is a suspending function. This is good for structured concurrency: if the scope is cancelled, so is the subscriber.

Send Values to the SharedFlow

A `MutableSharedFlow` exposes two methods to emit values—`emit` and `tryEmit`:

`emit`
: This suspends under some conditions (discussed shortly).

`tryEmit`
: This never suspends. It tries to emit the value immediately.

Why are there two methods to emit values? This is because, by default, when a `MutableSharedFlow` emits a value using `emit`, it suspends until *all* subscribers start processing the value. We will give an example of `emit` usage in the next section.

However, sometimes this isn't what you want to do. You'll find situations where you have to emit values from nonsuspending code (see "Using SharedFlow as an Event Bus" on page 270). So here comes `tryEmit`, which tries to emit a value immediately and returns `true` if it succeeded, and `false` otherwise. We'll provide more details on the nuances of `emit` and `tryEmit` in upcoming sections.

Using SharedFlow to Stream Data

Suppose you are developing a news app. One of the features of your app is that it fetches news from an API or a local database and displays this news (or newsfeed). Ideally, you should rely on a local database to avoid using the API when possible. In this example, we'll use the API as the only source of news, although you can easily extend on our example to add local persistence.

The architecture

In our architecture, a view-model relies on a repository to get the newsfeed. When the view-model receives news, it notifies the view. The repository is responsible for querying the remote API at regular intervals, and provides a means for view-models to get the newsfeed (see Figure 10-8).

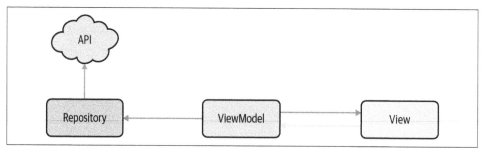

Figure 10-8. App architecture.

The implementation

To keep it simple, the following News data class represents news:

```
data class News(val content: String)
```

The repository reaches the API through a NewsDao. In our example, the data access object (DAO) is manually constructor-injected. In a real application, we recommend that you use a dependency injection (DI) framework such as Hilt or Dagger:

```
interface NewsDao {
    suspend fun fetchNewsFromApi(): List<News>
}
```

We now have enough material to implement the repository:

```
class NewsRepository(private val dao: NewsDao) {
    private val _newsFeed = MutableSharedFlow<News>()      ❶
    val newsFeed = _newsFeed.asSharedFlow()                ❷

    private val scope = CoroutineScope(Job() + Dispatchers.IO)

    init {
        scope.launch {                                     ❸
            while (true) {
                val news = dao.fetchNewsFromApi()
                news.forEach { _newsFeed.emit(it) }        ❹

                delay(3000)
            }
        }
    }

    fun stop() = scope.cancel()
}
```

❶ We create our private mutable shared flow. It will only be used inside the repository.

❷ We create the public nonmutable version of the shared flow.

❸ As soon as the repository instance is created, we start fetching news from the API.

❹ Every time we get a list of News instances, we emit those values using our Mutable SharedFlow.

All that's left is to implement a view-model that will subscribe to the repository's shared flow:

```
class NewsViewsModel(private val repository: NewsRepository) : ViewModel() {
    private val newsList = mutableListOf<News>()

    private val _newsLiveData = MutableLiveData<List<News>>(newsList)
    val newsLiveData: LiveData<List<News>> = _newsLiveData

    init {
        viewModelScope.launch {
            repository.newsFeed.collect {
                println("NewsViewsModel receives $it")
                newsList.add(it)
                _newsLiveData.value = newsList
            }
        }
    }
}
```

By invoking `repository.newsFeed.collect { .. }`, the view-model subscribes to the shared flow. Every time the repository emits a `News` instance to the shared flow, the view-model receives the news and adds it to its `LiveData` to update the view.

Notice how the flow collection happens inside a coroutine started with `viewModelScope.launch`. This implies that if the view-model reaches its end-of-life, the flow collection will automatically be cancelled, and that's a good thing.

 In our example, we manually constructor-inject an object (in this case, the repository). A DI framework would definitely help to avoid boilerplate code. As demonstrating DI frameworks isn't the primary focus of this chapter, we chose to go for a manual repository injection into the view-model.

Test of our implementation

In order to test the previous code, we need to mock the `NewsDao`. Our DAO will just send two dummy `News` instances and increment a counter:

```
val dao = object : NewsDao {
    private var index = 0

    override suspend fun fetchNewsFromApi(): List<News> {
        delay(100) // simulate network delay
        return listOf(
            News("news content ${++index}"),
            News("news content ${++index}")
```

```
            )
        }
    }
}
```

When we run our code using the preceding DAO, this is what we see in the console:

```
NewsViewsModel receives News(content=news content 1)
NewsViewsModel receives News(content=news content 2)
NewsViewsModel receives News(content=news content 3)
...
```

There is nothing surprising here: our view-model simply receives the news sent by the repository. Things become interesting when there's not one but several view-models that subscribe to the shared flow. We've gone ahead and created another view-model which also logs in the console. We created the other view-model 250 ms *after* the launch of the program. This is the output we get:

```
NewsViewsModel receives News(content=news content 1)
NewsViewsModel receives News(content=news content 2)
NewsViewsModel receives News(content=news content 3)
AnotherViewModel receives News(content=news content 3)
NewsViewsModel receives News(content=news content 4)
AnotherViewModel receives News(content=news content 4)
NewsViewsModel receives News(content=news content 5)
AnotherViewModel receives News(content=news content 5)
NewsViewsModel receives News(content=news content 6)
AnotherViewModel receives News(content=news content 6)
...
```

You can see that the other view-model *missed* the first two news entries. This is because, at the time the shared flow emits the first two news entries, the first view-model is the only subscriber. The second view-model comes after and only receives subsequent news.

Replay values

What if you need the second view-model to get previous news? A shared flow can *optionally* cache values so that new subscribers receive the last *n* cached values. In our case, if we want the shared flow to replay the last two news entries, all we have to do is to update the line in the repository:

```
private val _newsFeed = MutableSharedFlow<News>(replay = 2)
```

With that change, the two view-models receive *all* news. Replaying data is actually useful in other common situations. Imagine the user leaves the fragment that displays the list of news. Potentially, the associated view-model might also get destroyed, if its lifecycle is bound to the fragment (that wouldn't be the case if you chose to bound the view-model to the activity). Later on, the user comes back to the news fragment. What happens then? The view-model is re-created and immediately gets the last two news entries while waiting for fresh news. Replaying only two news entries might then be insufficient. Therefore, you might want to increase the replay count to, say, 15.

Let's recap. A SharedFlow can optionally replay values for new subscribers. The number of values to replay is configurable, using the replay parameter of the Mutable SharedFlow function.

Suspend or not?

There's one last thing about this replay feature that you should be aware of. A shared flow with replay > 0 internally uses a cache that works similarly to a Channel. For example, if you create a shared flow with replay = 3, the first three emit calls won't suspend. In this case, emit and tryEmit do exactly the same thing: they add a new value to the cache, as shown in Figure 10-9.

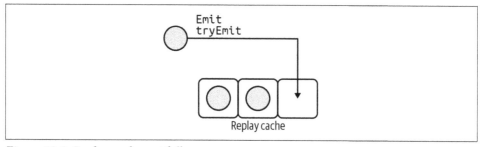

Figure 10-9. Replay cache not full.

When you submit a fourth value to the shared flow, then it depends on whether you use emit or tryEmit, as shown in Figure 10-10. By default, when the replay cache is full, emit suspends until all subscribers start processing the oldest value in the cache. As for tryEmit, it returns false since it can't add the value to the cache. If you don't keep track of that fourth value yourself, this value is lost.

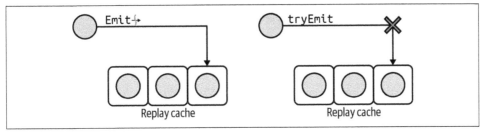

Figure 10-10. Replay cache full.

That behavior (when the replay cache is full) can be changed. You can also opt to discard either the oldest value in the cache or the value that is being added to the cache. In both cases, emit does not suspend and tryEmit returns true. Therefore, there are three possible behaviors on buffer overflow: suspend, drop oldest, and drop latest.

You apply the desired behavior while creating the shared flow, by using the onBufferOverflow parameter, as shown in the following:

```
MutableSharedFlow(replay = 3, onBufferOverflow = BufferOverflow.DROP_OLDEST)
```

BufferOverflow is an *enum* with three possible values: SUSPEND, DROP_OLDEST, and DROP_LATEST. If you don't specify a value for onBufferOverflow, SUSPEND is the default strategy.

Buffer values

In addition to being able to replay values, a shared flow can *buffer* values without replaying them, allowing slow subscribers to lag behind other, faster subscribers. The size of the buffer is customizable, as shown in the following:

```
MutableSharedFlow(extraBufferCapacity = 2)
```

By default, extraBufferCapacity equals zero. When you set a strictly positive value, emit doesn't suspend while there is buffer space remaining—unless you explicitly change the buffer overflow strategy.

You might be wondering in what situations extraBufferCapacity can be useful. One immediate consequence of creating a shared flow with, for example, extraBufferCapacity = 1 and onBufferOverflow = BufferOverflow.DROP_OLDEST, is that you're guaranteed that tryEmit will *always* successfully insert a value into the shared flow. It's sometimes really convenient to insert values in a shared flow from nonsuspending code. A good example of such a use case is when using a shared flow as an event bus.

Using SharedFlow as an Event Bus

You need an event bus when all the following conditions are met:

- You need to broadcast an event across one or several subscribers.
- The event should be processed *only once*.
- If a component isn't registered as a subscriber at the time you emit the event, the event is lost for that component.

Notice the difference with LiveData, which keeps in memory the last emitted value and replays it every time the fragment is re-created. With an event bus, the fragment would only receive the event *once*. For example, if the fragment is re-created (the user rotates the device), the event won't be processed again.

An event bus is particularly useful when you want, for example, to display a message as a Toast or Snackbar. It makes sense to display the message only once. To achieve this, a repository can expose a shared flow as shown in the following code. In order to make the exposed flow accessible for view-models, or even fragments, you can use a DI framework such as Hilt or Dagger:

```
class MessageRepository {
    private val _messageFlow = MutableSharedFlow<String>(
        extraBufferCapacity = 1,
        onBufferOverflow = BufferOverflow.DROP_OLDEST
    )
    val messageEventBus = _messageFlow.asSharedFlow()

    private fun someTask() {
        // Notify subscribers to display a message
        _messageFlow.tryEmit("This is important")
    }
}
```

We've set extraBufferCapacity to 1 and onBufferOverflow to DROP_OLDEST so that _messageFlow.tryEmit always emits successfully. Why do we care about tryEmit? In our example, we use _messageFlow from a nonsuspending function. Therefore, we can't use emit inside someTask.

If you use _messageFlow from inside a coroutine, you can use emit. The behavior would be exactly the same, since emit wouldn't suspend because of the presence of the buffer and the buffer overflow policy.

An event bus is appropriate for dispatching one-time events that some components might miss if they're not ready to receive those events. For example, say you fire a "recording-stopped" event while the user hasn't navigated to the fragment displaying recordings yet. The result is that the event is lost. However, your application can be designed to update the state of the fragment anytime the fragment resumes. Consequently, receiving "recording-stopped" is only useful when the fragment is in the resumed state, as this should trigger a state update. This is just an example of when losing events is totally acceptable and part of your application's design.

Sometimes, however, this isn't what you want to achieve. Take, for example, a service that can perform downloads. If the service fires a "download-finished" event, you don't want your UI to miss that. When the user navigates to the view displaying the status of the download, the view should render the updated *state* of the download.

You will face situations where sharing a *state* is required. This situation is so common that a type of shared flow was specifically created for it: StateFlow.

StateFlow: A Specialized SharedFlow

When sharing a state, a state flow:

- Shares only one value: the current *state*.
- Replays the state. Indeed, subscribers should get the last state even if they subscribe afterward.
- Emits an initial value—much like LiveData has an initial value.
- Emits new values only when the state changes.

As you've learned previously, this behavior can be achieved using a shared flow:

```
val shared = MutableSharedFlow(
    replay = 1,
    onBufferOverflow = BufferOverflow.DROP_OLDEST
)
shared.tryEmit(initialValue) // emit the initial value
val state = shared.distinctUntilChanged() // get StateFlow-like behavior
```

StateFlow[7] is a shorthand for the preceding code. In practice, all you have to write is:

```
val state = MutableStateFlow(initialValue)
```

---

7. Actually, StateFlow *is* a SharedFlow under the hood.

An Example of StateFlow Usage

Imagine that you have a download service that can emit three possible download states: download started, downloading, and download finished, as shown in Figure 10-11.

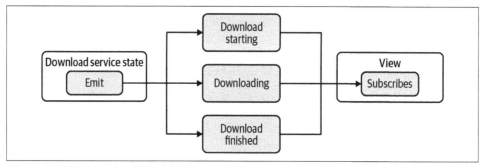

Figure 10-11. Download state.

Exposing a flow from an Android service can be done in several ways. If you need high decoupling for, say, testability purposes, a DI-injected "repository" object can expose the flow. The repository is then injected in all components that need to subscribe. Or the service can statically expose the flow in a companion object. This induces tight coupling between all components that use the flow. However, it might be acceptable in a small app or for demo purpose, such as in the following example:

```
class DownloadService : Service() {
    companion object {
        private val _downloadState =
            MutableStateFlow<ServiceStatus>(Stopped)
        val downloadState = _downloadState.asStateFlow()
    }
    // Rest of the code hidden for brevity
}

sealed class ServiceStatus
object Started : ServiceStatus()
data class Downloading(val progress: Int) : ServiceStatus()
object Stopped : ServiceStatus()
```

Internally, the service can update its state by using, for example, _downloadState.tryEmit(Stopped). When declared inside a companion object, the state flow can be easily accessed from a view-model, and exposed as a LiveData using asLiveData():

```
class DownloadViewModel : ViewModel() {
    val downloadServiceStatus = DownloadService.downloadState.asLiveData()
}
```

Subsequently, a view can subscribe to the LiveData:

```
class DownloadFragment : Fragment() {
    private val viewModel: DownloadViewModel by viewModels()

    override fun onCreate(savedInstanceState: Bundle?) {
        super.onCreate(savedInstanceState)

        viewModel.downloadServiceStatus.observe(this) {      ❶
            it?.also {
                onDownloadServiceStatus(it)
            }
        }
    }

    private fun onDownloadServiceStatus(
        status: ServiceStatus
    ): Nothing = when (status) {                             ❷
        Started -> TODO("Show download is about to start")
        Stopped -> TODO("Show download stopped")
        is Downloading -> TODO("Show progress")
    }
}
```

❶ We subscribe to the LiveData. If we receive a nonnull value, then we invoke onDownloadServiceStatus method.

❷ We are purposely using when as an expression so that the Kotlin compiler guarantees that all possible types of ServiceStatus are taken into account.

You might be wondering why we used a state flow, and why we haven't used a Live Data in the first place—eliminating the need of asLiveData() in the view-model.

The reason is simple. LiveData is Android-specific. It's a lifecycle-aware component which is meaningful when used within Android views. You might design your application with Kotlin multiplatform code in mind. When targeting Android and iOS, only multiplatform code can be shared as common code. The coroutine library is multiplatform. LiveData isn't.

However, even when not considering Kotlin multiplatform, the Flows API makes more sense since it provides greater flexibility with all its flows operators.

Summary

- The Flows API allows for *asynchronous data stream transformation*. A lot of operators are already available out of the box and cover most use cases.

- Thanks to the *composable* nature of flow operators, you can fairly easily design your own, if you need to.

- Some parts of the flow can be offloaded to a background thread or thread pool, and yet keep a high-level view of data transformation.

- A shared flow broadcasts values to all its subscribers. You can enable buffering and/or replay of values. Shared flows really are a toolbox. You can use them as an event bus for one-time events, or in more complex interactions between components.

- When a component shares its state, a special kind of shared flow is appropriate for use: state flow. It replays the last state for new subscribers and only notifies subscribers when the state changes.

CHAPTER 11

Performance Considerations with Android Profiling Tools

Using proficient concurrency in Android leads to better performance in your application. This is why we have made Kotlin concurrency in Android the primary focus of this book. In order to provide a solution for performance bottlenecks, you have to be able to spot them in the first place. Have no worry: this chapter looks at popular Android tooling commonly used to check for potential problems in performance.

Out in the wild, Android faces real-life challenges that affect performance and battery life. For example, not everyone has unlimited data in their mobile plans, or reliable connectivity. The reality is that Android apps must compete with one another for limited resources. Performance should be a serious consideration for any Android application. Android development doesn't stop at creating an app. Effective development also ensures a smooth and seamless user experience. Even if you have a deep understanding of Android development, your application may have issues such as:

- Decrease in performance
- Slow startup/slow response to user interactions
- Battery drain
- Wasteful use of resources, and clogged memory
- UI bugs that don't force a crash or generate an exception, but nevertheless affect user experience

This list of sudden, strange behaviors in an app is by no means exhaustive. As previous chapters showed, managing multithreading can become complex when there are also interacting Android components to keep track of. Even if you have a solid understanding of multithreading, it's hard to say how an application really works until we analyze performance with profiling tools. To answer these kinds of ambiguities, there are several useful tools for profiling various aspects of Android. Four of them can be retrieved and used right in Android Studio, as diagrammed in Figure 11-1.

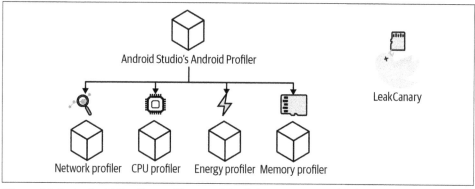

Figure 11-1. Android Studio profilers and LeakCanary are useful for identifying performance bottlenecks.

In this chapter, we look at profiling tools in Android Studio's *Android Profiler* and a popular open source library called *LeakCanary*. We explore each one by profiling a real-life application for potential performance bottlenecks. Remember the hiking application described in previous chapters? Surprise! It was inspired by *TrekMe*. TrekMe is an Android trail-trekking app, an open source Android project where users download interactive topographical hiking routes to use offline later while on hikes. TrekMe started as a Java project, but its codebase is currently 80%+ Kotlin. Here are some important features of TrekMe that users of the application can enjoy:

- Download topographical maps for offline use.
- Get the device's live position even when there's no network, while the app tries its best to preserve battery life.
- Track hikes in great detail without draining the device's battery when you need it most.
- Access other useful information without needing an internet connection (save for creating the map).

We encourage you to explore TrekMe so you can follow along with this chapter. You can retrieve the source code from GitHub (*https://oreil.ly/j7KbY*). Once you've cloned the project, open it with Android Studio. Finally, run an instance of an emulator from the *Android Virtual Device (AVD) Manager* that you intend to run TrekMe on.

Performance considerations are crucial. It;s not uncommon to find performance lag in any application, but such a "fishing expedition" must be approached with care. It's up to the developer to decide on the most relevant tooling, and which optimizations outweigh in benefits the cost of their creation. Profiling your app allows you to investigate application performance objectively. To give some examples of the kinds of surprises you might encounter, we'll look at TrekMe with Android Profiler.

Android Profiler

Android Profiler analyzes an application's session to generate real-time feeds for CPU usage and memory usage, as well as network and energy profiling. Figure 11-2 shows Android Studio with the TrekMe application runtime showing in the bottom half of the console.

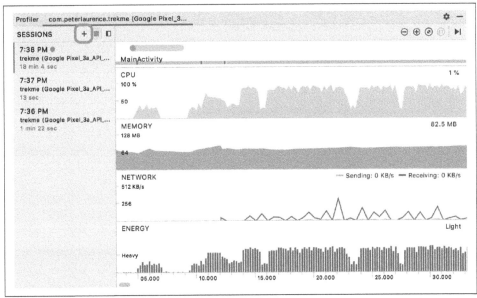

Figure 11-2. A profiling session records profiling data. The active session attaches to the running app in the emulator (not pictured).

Android profiling can be instantiated in three ways:

1. If your application is not running, click the Profile app icon in the upper-right corner to instantiate the app and the profiler at once. This action builds and compiles a new running instance of the application. Android Studio will then open a new session giving you a stream of your data in real time.

2. If your application is already running, click the + icon and select the running emulator.

3. You can also import a previously saved profiling session with the + icon. From there, you can load the previously saved *.hprof* file.

You can record and store data in each session. In Figure 11-3, we show a screenshot of saved profiling sessions with different kinds of data that can be recorded with Android Profiler.

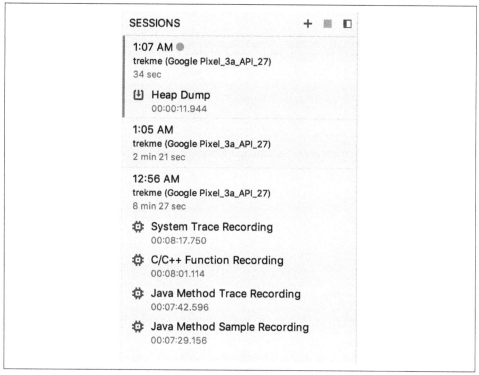

SESSIONS   + ▩ ▢

1:07 AM ●
trekme (Google Pixel_3a_API_27)
34 sec

⤓ Heap Dump
     00:00:11.944

1:05 AM
trekme (Google Pixel_3a_API_27)
2 min 21 sec

12:56 AM
trekme (Google Pixel_3a_API_27)
8 min 27 sec

⚙ System Trace Recording
     00:08:17.750

⚙ C/C++ Function Recording
     00:08:01.114

⚙ Java Method Trace Recording
     00:07:42.596

⚙ Java Method Sample Recording
     00:07:29.156

Figure 11-3. Save heap dumps, or different kinds of CPU traces.

Both *method traces* and *heap dumps* can be saved as separate entries within a running session. Method traces show a stacktrace of methods and functions that can be recorded in CPU profiling. Meanwhile, a heap dump refers to the data collected from *garbage collection*, allowing us to analyze what objects are taking up unnecessary space in memory.

Android Profiler records one application session at a time. However, you can save multiple recordings and switch between them to compare the data. A bright dot indicates the recording of an active session. In Figure 11-3, there are three recorded sessions. The last recorded session has a saved heap dump, which refers to a log of stored memory in the JVM at the time of the snapshot. We'll cover this in more detail in "Memory Profiler" on page 299. The first recorded session saved different kinds of CPU recordings. This will be discussed in "CPU Profiler" on page 286.

Android Studio caches sessions only for the lifetime of the Android Studio instance. If Android Studio is restarted, the recorded sessions will not save.

The following sections show in more detail how Android Profiler evaluates device resources in the virtual machine at runtime. There are four profilers we'll use: *Network Profiler*, *CPU Profiler*, *Energy Profiler*, and *Memory Profiler*. All of these profilers record streams of data during an application's runtime, which can be accessed in greater detail in their own special views.

By design, TrekMe encourages users to download detailed topographical maps directly to their devices while they're at home and can do so easily. Creating new topographical maps in TrekMe is the feature that consumes the most resources in this process. The maps can then be rendered when the user is hiking, even if mobile coverage is unreliable. TrekMe's map creation feature allows you to select an official map generator like the *Instituto Geografico Nacional* (IGN) or *U.S. Geological Survey* (USGS) or some other map provider, as shown in Figure 11-4. TrekMe will then load the selected service's map in square tiles, one by one.

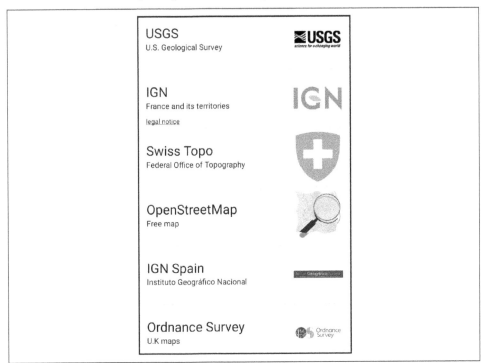

Figure 11-4. TrekMe allows you to create and download a map from different services.

For the remainder of this chapter, we'll profile TrekMe while creating a map via IGN to study the time it takes to load a map, and to ensure that it is optimal. With Android profiling, we can explore questions like:

- Are we making fast network calls?
- Is the data we get in our response returned in the most efficient format?
- What parts of the application are the most CPU-intensive?
- Which Android actions drain the most battery?
- What objects are eating up the most memory in heap?
- What consumes the most memory?

In the next section, we answer the first two questions with Network Profiler. We explore the remainder of these questions in later sections.

Network Profiler

When a network call is made, the radio in the Android device powers up to allow for network communication. This radio then stays powered on for a short time to ensure there are no additional requests to listen for. On some phones, using the network every two minutes keeps the device at full power forever. Too many network calls can be expensive for Android resources, so it is important to analyze and optimize network use in an application.

Network Profiler generates connection breakdowns used by *HttpURLConnection* or *OkHttp* libraries. It can give you information like network request/response time, headers, cookies, data formats, the call stack, and more. When you record a session, Network Profiler generates interactive visual data while you continue to interact with the application.

When we create a map using IGN, TrekMe renders the map on the screen in square tiles, one by one. Sometimes, though, the tile rendering seems to take a long time. Figure 11-5 shows the profiler capturing incoming/outgoing network requests, and shows the connections that are available while creating a map on TrekMe via IGN:

You can highlight a selected range of the timeline to drill into these connections further, which will expand a new view of the Network Profiler workspace, allowing you to access the *Connection View* and *Thread View* tabs to analyze these network calls further.

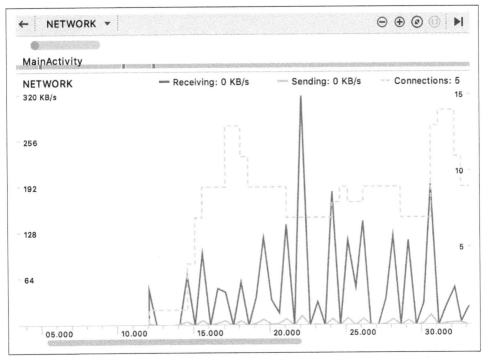

Figure 11-5. Network Profiler timeline records IGN Spain map creation on TrekMe. In the upper-left corner of the chat, the long line under the label MainActivity *represents an active* Activity *session while the short, thick line above the* MainActivity *label with a dot at the left represents user touch events.*

Viewing network calls with Connection View and Thread View

Connection View shows the data that was sent/received. You can see this in Figure 11-6 in the highlighted portion of the timeline. Perhaps what is most notable is Connection View's ability to sort resource files by size, status, and time. Clicking the header of each section will organize the ordering of the desired filter. The timeline section represents the timing of the request/response bars split into two colors. The lighter portion represents the duration of the request, while the darker portion represents the duration of the response.

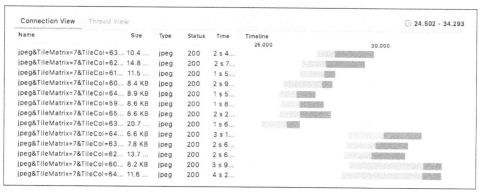

Connection View	Thread View							⏱ 24.502 - 34.293
Name	Size	Type	Status	Time	Timeline			
					25.000		30.000	
jpeg&TileMatrix=7&TileCol=63...	10.4 ...	jpeg	200	2 s 4...				
jpeg&TileMatrix=7&TileCol=62...	14.8 ...	jpeg	200	2 s 7...				
jpeg&TileMatrix=7&TileCol=61...	11.5 ...	jpeg	200	1 s 5...				
jpeg&TileMatrix=7&TileCol=60...	8.4 KB	jpeg	200	2 s 9...				
jpeg&TileMatrix=7&TileCol=64...	8.9 KB	jpeg	200	1 s 5...				
jpeg&TileMatrix=7&TileCol=59...	8.6 KB	jpeg	200	1 s 8...				
jpeg&TileMatrix=7&TileCol=65...	8.6 KB	jpeg	200	2 s 2...				
jpeg&TileMatrix=7&TileCol=63...	20.7 ...	jpeg	200	1 s 6...				
jpeg&TileMatrix=7&TileCol=64...	6.6 KB	jpeg	200	3 s 1...				
jpeg&TileMatrix=7&TileCol=63...	7.8 KB	jpeg	200	2 s 6...				
jpeg&TileMatrix=7&TileCol=62...	13.7 ...	jpeg	200	2 s 6...				
jpeg&TileMatrix=7&TileCol=60...	8.2 KB	jpeg	200	3 s 9...				
jpeg&TileMatrix=7&TileCol=64...	11.6 ...	jpeg	200	4 s 2...				

Figure 11-6. Connection View shows a list of individual network calls.

Connection View looks similar to the timeline in Thread View, but they're not quite the same. Thread View shows the network calls being made within the designated initiating threads, which can show multiple network calls running in parallel time. The screenshot shown in Figure 11-7 is the complement of the previous image, using the same data set.

Initiating thread	Timeline		
	25.000	30.000	
Thread-14	eRo¡ jpeg&TileMatrix=7&TileCol=5... Matrix=7&T...	jpeg&TileMatrix=7&TileCol=65&Til¡ jpeg&TileMatrix=7...	
Thread-15	jpeg&TileMatrix=7&TileC...	jpeg&TileMatrix=7&TileCol=64&TileRow=51	
Thread-16	·eg&TileMatrix=7&Tile... jpeg&TileMatrix=7&TileCol=6...	jpeg&TileMatrix=7&TileCol=64&TileRow=51 eMat...	
Thread-17	ow=4 jpeg&TileMatrix=7&TileCol=... ·Matrix=7&TileC... jpeg&TileMa	3.19 s	
Thread-18		**Also accessed by:**	eMat...
Thread-19	jpeg&TileMatrix=7&TileCol=61... ·rix=7&TileCol=65...)Matrix=} jpeg&	Thread-21	
Thread-21		jpeg&TileMatrix=7&TileCol=62&TileRow=...	
Thread-23		jpeg&TileMatrix=7&TileCol=59&TileRow=52	jpeg... ¡
Thread-24	jpeg&TileMatrix=7&Ti... jpeg&TileMatrix=7&78 jpeg&TileMatrix=7&TileCol· jpeg&TileMatrix=7&1 jpeg&TileMat...		
Thread-25	Matrix=7&TileCol=62... ·eMatrix=7&TileCol=62&...	jpeg&TileMatrix=7&TileCol=53&TileRo...	

Figure 11-7. Thread View shows a list of network calls made within each thread.

Seeing how worker threads divide labor in real time can help to reveal areas for improvement. TrekMe's pooled threads are responsible for automatically breaking up, as needed, the work of downloading all these images.

Both images show roughly 23 seconds of network calls, with response times showing a similar trend. Compared to the requests, responses appear to take up a disproportionate amount of the time it takes to complete an entire network call. There could be several reasons for this: for example, the server connection might be weaker if a device attempts to pull this data from a distant country. Perhaps there are inefficiencies with the query call in the backend. Regardless of the reason, we can say that our network calls may not be fastest. However, the presence of fast request times *and* slow response times indicates external factors that are out of the device's control.

We now turn to our second question: are we using the most efficient data format? Let's look at the connection type in the Connection View tab as pictured in Figure 11-6. If you don't need transparency in your images, avoid using PNG files since the file format doesn't compress as well as JPEG or WebP. In our case, the network calls return a JPEG-formatted payload. We want files that provide consistent and good image quality to enable users to zoom in to the details of those images as much as they need to. Using a JPEG file also takes up less memory than a PNG file would.

We can get more granular detail on each network call and its payload by selecting any item: this opens a new view within Network Profiler on the right side, showing tabs for Overview, Response, Request, and Callstack. In the next section, we'll be able to look into the specifics of a single network call and locate where the network call is made in the code.

Network call, expanded: Overview | Response | Request | Callstack

Android developers are used to working with other platforms in order to achieve feature parity and more. Suppose a network call starts returning the wrong kind of information for a network request. The API team is in need of specifics for the network request and response you're getting on the client side. How can you send them over the necessary request parameters and content headers they need to investigate on their side?

Network Profiler gives us the ability to inspect network responses and requests on the right-side panel in Connection View or Thread View, as shown in Figure 11-8.

The *Overview* tab details notable highlights captured in the request and response:

Request
　　The path and potential query parameters

Status
　　The HTTP status code returned within the resulting response

Method
　　The type of method used

Content type
　　The media type of the resource

Size
　　The size of the resource returned in the resulting response

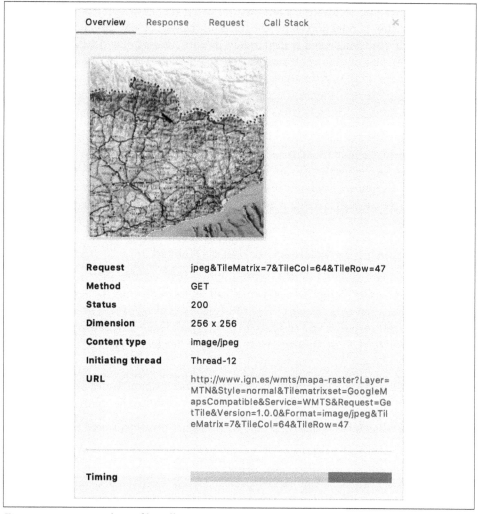

Figure 11-8. Network Profiler allows you to inspect response and request information.

The *Request* and *Response* tabs show a breakdown of headers, parameters, body data, etc. In Figure 11-9, we show the exact network call as in the previous image, except with the Response tab selected.

As you can see in the network response, TrekMe uses a basic HTTP API. Other types of API data formats return HTML, JSON, and other resources. When applicable, the Request and Response tabs offer body data as a formatted or raw representation. In our case, the resource media returns JPEGs.

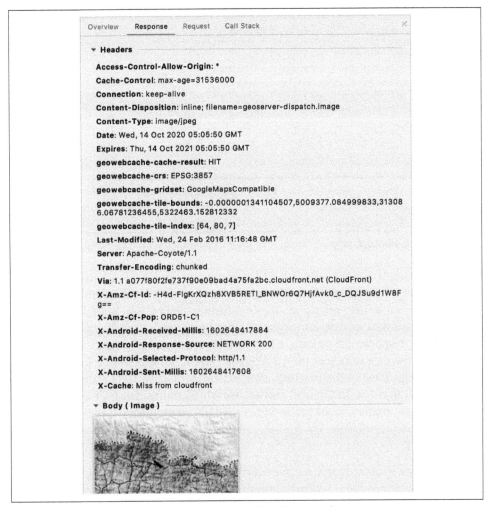

Figure 11-9. Network Profiler captures network calls to render map.

Finally, the *Call Stack* tab, shows the stacktrace for the relevant calls made to execute a network connection, as pictured in Figure 11-10. The calls that are not faded represent the method calls within the call stack coming from your own code. You can right-click the calls indicated to be able to jump to the source code with ease.

Network Profiler is useful for more than just analytics. As you can see for yourself, you're able to process a lot of information quickly. From caching repetitive calls to confirming API contracts, Network Profiler is a tool worth keeping in your toolbox.

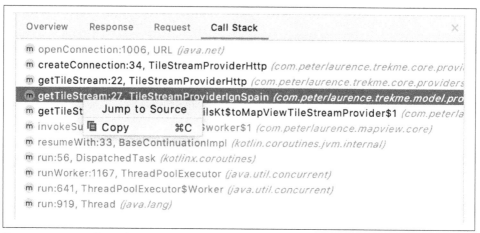

Figure 11-10. Call Stack tab.

Poor networking is not the only culprit when it comes to slow rendering times. The task of creating a brand new topographical map is heavy in itself, but as we have determined from a networking stance, no further action is required to improve loading times or data format. However, we would be remiss to chalk up slow loading times to slow response time alone. After TrekMe receives the network data, it must then process the data to render the UI. For this reason, we should check for potential inefficiencies in drawing the map out after the network calls. *CPU Profiler* is able to provide insight for this. In the next section, we will examine, using CPU Profiler, the processing consumption of the rendering of the IGN Spain map.

CPU Profiler

While Network Profiler is able to give information about network calls, it is not able to paint a full picture about where the time goes. We have a call stack for our network calls, but we don't know how long certain methods actually run. This is where CPU Profiler comes in. CPU Profiler helps identify greedy consumption of resources by analyzing how much time has passed on function execution and tracks which thread a call executes on. Why does this matter? If TrekMe consumes too much processing, the application slow downs, impacting the user experience. The more CPU power that is used, the more quickly the battery drains.

CPU Profiler allows you to examine CPU recordings and livestream data by examining the call stack by the thread, as shown in Figure 11-11.

In the following sections, we break down the CPU timeline, Thread activity timeline, and Analysis panels. Because TrekMe seems to spend a lot of time offloading work to background threads, we will select one to look into more closely.

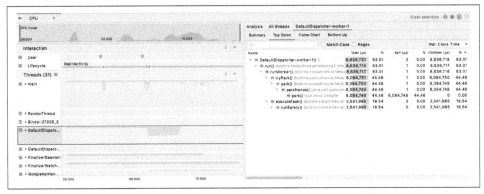

Figure 11-11. CPU Profiler shows the call stack and recorded times for methods executed.

CPU timeline

The CPU timeline organizes regional call stacks into recorded threads in the Threads pane. The graph in Figure 11-12 shows spikes of CPU usage, where the number is a percentage of available CPU. If you have made a trace recording, you should be able to highlight the CPU timeline to see more information.

Figure 11-12. CPU timeline.

Android Studio allows you to drag-and-click over a recorded sample from the CPU timeline to show the Call Chart. Clicking on Record brings you to a separate trace CPU recording screen (covered in greater detail in *Record Traces*). To create the more granular call charts we explore in the next section, it helps to highlight smaller portions of the recorded CPU trace.

Thread activity timeline

The Thread activity timeline accompanies the CPU timeline showing every running thread in the app. If a section was trace-recorded, you should be able to select a thread to view the call stack captured within the selected time range. In Figure 11-13, 31 threads have been created and used within the application. These threads have been created either by your code, the Android OS, or a third-party library.

Figure 11-13. Thread activity timeline.

The lightest-colored blocks represent a running or active thread. There's not a lot to see on the Main thread, but remember, this image captures a CPU trace of the network request downloading the map images. In this case, we expect background threads to do the necessary work to download the network data. It seems we have the main thread waiting on one of the DefaultDispatcher threads for half the time. Double-clicking on an individual thread expands the call stack.

Below the Thread activity timeline is the Call Chart (see Figure 11-14).

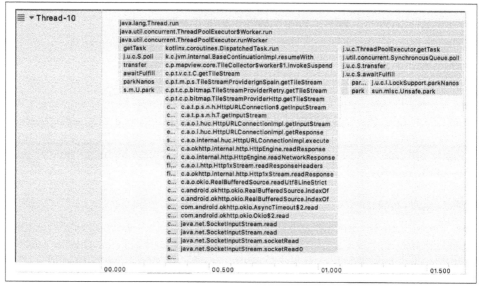

Figure 11-14. The Call Chart shows a top-down representation of captured methods.

The Call Chart shows a call stack of the segmented range of time for CPU usage. The top boxes represent the encapsulating parent method, while the methods below are child methods that were called. The parent method waits on the child methods to finish executing, so this is a good place to see which of TrekMe's methods could be executing for a long time, like the method TileStreamProviderHttp.

If you're reading the printed book, be aware that the bars are color coded. Android OS methods are orange, methods you've written are green, and third-party libraries are blue. Within this coroutine, the longest amount of execution time is with TileStreamProviderHttp.getTileStream(...). This is expected, given that this call makes individual network requests per tile.

Analysis panel

The *Analysis panel* presents a layered tab view. The top of the pane highlights the active set of thread(s). Beneath the tabbed menu sits a search bar above the stack-trace. You can use the search bar to filter trace data related to a particular call. Below that is a set of tabs intended to render visual data from method tracing in three views: *Top Down*, *Bottom Up*, and *Flame Chart*.

Top Down renders a graphical representation of method traces from the top to the bottom of the chart. Any call made within a method renders as a child underneath the original method. Shown in Figure 11-15, the method getTileStream used in TrekMe waits for a series of calls for internet connection and reading from a data stream.

The Top Down view shows how CPU time breaks down in three ways:

Self
> The method execution time itself

Children
> The time it takes to execute callee methods

Total
> Combined time of self and children

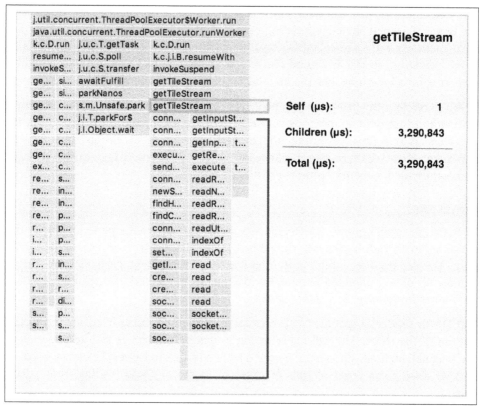

Figure 11-15. Top Down view.

In the case of `getTileStream`, the majority of the time is spent on the network calls themselves: in particular, the connection request and `getInputStream` to receive incoming data from the network. For the IGN Spain server, these times can vary when accessed in another country and at different times of the day. Because it is the client consuming server data, TrekMe has no control over how the server performs.

Contrary to Top Down, Bottom Up (shown in Figure 11-16) shows an inverse representation of *leaf elements* of the call stack. In comparison, such a view renders a substantial number of methods, which can be useful in identifying methods that are consuming the most CPU time.

The final tab provides a Flame Chart view. A Flame Chart provides an aggregated visual of operations from the bottom up. It provides an inverted call chart to better see which functions/methods are consuming more CPU time.

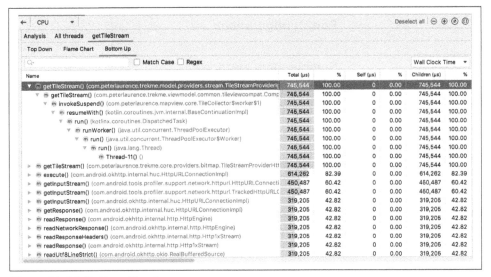

Name	Total (μs)	%	Self (μs)	%	Children (μs)	%
▼ getTileStream() (com.peterlaurence.trekme.model.providers.stream.TileStreamProviderI|	745,544	100.00	0	0.00	745,544	100.00
▼ getTileStream() (com.peterlaurence.trekme.viewmodel.common.tileviewcompat.Comp	745,544	100.00	0	0.00	745,544	100.00
▼ invokeSuspend() (com.peterlaurence.mapview.core.TileCollector$worker$1)	745,544	100.00	0	0.00	745,544	100.00
▼ resumeWith() (kotlin.coroutines.jvm.internal.BaseContinuationImpl)	745,544	100.00	0	0.00	745,544	100.00
▼ run() (kotlinx.coroutines.DispatchedTask)	745,544	100.00	0	0.00	745,544	100.00
▼ runWorker() (java.util.concurrent.ThreadPoolExecutor)	745,544	100.00	0	0.00	745,544	100.00
▼ run() (java.util.concurrent.ThreadPoolExecutor$Worker)	745,544	100.00	0	0.00	745,544	100.00
▼ run() (java.lang.Thread)	745,544	100.00	0	0.00	745,544	100.00
Thread-11() ()	745,544	100.00	0	0.00	745,544	100.00
▶ getTileStream() (com.peterlaurence.trekme.core.providers.bitmap.TileStreamProviderHtt	745,544	100.00	0	0.00	745,544	100.00
▶ execute() (com.android.okhttp.internal.huc.HttpURLConnectionImpl)	614,262	82.39	0	0.00	614,262	82.39
▶ getInputStream() (com.android.tools.profiler.support.network.httpurl.HttpURLConnecti	450,487	60.42	0	0.00	450,487	60.42
▶ getInputStream() (com.android.tools.profiler.support.network.httpurl.TrackedHttpURLC	450,487	60.42	0	0.00	450,487	60.42
▶ getInputStream() (com.android.okhttp.internal.huc.HttpURLConnectionImpl)	319,205	42.82	0	0.00	319,205	42.82
▶ getResponse() (com.android.okhttp.internal.huc.HttpURLConnectionImpl)	319,205	42.82	0	0.00	319,205	42.82
▶ readResponse() (com.android.okhttp.internal.http.HttpEngine)	319,205	42.82	0	0.00	319,205	42.82
▶ readNetworkResponse() (com.android.okhttp.internal.http.HttpEngine)	319,205	42.82	0	0.00	319,205	42.82
▶ readResponseHeaders() (com.android.okhttp.internal.http.Http1xStream)	319,205	42.82	0	0.00	319,205	42.82
▶ readResponse() (com.android.okhttp.internal.http.Http1xStream)	319,205	42.82	0	0.00	319,205	42.82
▶ readUtf8LineStrict() (com.android.okhttp.okio.RealBufferedSource)	319,205	42.82	0	0.00	319,205	42.82

Figure 11-16. Bottom Up view.

To summarize, CPU profiling can render three different kinds of views, depending on the kind of deep dive you wish to pursue:

- Top Down graphical representation shows each method call's CPU time along with the time of its callees.

- Bottom Up inverts the Top Down representation and is most useful to sort methods consuming the most or the least amount of time.

- The Flame Chart inverts and aggregates the call stack horizontally with other callees of the same level to show which ones consume the most CPU time first.

Not only are there three different ways to render data, but there are different kinds of call stacks you can record. In the upcoming sections, we cover different kinds of method tracing in CPU Profiler. As you're starting to get the picture of what kind of information CPU Profiler tries to capture, we'll turn to *method tracing* with CPU Profiler and record a segment of TrekMe creating a new map.

Method tracing

CPU Profiler allows you to *record a trace* to analyze and render its status, duration, type, and more. Tracing relates to recording device activity over a short period of time. Method tracing doesn't occur until the recording button is clicked twice: once to start the recording, and another time to end the recording. There are four configurations for samples and traces, as shown in Figure 11-17.

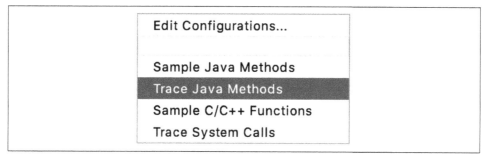

Figure 11-17. Configurations are available for Android developers for samples and traces.

Sample Java Methods captures the application call stack, or a Call Chart (also seen in previous sections). The Call Chart renders under the Thread activity timeline, which shows which threads are active at a particular time. These traces store individual sessions to the right pane for comparison with others' saved sessions.

By choosing the Sample Java Methods configuration, you can examine TrekMe's call stack by hovering the mouse pointer over particular methods, as shown in Figure 11-18.

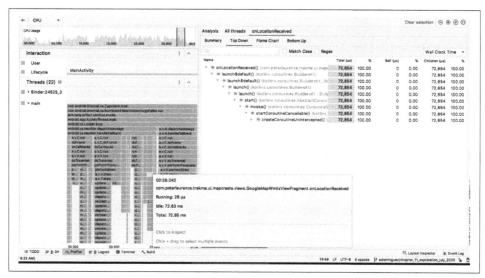

Figure 11-18. Sample Java Methods.

 Don't let your recording run too long. Once a recording reaches its size limit, the trace stops collecting data even if the current session continues to record.

Unlike Sample Java Methods, *Trace Java Methods* strings together a series of time-stamps recorded for the start and end of a method call. Should you wish, you can monitor *Sample C/C+ Functions* to gain insight into how the app is interacting with the Android OS. Recording sample traces for native threads is available for Android API 26 and up.

The terms "method" and "function" tend to be used in everyday conversation interchangeably when talking about method-tracing analysis. At this point, you might be wondering why Java methods and C/C++ functions differentiate enough to matter in CPU profiling.

In the CPU-recording configurations, Android Profiler uses "method" to refer to Java-based code, while "function" references threads. The difference between the two is the order of method execution preserved via a call stack while threads are created and scheduled by the Android OS itself.

Finally, there is Trace System Calls in the configurations shown in Figure 11-17. System Trace is a powerful CPU-recording configuration made available for Android developers. It gives back graphical information on frame-rendering data.

Trace System Calls records analytics on *CPU Cores* to see how scheduling occurs across the board. This configuration becomes more meaningful for detecting CPU bottlenecks across the CPU Cores. These kinds of bottlenecks can jump out in places where the RenderThread chokes, especially for red-colored frames. Unlike other configurations, Trace System Calls shows thread states and the CPU core it currently runs on, as shown in Figure 11-19.

One of the key features in a system trace is having access to the *RenderThread*. RenderThread can show where performance bottlenecks might be occurring when rendering the UI. In the case of Figure 11-19, we can see that much of the idle time occurs around the actual drawing of the tiles themselves.

The Android system tries to redraw the screen depending on the refresh rate on the screen (between 8 ms and 16 ms). Work packets taking longer than the frame rate can cause *dropped frames*, indicated by red slots in Frames. Frames drop when some task does not return before the screen redraws itself. In the case of this system trace recording, it appears that we indeed have some dropped frames indicated by the numbers labeling boxes inside the Frame subsection under the Display section.

TrekMe saves each frame into a JPEG file and loads the image into a bitmap for decoding. However, in Figure 11-19, we see that in the RenderThread, the length of DrawFrame doesn't quite match up with the draw rate intervals. A bit farther below that, some of that idle time is tied to various long-running decodeBitmap methods in the pooled threads.

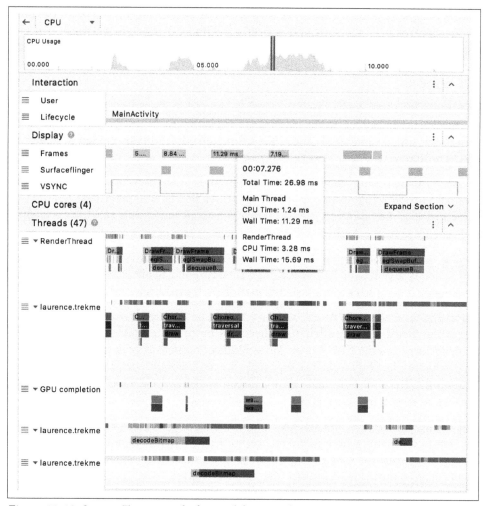

Figure 11-19. System Trace reveals dropped frames where times are labeled within Frames.

From here, there are some options that could potentially be considered for faster drawing; that is, caching network responses for images, or even *prefetching*. For users in need of a few megabytes of data, prefetching is a nice-to-have in the case a device has access to at least a 3G network. The problem with that is that it may not be the best option to render those bitmaps before we *know* what must be rendered. Another option is potentially encoding the data into a more compressed format for easier decoding. Whatever the decision, it's up to the developer to evaluate the trade-offs and the effort of implementing certain optimizations.

The concept of prefetching refers to predicting what kind of data would come in a future request, and grabbing that data preemptively while there's an active radio connection. Each radio request has overhead in terms of the time it takes to wake up the radio and the battery drainage that occurs to keep the radio awake, so Android developers can take advantage of making additional calls while the radio is already awake.

Recording a sample method trace

Now that you are more familiar with what the recording configurations offer, we turn to *Sample Method Trace* on TrekMe. CPU recordings are separated from the CPU Profiler timeline. To begin, click the Record button at the top of the screen to analyze CPU activity while interacting with TrekMe.

Ending the recording renders a tabbed right pane of execution times for sample or trace calls. You can also highlight multiple threads at once for analysis. The average Android developer may not use all these tabs all the time; still, it's good to be cognizant of what tools are at your disposal.

In TrekMe, there's a predefined set of iterable tiles to download. A number of coroutines concurrently read the iterable and perform a network request per tile. Each coroutine decodes a bitmap right after the network request succeeded. These coroutines are sent to some dispatcher such as `Dispatchers.IO`, and the rendering happens when the result is sent back to the UI thread. The UI thread is never blocked waiting for bitmap decoding, or waiting for a network request.

The shrunken CPU timeline in Figure 11-20, at first glance, appears to be nothing more than a reference to the previous screen view. However, you can interact with this data to drill down further by highlighting a chunk of time via the range selector, as shown in Figure 11-21.

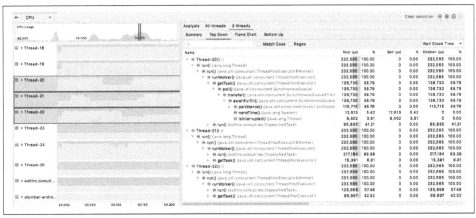

Figure 11-20. CPU Profiler separates the recorded trace.

Figure 11-21. The range selector helps to manage sections of highlighted ranges.

In Figure 11-22, we look at one of the longer-running methods, getTileStream. Below the timeline, the left panel allows you to organize *threads* and *interactions* via drag-and-drop functionality. Being able to group threads together also means you can highlight groups of stacktraces. You can expand a thread in a recorded trace by double-clicking the thread twice to show a drop-down visual of a call stack.

Selecting an item also opens an additional pane to the right. This is the *Analysis Panel*, which allows you to examine stacktrace and execution time in more granular detail. Tracking CPU usage is important, but perhaps you'd like to be able to analyze how an application interacts with Android hardware components. In the next section, we look into Android Studio's *Energy Profiler*.

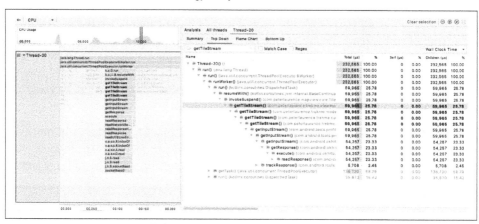

Figure 11-22. You can search for a specific method via the search function.

Excessive networking calls on Android devices are also *power-hungry*. The longer the device radio stays awake for network communication, the more CPU consumption and battery drainage there is. By this logic, it would be fair to assume that networking accounts for most energy consumption. We can confirm this by using Energy Profiler.

Energy Profiler

Energy Profiler is best used for determining heavy energy consumption. When an application makes a network request, the application turns on the mobile radio hardware component. CPU consumption accelerates as the Android device communicates with the network, draining battery at a faster rate.

TrekMe prescales bitmaps to ensure consistent memory and energy usage when the user is zooming in and out. When the user is creating and downloading a map, the details of the map are, by default, downloaded with the highest-resolution detail. The event pane shows higher levels of consumption when downloading large chunks of data.

A drag-and-click can select a range of the timeline to show details for events for the Android OS. In Figure 11-23, we can see a pop-up rendering of a breakdown of the energy graph. The first half of the pop-up legend contains the categories CPU, Network, and Location, which relay to each category provided in the stacked graph. It is a good sign to see that CPU and networking usage is light despite the relatively heavy job of making a network call to request large pieces of data and draw them on the screen.

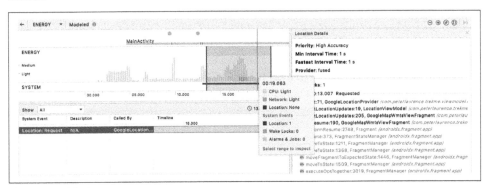

Figure 11-23. System event pane.

The second half of the pop-up legend describes the kinds of system events captured from the device. Energy Profiler works to capture certain kinds of system events and their energy consumption on a device:

- *Alarms* and *Jobs* are system events designed to wake up a device at a specified time. As a best practice, Android now recommends using *WorkManager* or *JobScheduler* whenever possible, especially for background tasks.

- *Location* requests use Android GPS Sensor, which can consume a large amount of battery. It's a good practice to make sure accuracy and frequency are gauged correctly.

Although Figure 11-23 shows only one location request, there are other types of system events that contain their own unique set of states. A request event may possess the state of *Active*, as pictured in Figure 11-23, *Requested*, or *Request Removed*. Likewise, if Energy Profiler captures a *Wake Lock* type of system event, the timeline would be able to show state(s) for the duration of the wake lock event such as *Acquired*, *Held*, *Released*, and so on.

Selecting a particular system event opens a right pane in Energy Profiler to see more details. From here, you can jump directly to the source code for that particular location request. In TrekMe, `GoogleLocationProvider` is a class that polls for user location every second. This isn't necessarily an issue—the polling is intended to enable the device to constantly update your location. This proves the power of this profiling tool: you can get precise information without looking at the source code. Requests are made one at a time, removing existing requests in order to make a new one when a new image block has been downloaded.

In comparison to location polling, we can expect decreased energy consumption when a user is zooming in on a rendered map. There are no requests made for downloading large chunks of data. We do expect some energy consumption for keeping track of the user's location, which also uses `GoogleLocationProvider`.

In Figure 11-24, we can see the excessive and rapid touch events indicated by the circular dots above the stacked overlay graph. Because TrekMe has downloaded all the information it needed, no network calls are made at this time. However, we do notice how CPU usage spikes back up to high levels. To avoid overwhelming the system, it is a good practice to limit touch events to avoid spinning off duplicate zoom-drawing functions.

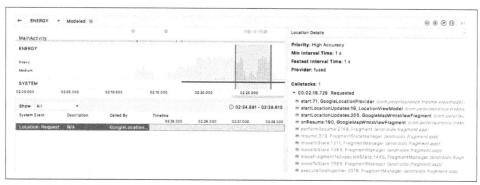

Figure 11-24. TrekMe opens and zooms in on an existing map.

So far, we've covered evaluating performance by looking at processing power. But examining battery/CPU usage does not always diagnose performance problems. Sometimes, slow behavior can be attributed to clogged memory. In the next section, we explore the relationship between CPU and memory and use Memory Profiler on TrekMe's GPX recording feature.

Memory Profiler

In TrekMe, you can navigate to *GPX Record* in the pullout drawer. GPX stands for *GPS Exchange Format* and is a set of data used with XML schema for GPS formatting in software applications. Hikers can click the play icon under Control. The app then tracks and records the movements of the hikers and their devices, which can be saved as a GPX file to be rendered as a line drawing later on to indicate the path traveled. Figure 11-25 shows TrekMe's GPX recording feature.

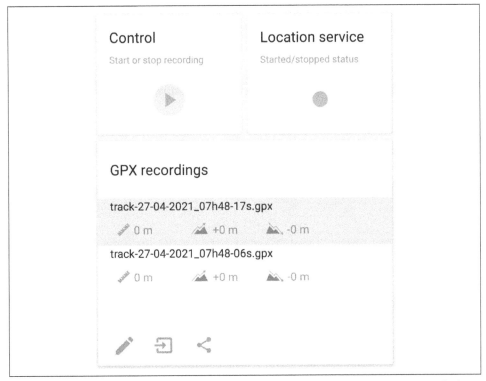

Figure 11-25. TrekMe's GPX recording feature uses `GpxRecordingService` *to track the GPS coordinates of a user on a hike.*

We know that using location in the system *can* be heavy for CPU processing. But sometimes, slowdowns can be attributed to memory problems. CPU processing uses RAM as its capacity for workspace, so when RAM fills up, the Android system must execute a heap dump. When memory usage is severely restricted, the ability to execute many tasks at once becomes limited. The more time it takes to execute fewer application operations, the slower Android gets. RAM is shared across all applications: if too many applications are consuming too much memory, it can slow the performance of the device or, worse, cause `OutOfMemoryException` crashes.

Memory Profiler allows you to see how much memory is consumed out of the memory allocated for your application to run. With Memory Profiler, you can manually trigger a heap dump in a running session to generate analysis to determine which objects are held in the heap and how many there are.

As shown in Figure 11-26, Memory Profiler offers powerful features:

- Triggering garbage collection
- Capturing a Java heap dump
- Allocation tracking
- An interactive timeline of the fragments and activities available in the Android application
- User-input events
- Memory count to divide memory into categories

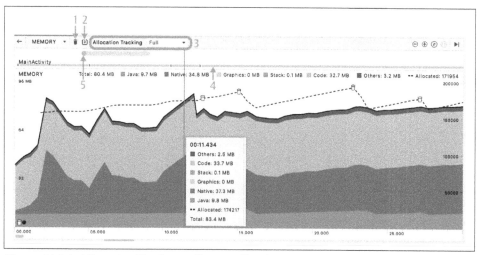

Figure 11-26. Allocation Tracking offers a Full Italicized Text configuration, which captures all object allocations in memory, while a Sampled configuration records objects at regular intervals.

Like recording samples and traces in CPU Profiler, capturing Java heap dumps saves the results within the session panel in Android Profiler for comparison for the life of your Android Studio instance.

Initiating too much garbage collection (GC) can affect performance: for example, executing a ton of GC can slow the device down, depending on how frequent and how large generational object allocation is in memory. At a minimum, Android developers should try to run memory profiling of every application to ensure that nothing is being held in the heap past its use, otherwise known as "memory leaks." Detecting memory leaks can be life-saving, especially for Android users depending on longer battery life. What you are about to see is a variation of a common memory management mistake developers often make while working with services: leaving a service accidentally running.

TrekMe uses a foreground service to gain stats of the user's hike, which is a natural choice for tracking the user's location. Services, like other Android components, run in the UI thread of the application. However, persisting services tend to drain battery and system resources. Hence, it is important to limit the use of foreground services so as not to impair overall device performance and to kill them off as soon as possible if the app must use one.

We can run a couple of GPX recordings against Memory Profiler and trigger the heap dump to see which objects held in heap consume the most memory, as shown in Figure 11-27.

Class Name	Allocations ▼	Native Size	Shallow Size	Retained Size
▣ app heap	58,907	10,300,551	2,526,327	54,077,138
ⓒ Rect (android.graphics)	5,759	0	138,216	138,216
ⓒ HashMap$Node (java.util)	5,639	0	135,336	150,419
ⓒ byte[]	5,373	0	414,472	414,472
ⓒ HashMap$KeyIterator (java.util)	4,818	0	154,176	154,176
ⓒ int[]	3,407	0	92,108	92,108
ⓒ String (java.lang)	3,392	0	54,272	147,277
ⓒ Object[] (java.lang)	3,055	0	92,840	3,609,432
ⓒ Class (java.lang)	2,467	0	343,519	807,954
ⓒ AccessibilityNodeInfo (android.view.accessibility)	2,400	0	396,000	396,000
ⓒ ArrayList (java.util)	2,263	0	45,260	3,375,023
ⓒ WindowInsetsCompat$Impl21 (androidx.core.view)	878	0	21,072	21,202
ⓒ WindowInsetsCompat (androidx.core.view)	878	0	10,536	10,714
ⓒ CombinedContext (kotlin.coroutines)	712	0	11,392	11,460
ⓒ HashMap (java.util)	693	0	27,720	50,411
ⓒ WeakHashMap$Entry (java.util)	683	0	24,588	26,555
ⓒ WindowInsets (android.view)	661	0	19,169	19,289
ⓒ ArrayList$Itr (java.util)	614	0	17,192	17,192
ⓒ HashSet (java.util)	508	0	6,096	10,408
ⓒ AndroidLeakFixes$FLUSH_HANDLER_THREADS$apply$1$3$2$1 (leakcanary)	480	0	5,760	5,760

MEMORY ▾ Heap Dump: 57:03.180
View app heap ▾ Arrange by class ▾ Show all classes ▾ Match Case Regex
1,656 Classes / 0 Leaks / 58,907 Count / 10,300,551 Native Size / 2,526,327 Shallow Size / 54,077,138 Retained Size

Figure 11-27. You can use the CTRL + F function to search for "GpxRecordingService" to narrow your results.

A heap dump shows you a list of classes, which can be organized by heap *allocations*, *native size*, *shallow size*, or *retained size*. Shallow size is a reference to the total Java memory used. Native size is a reference to the total memory used in native memory. Retained size is made of both shallow size and retained size (in bytes).

Within a recorded heap dump, you can organize your allocation record by *app heap*, *image heap*, or *zygote heap*. The zygote heap refers to the memory that is allocated for a zygote process, which might include common framework code and resources. The image heap stores memory allocation from the OS itself and contains references to classes used in an image containing our application for a system boot. For our use case, we're more concerned with the app heap, which is the primary heap the app allocates memory to.

In Memory Profiler, triggering a heap dump will render a list of objects still held in memory after GC. This list can give you:

- Every object instance of a selected object displayed in the *Instance View* pane, with the option to "Jump to Source" in the code

- The ability to examine instance data by right-clicking an object in *References* and selecting *Go to Instance*

Remember, a memory leak occurs when caching holds references to objects that are no longer needed. In Figure 11-28, we search for "Location" with the same heap dump to locate our service and be able to view total memory allocation. `LocationSer vice` appears to have separate allocations when it should only have one running at a time.

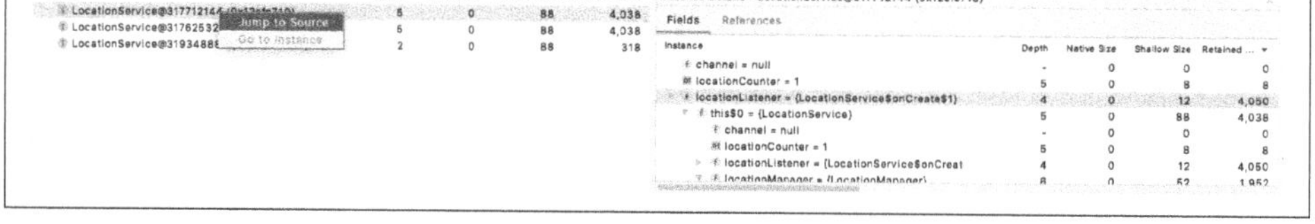

Figure 11-28. A suspicious number of `LocationService` *instances appears to be held in memory.*

It appears that every time we press Record, a new `LocationService` in TrekMe is instantiated and then held in memory even after the service dies. You can start-and-stop a service, but if you are holding a reference to that service in a background thread, even if it is dead, the instance continues to be held in the heap even after GC occurs.

Let's just run a couple more recordings in TrekMe to confirm the behavior we suspect. We can right-click one of these instances to "Jump to Source" and see. In *RecordingViewModel.kt*, we see the following code:

```
fun startRecording() {
    val intent = Intent(app, LocationServices::class.java)
    app.startService(intent)
}
```

We want to check whether these services are indeed stopping before starting a new one. A started service stays alive as long as possible: until a `stopService` call is made outside the service or `stopSelf` is called within the service. This makes the use of persistent services expensive, as Android considers running services always in use, meaning that the memory a service uses up in RAM will never be made available.

When a GPX recording stops, `LocationService` propagates a series of events, pinging the GPS location, which is then recorded and saved as a set of data. When a GPX file has just been written, the service subscribes to the main thread to send a status. Because `LocationService` extends Android `Service`, we can call `Service::stopSelf` to stop the service:

```
@Subscribe(threadMode = ThreadMode.MAIN)
fun onGpxFileWriteEvent(
    event: GpxFileWriteEvent
) {
    mStarted = false
    sendStatus()
    stopSelf()    // <--- fix will stop the service and release the refer
ence at GC
}
```

We can use Memory Profiler and check the heap dump to ensure we hold reference to only one service in memory. Actually, since GPX recordings are done through `LocationService`, it makes sense to stop the service when the user stops recording. This way, the service can be deallocated from memory on GC: otherwise, the heap continues to hold an instance of `LocationService` past its life.

Memory Profiler can help you detect possible memory leaks through the process of sifting through the heap dump. You can also filter a heap dump by checking the *Activities/Fragments Leaks* box in the heap dump configurations in Memory Profiler. Hunting for memory leaks can be…a manual process, and even then, hunting for memory leaks yourself is only one way of catching them. Luckily, we have LeakCanary, a popular memory leak detection library that can attach to your app in debug mode and idly watch for memory leaks to occur.

Detecting Memory Leaks with LeakCanary

LeakCanary automatically detects at runtime explicit and implicit memory leaks that might be hard to detect manually. This is a great benefit, since Memory Profiler requires manually triggering a heap dump and checking for retained memory. When crash analytics are unable to detect crashes coming from an OutOfMemoryException, LeakCanary serves as a viable alternative to keep an eye on issues detected at runtime, and offers better coverage in discovering memory leaks.

Memory leaks commonly come from bugs related to the lifecycle of objects being held past their use. LeakCanary is able to detect various mistakes such as:

- Creating a new Fragment instance without destroying the existing version first
- Injecting an Android Activity or Context reference *implicitly* or *explicitly* into a non-Android component
- Registering a listener, broadcast receiver, or RxJava subscription and not remembering to dispose of the listener/subscriber at the end of the parent lifecycle

For this example, we have installed LeakCanary in TrekMe. LeakCanary is used organically in development until a heap dump with potential leaks has been retained. You can install LeakCanary by adding the following dependency to Gradle:

```
debugImplementation 'com.squareup.leakcanary:leakcanary-android:2.*'
```

Once installed in your application, LeakCanary automatically detects leaks when an Activity or Fragment has been destroyed, clears the ViewModel, and more. It does this by detecting retained objects passed through some ObjectWatcher. LeakCanary then dumps the heap, analyzes the heap, and categorizes those leaks for easy consumption. After installing LeakCanary, you can use the application like normal. Should LeakCanary detect retained instances in a heap dump that occurs, it sends a notification to the system tray.

In the case of TrekMe, it appears LeakCanary has detected a memory leak within a RecyclerView instance of `MapImportFragment`, as shown in Figure 11-29.

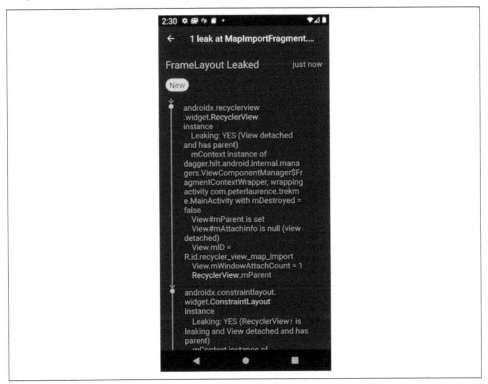

Figure 11-29. LeakCanary shows a RecyclerView leaking in its stacktrace.

The error message is telling us that a `RecyclerView` instance is "leaking." LeakCanary indicates that this view instance holds a reference on a `Context` instance which wraps the activity. Something prevents the `RecyclerView` instance from being garbage-collected—either an implicit or explicit reference to the `RecyclerView` instance passed to the component outliving the activity.

We're not sure what we're dealing with quite yet, so we start by looking at the *MapImportFragment.kt* class holding the RecyclerView mentioned in Figure 11-29. Tracing back to the UI element `recyclerViewMapImport` referenced from the layout file, we bring your attention to something curious:

```
class MapImportFragment: Fragment() {

    private val viewModel: MapImportViewModel by viewModels()

    /* removed for brevity */
```

```
override fun onViewCreated(view: View, savedInstanceState: Bundle?) {
    /* removed for brevity */
    recyclerViewMapImport.addOnItemTouchListener(
        RecyclerItemClickListener(
            this.context,                                    ❶
            recyclerViewMapImport,
            object: RecyclerItemClickListener.onItemClickListener {
                override fun onItemClick(view: View, position: Int) {
                    binding.fab.activate()
                    single.fab(position)
                }
            })
    )
}

/* removed for brevity */

private fun FloatingActionButton.activate() {
    /* removed for brevity */
    fab.setOnClickListener {
        itemSelected?.let { item ->
            val inputStream = context.contentResolver.
                openInputStream(item.url)
            inputStream?.let {
                viewModel.unarchiveAsync(it, item)          ❷
            }
        }
    }
}
}
```

❶ In the MapImportFragment, we attach a custom click listener to every ViewHolder in the RecyclerView.

❷ The Context then is used to get a ContentResolver and create an InputStream to feed as an argument for MapImportViewModel::unarchiveAsync.

When a user clicks on a particular item in the RecyclerView, the Kotlin extension function FloatingActionButton::activate is called. Remember, a common cause for a memory leak is when we accidentally inject an Activity or a Context into a non-Android component.

If you look closely at the FloatingActionButton::activate implementation, you can see that we create an implicit reference to the enclosing class, which is the MapIm portFragment instance.

How is an implicit reference created? We add a click listener to a button. The listener holds a reference to the parent Context (returned by the getContext() method of the fragment). To be able to access the `Context` from inside the listener, the Kotlin compiler creates an implicit reference to the enclosing class.

Following the code to the `MapImportViewModel` method, we see the `InputStream` passed down to be able to call another private method in the `ViewModel`:

```kotlin
class MapImportViewModel @ViewModelInject constructor(
    private val settings: Settings
) : ViewModel() {
    /* removed for brevity */

    fun unarchiveAsync(inputStream: InputStream, item: ItemData) {
        viewModelScope.launch {
            val rootFolder = settings.getAppDir() ?: return@launch
            val outputFolder = File(rootFolder, "imported")
            /* removed for brevity */
        }
    }
}
```

A `ViewModel` object has a lifecycle of its own and is intended to outlive the lifecycle of the view it is tied to until the `Fragment` is detached. Rather than using an `Input Stream` as an argument, it is better to use an application `context`, which is available throughout the life of the application and which can be injected via constructor parameter injection in `MapImportViewModel`.[1] We can then create the `InputStream` right in `MapImportViewModel::unarchiveAsync`:

```kotlin
class MapImportViewModel @ViewModelInject constructor(
    private val settings: Settings,
    private val app: Application
): ViewModel() {
    /* removed for brevity */

    fun unarchiveAsync(item: ItemData) {
        viewModelScope.launch {
            val inputStream = app.contentResolve.
                openInputStream(item.uri) ?: return@launch
            val rootFolder = settings.getAppDir() ?: return@launch
            val outputFolder = File(rootFolder, "imported")
            /* removed for brevity */
        }
```

---

1. The `@ViewModelInject` annotation is special to Hilt, which is a dependency injection framework. However, constructor parameter injection can also be achieved with manual DI or with DI frameworks like Dagger and Koin.

```
        }
    }
```

Of course, turning on LeakCanary can be disrupting for development if an existing application has many memory leaks. In this case, the temptation might be to turn off LeakCanary to prevent disruption to current work. Should you choose to put Leak-Canary on your application, it is best to do it only when you and your team have the capacity to "face the music."

Summary

There is no doubt that Android benchmarking and profiling tools are powerful. To ensure that your application is getting the most out of analytics, it's best to choose one or two tools as appropriate. It can be easy to get lost in the world of optimizations, but it's important to remember that the largest wins come from making optimizations with the least effort and the largest impact. Likewise, it's important to take current priorities and team workload into consideration.

Approach Android optimizations like a nutritionist, encouraging incremental, habitual changes instead of "crash dieting." Android profiling is intended to show you what's really happening under the hood, but it's important to remember that the average Android developer must prioritize which issues must be addressed in a world where their time and manpower may be limited.

The hope is that you feel more equipped to handle any potential bugs that may come your way, and that this chapter gives you confidence to start exploring some of these tools on your own applications to see how things are working under the hood:

- Android Profiler is a powerful way to analyze application performance, from networking and CPU to memory and energy analytics. Android Studio caches recorded sessions along with heap dumps and method traces for the lifespan of an Android Studio instance so that you can compare them with other saved sessions.

- Network Profiler can help solve Android problems specific to API debugging. It can provide information useful to both the client device and the server where the data comes from, and can help us ensure optimal data formatting within a network call.

- CPU Profiler can give insight as to where most of the time is being spent executing methods, and is particularly useful for finding bottlenecks in performance. You can record different kinds of CPU traces to be able to drill down into specific threads and call stacks.

- Energy Profiler looks at whether CPU processes, networking calls, or GPS locations in an application could be draining a device's battery.

- Memory Profiler looks at how much memory is allocated in the heap. This can help give insight about areas of code that could use improvements in memory.
- LeakCanary is a popular open source library created by Square. It can be helpful to use LeakCanary to detect memory leaks that are harder to detect at runtime.

CHAPTER 12

Trimming Down Resource Consumption with Performance Optimizations

In the previous chapter, you became familiar with ways to examine what's going on "under the hood" using popular Android profiling tools. This final chapter highlights a medley of performance optimization considerations. There's no one-size-fits-all approach, so it is helpful to become aware of potential performance pitfalls (and solutions). However, performance issues can sometimes be the result of many compounding problems that individually may not seem noteworthy.

Performance considerations allow you to examine concerns that may impact your application's ability to scale. If you can use any of these strategies as "low-hanging fruit" in your code base, it's well worth going for the biggest win with the smallest amount of effort. Not every section of this chapter will be suitable for every project you work on, but they are still useful considerations to be aware of when writing any Android application. These topics range from view system performance optimizations to network data format, caching, and more.

We are aware that the View system is to be replaced by Jetpack Compose: however, the View system is not going anywhere for years, even with Jetpack. The first half of this chapter is dedicated to view topics every project could benefit from: potential optimizations for the Android View system. The way you set up view hierarchies can end up having a substantial impact on performance if you are not careful. For this reason, we look at two easy ways to optimize view performance: reducing view hierarchy complexity with `ConstraintLayout`, and creating drawable resources for animation/customized backgrounds.

Achieving Flatter View Hierarchy with ConstraintLayout

As a general rule, you want to keep your view hierarchies in Android as flat as possible. Deeply nested hierarchies affect performance, both when a view first inflates and when the user interacts with the screen. When view hierarchies are deeply nested, it can take longer to send instructions back up to the root ViewGroup containing all your elements and traverse back down to make changes to particular views.

In addition to the profiling tools mentioned in Chapter 11, Android Studio offers *Layout Inspector*, which analyzes your application at runtime and creates a 3D rendering of the view elements stacked on the screen. You can open Layout Inspector by clicking the bottom corner tab of Android Studio, as shown in Figure 12-1.

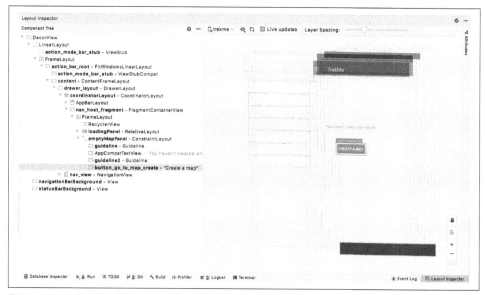

Figure 12-1. Layout Inspector allows you to rotate the 3D rendering for devices running API 29+.

When child components are drawn, they are drawn on top of the parent View, stacking one on top of the other. Layout Inspector does provide a *Component Tree* pane to the left so that you are able to drill down the elements and inspect their properties. To better understand what happens when users interact with Android UI widgets, Figure 12-2 shows a bird's-eye view of the very same layout hierarchy provided in the Component Tree.

Even for a relatively simple layout, a view hierarchy can grow in complexity pretty quickly. Managing many nested layouts can come with additional costs such as increased difficulty managing touch events, slower GPU rendering, and difficulty guaranteeing the same spacing/size of views across different-sized screens.

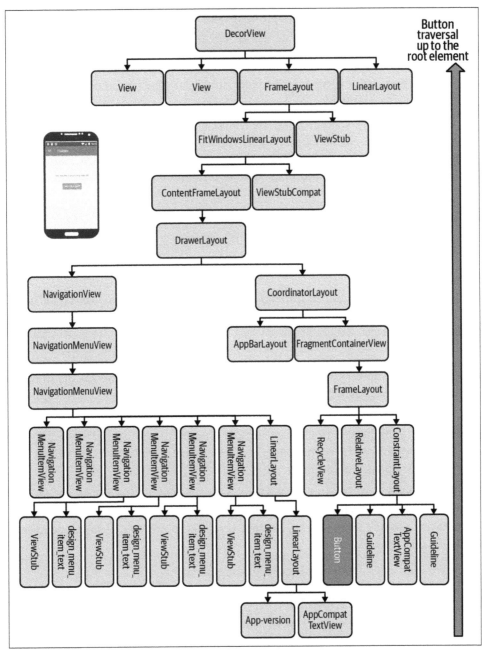

Figure 12-2. The elements of a running activity stretched out in their entirety.

On top of the visual changes your app might call for, the Android OS could also be affecting view properties on its own. Changes on view properties, called by either you or the OS, could trigger a re-layout of your view hierarchy. Whether this happens or not depends on how views are implemented (by yourself or by an external dependency), how often layout components trigger dimension resizing, and where they are located in the view hierarchy.

Not only must we worry about hierarchy complexity, but we also must be mindful of avoiding certain types of views that could end up costing our application twice the number of traversals necessary to send instructions to the Android OS. Some older layout types in Android are prone to "double taxation" when relative positioning is enabled:

RelativeLayout
: Without fail, this always traverses its child elements at least twice: once for layout calculations for each position and size and once to finalize positioning.

LinearLayout
: This sets its orientation to horizontal or sets `android:setMeasureWithLargest ChildEnabled="true"` while in vertical orientation; both cases make two passes for each child element.

GridLayout
: This can end up making double traversals if the layout uses weight distribution or sets `android:layout_gravity` to any valid value.

The cost of double taxation can become far more severe when any one of these cases is located closer to the root of the tree, and can even cause exponential traversals. The deeper the view hierarchy is, the longer it takes for input events to be processed and for views to be updated accordingly.

As a good practice, it's best to lower the negative impact of view re-layout on app responsiveness. To keep hierarchies flatter and more robust, Android advocates using `ConstraintLayout`. `ConstraintLayout` helps create a responsive UI for complex layouts with a flat-view hierarchy.

There are a few rules of `ConstraintLayout` to remember:

- Every view must have at least one horizontal and one vertical constraint.
- The Start/End of a view may only chain itself to the Start/End of other views.
- The Top/Bottom of a view may only chain itself to the Top/Bottom of other views.

Android Studio's design preview shows how the parent ties the view to the designated end of the screen, as shown in Figure 12-3.

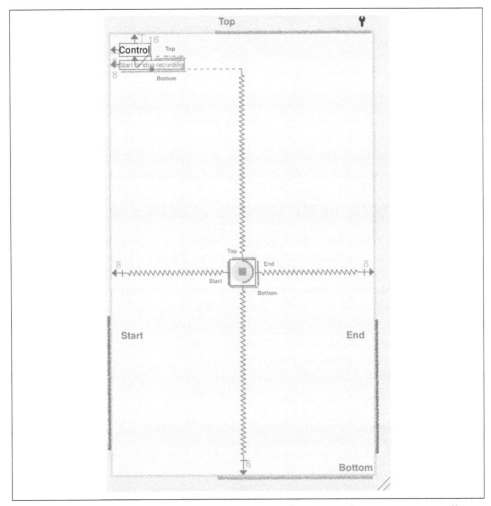

Figure 12-3. In this particular `ConstraintLayout`, *the spinner button constrains all parent sides to the center of the screen. The text elements in the upper-left corner are only constrained to the top and left sides of the parent.*

When highlighted, the zigzagged lines appear on a view to indicate where a side is constrained to. A zigzag indicates a constraint one way to a view while a squiggly line indicates that the two views constrain each other.

This book does not cover additional useful features of `ConstraintLayout`, like barriers, guidelines, groups, and creating constraints. The best way to get to know `ConstraintLayout` is to experiment with the elements yourself in *Split View* within the design panel, as shown in Figure 12-4.

Figure 12-4. The Split View of the design panel shows half code and half design for layout files.

Using `ConstraintLayout`, especially when `ViewGroup` elements might be deeply nested or inefficient, is an easy way to address potential performance bottlenecks at runtime for any Android application. In the next section, we shift focus on performance optimizations from views themselves to view animations.

Reducing Programmatic Draws with Drawables

Another potential performance issue for any Android project is programmatic draws at runtime. Once in a while, Android developers run into a view element which does not have access to certain properties in a layout file. Suppose you wanted to render a view with rounded corners only on the top two corners. One way to approach this is with a programmatic draw via a Kotlin extension function:

```
fun View.roundCorners(resources: Resources, outline: OutLine?) {
    val adjusted = TypedValue.applyDimension(
        TypedValue.COMPLEX_UNIT_SP,
        25,
        resources?.displayMetrics
    )
    val newHeight =
        view.height.plus(cornerRadiusAdjusted).toInt()
    this.run { outline?.setRoundRect(0, 0, width, newHeight, adjusted)}
}
```

This is fine and valid; however, too many programmatic draws can end up choking the RenderThread and subsequently block the UI thread from being able to process further events until runtime drawings complete. Furthermore, the cost of altering views programmatically becomes higher if a particular view needs to resize to meet constraints. Resizing a view element at runtime means you won't be able to use the `LayoutInflater` to adjust how the elements fit with the new dimensions of the original altered view.

You can offload overhead that would otherwise occur by using drawables, which are stored in the */drawables* folder in your resource assets. The following code shows how a `Drawable` XML file achieves the same goal of rounding the top two corners of a view element:

```
<?xml version="1.0" encoding="utf-8"?>
<shape xmlns:android="http://schemas.android.com/apk/res/android"
    android:shape = "rectangle">
    <corners android:topLeftRadius="25dp" android:topRightRadius="25dp"/>
    <stroke android:width="1dp" android:color="#FFF"/>
    <solid android:color="#FFF"/>
</shape>
```

You can then add the name of the file as a `Drawable` type to the background attribute in the View's layout file the name of the `Drawable` file:

```
android:background="@drawable/rounded_top_corners_background"
```

In the previous section, we briefly touched on the initial stages of how user interaction sends instructions to the Android OS. To understand where animations come in, we will now dive a little further into the full process of how Android renders the UI. Let's consider the case where a user in TrekMe presses the "Create a Map" button.

The stages we cover in the remainder of this section show how the OS processes user events with a screen and how it is able to execute draw instructions from software to hardware. We explain all the phases the Android OS performs in a draw up to where animations occur in the *Sync* stage, as shown in Figure 12-5.

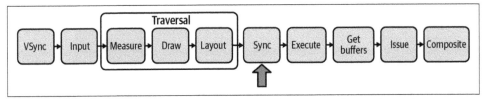

Figure 12-5. Animation occurs at the Sync stage, after traversal is performed.

VSync represents the time given between frame draws on the screen. In an app, when a user touches a view element on the screen, *input handling* occurs. In the *Input* stage, the Android OS makes a call to *invalidate* all the parent view element nodes up the tree by copying a set of instructions to keep track of dirtied state. Invalidation does not redraw the view itself, but rather, indicates to the system later on which marked view must be redrawn later. This is done by propagating the copied information up the view hierarchy so that it can all be executed on the way back down at a later stage. Figure 12-6 shows what invalidation looks like after user input occurs when someone touches a button: traversing up the node, then copying a set of `DisplayList` instructions up each parent view. Even though the arrow points down the elements, indicating child elements, the traversal and the copying of `getDisplayList()` actually goes up to the root before going back down.

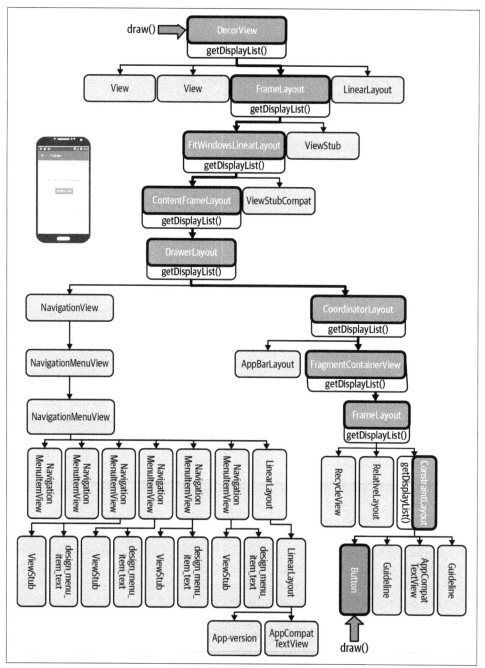

Figure 12-6. The `DisplayList` *object is a set of compact instructions used to instruct which views need to be redrawn on the Canvas. These instructions are copied up every parent view element to the root hierarchy during invalidation and then executed during traversal.*

The Android UI system then schedules the next stage, known as *traversal*, which contains its own subset of rendering stages:

Measure

This calculates `MeasureSpecs` and passes it to the child element for measuring. It does this recursively, all the way down to the leaf nodes.

Layout

This sets the view position and sizing of a child layout.

Draw

This renders the views using a set of instructions given by a set of `DisplayList` instructions.

In the next stage, *Sync*, the Android OS syncs the `DisplayList` info between the CPU and GPU. When the CPU starts talking to the GPU in Android, the JNI takes its set of instructions in the Java Native layer within the UI thread and sends a synthetic copy, along with some other information, to the GPU from the RenderThread. The RenderThread is responsible for animations and offloading work from the UI thread (instead of having to send the work to the GPU). From there, the CPU and GPU communicate with each other to determine what instructions ought to be executed and then combined visually to render on the screen. Finally, we reach the *Execute* stage, where the OS finally executes `DisplayList` operations in optimized fashion (like drawing similar operations together at once). "Drawn Out: How Android Renders" (*https://oreil.ly/P5WbO*) is an excellent talk that provides more detail on Android rendering at the system level.[1]

As of Android Oreo, animations, such as circular reveals, ripples, and vector drawable animations, live only in the `RenderThread`, meaning that these kinds of animations are nonblocking for the UI thread. You can create these animations with custom drawables. Consider the case where we wish to animate a shadowed ripple in the View background whenever a user presses some kind of `ViewGroup`. You can combine a set of drawables to make this happen, starting with `RippleDrawable` type `Drawable` to create the ripple animation itself:

```xml
<?xml version="1.0" encoding="utf-8"?>
<ripple xmlns:android="http://schemas.android.com/apk/res/android"
        android:color="@color/primary">
    <item android:id="@android:id/mask">
        <shape android:shape="rectangle">
            <solid android:color="@color/ripple_mask" />
        </shape>
```

---

1. Chet Haase and Romain Guy. "Drawn Out: How Android Renders." Google I/O '18, 2017.

```
    </item>
  </ripple>
```

RippleDrawable, whose equivalent on XML is ripple, requires a color attribute for ripple effects. To apply this animation to a background, we can use another drawable file:

```xml
<?xml version="1.0" encoding="utf-8"?>
<shape xmlns:android="http://schemas.android.com/apk/res/android"
       android:shape="rectangle">
    <solid android:color="@color/background_pressed" />
</shape>
```

We can use DrawableStates, a set of framework-provided states that can be specified on a Drawable. In this case, we use DrawableStates on a selector to determine the animation as well as whether the animation occurs on press or not. Finally, we create a Drawable used to render different states. Each state is represented by a child drawable. In this case, we apply the ripple drawable animation only when the view has been pressed:

```xml
<?xml version="1.0" encoding="utf-8"?>
<selector xmlns:android="http://schemas.android.com/apk/res/android"
    android:enterFadeDuration="@android:integer/config_shortAnimTime"
    android:exitFadeDuration="@android:integer/config_shortAnimTime">
    <item
        android:state_pressed="true" android:state_enabled="true"
        android:drawable="@drawable/background_pressed_ripple"/>
    <item
        android:state_pressed="false"
        android:drawable="@android:color/transparent"/>
</selector>
```

Android Jetpack

As mentioned in the beginning of the chapter, the view system build around Jetpack Compose is completely different from the view system in Android, with its own sets of UI management, graphics, runtime/compile time behavior, and more. If Jetpack Compose is done with programmatic draws, would that mean using Jetpack Compose is not efficient for drawing? While XML currently renders faster than Compose rendering itself, optimizations are underway for closing the gap on render time. However, you should keep in mind the major advantage Compose holds is the ability to update, or recompose, Composable views quickly and far more efficiently than the current Android view framework.

We're done talking about view performance optimizations, and we'll move on to more performance optimization tips around various parts of an Android application for the remainder of the chapter.

Minimizing Asset Payload in Network Calls

In Android, it's important to use minimal payload to avoid slower loads, battery drainage, and using too much data. In the previous chapter, we started looking at network payload data formats. Both images and serialized data formats are the usual suspects for causing the most bloat, so it's important to check your payload's data format.

If you don't need transparency for the images you work with in your Android project, it's better to work with JPG/JPEG since this format intrinsically doesn't support transparency and compresses better than PNG. When it comes to blowing up bitmaps for thumbnails, it probably makes sense to render the image in much lower resolution.

In the industry, JSON is commonly used as the data payload in networking. Unfortunately, JSON and XML payloads are horrible for compression since the data format accounts for spaces, quotes, returns, acmes, and more. Binary serialization formats like *protocol buffers*, an accessible data format in Android which might serve as a cheaper alternative. You can define the data structs, which Protobuf is able to compress much smaller than XML and JSON data. Check out Google Developers (*https://oreil.ly/6dUL0*) for more on protocol buffers.

Bitmap Pooling and Caching

TrekMe uses Bitmap pooling to avoid allocating too many `Bitmap` objects. Bitmap pooling reuses an existing instance, when possible. Where does this "existing instance" come from? After a `Bitmap` is no longer visible, instead of making it available for garbage collection (by just not keeping a reference on it), you can put the no-longer-used `Bitmap` into a "bitmap pool." Such a pool is just a container for available bitmaps for later use. For example, TrekMe uses a simple in-memory dequeue as a bitmap pool. To load an image into an existing bitmap, you have to specify which bitmap instance you want to use. You can do that using the `inBitmap` parameter[2] of `BitMapFactory.Options`:

```
// we get an instance of bitmap from the pool
BitmapFactory.Options().inBitmap = pool.get()
```

---

2. The instance of `Bitmap` that you supply must be a mutable bitmap.

It's worth noting that image-loading libraries like Glide can save you from having to handle bitmap craziness yourself. Using these libraries results in bitmap caching for free in your applications. In cases where network calls are slow, fetching a fresh instance of a Bitmap could be costly. This is when fetching from a bitmap cache can save a lot of time and resources. If a user revisits a screen, the screen is able to load almost immediately instead of having to make another network request. We can distinguish two kinds of caches: *in-memory* and *filesystem* caches. In-memory caches provide the fastest object retrieval, at the cost of using more memory. Filesystem caches are typically slower, but they do have a low memory footprint. Some applications rely on in-memory LRU cache,[3] while others use filesystem-based cache or a mix of the two approaches.

As an example, if you perform HTTP requests in your application, you can use *OkHttp* to expose a nice API to use a filesystem cache. *OkHttp* (which is also included as a transitive dependency of the popular library, *Retrofit*) is a popular client library widely used in Android for networking. Adding caching is relatively easy:

```
val cacheSize = 10 * 1024 * 1024
val cache = Cache(rootDir, cacheSize)

val client = OkHttpClient.Builder()
                .cache(cache)
                .build()
```

With *OkHttp* client building, it is easy to create configurations with custom interceptors to better suit the use case of an application. For example, interceptors can force the cache to refresh at a designated interval. Caching is a great tool for a device working with limited resources in its environment. For this reason, Android developers ought to use cache to keep track of calculated computations.

 A nice open source library that supports both *in-memory* and *filesystem* cache is Dropbox Store (*https://oreil.ly/urfwv*).

---

3. LRU stands for Least Recently Used. As you can't cache objects indefinitely, caching is always related to an eviction strategy to maintain the cache at a target or acceptable size. In an LRU cache, the "oldest" objects are evicted first.

Reducing Unnecessary Work

For your application to consume resources frugally, you want to avoid leaving in code that is doing unnecessary work. Even senior developers commonly make these kinds of mistakes, causing extra work and memory to be allocated unnecessarily. For example, custom views in Android require particular attention. Let's consider a custom view with a circular shape. For a custom view implementation, you can subclass any kind of View and override the onDraw method. Here is one possible implementation of CircleView:

```kotlin
// Warning: this is an example of what NOT to do!
class CircleView @JvmOverloads constructor(
    context: Context,
) : View(context) {

    override fun onDraw(canvas: Canvas) {
        super.onDraw(canvas)
        canvas.save()
        // Never initialize object allocation here!
        val paint: Paint = Paint().apply {
            color = Color.parseColor("#55448AFF")
            isAntiAlias = true
        }
        canvas.drawCircle(100f, 100f, 50f, paint)
        canvas.restore()
    }
}
```

The onDraw method is invoked every time the view needs to be redrawn. That can happen quite frequently, especially if the view is animated or moved. Therefore, you should never instantiate new objects in onDraw. Such mistakes result in unnecessarily allocating a lot of objects, which puts high pressure on the garbage collector. In the previous example, a new Paint instance is created every time the rendering layer draws CircleView. You should never do that.

Instead, it is better to instantiate the Paint object once as a class attribute:

```kotlin
class CircleView @JvmOverloads constructor(
    context: Context,
) : View(context) {

    private var paint: Paint = Paint().apply {
        color = Color.parseColor("#55448AFF")
        isAntiAlias = true
    }
        set(value) {
            field = value
```

```
        invalidate()
    }

    override fun onDraw(canvas: Canvas) {
        super.onDraw(canvas)
        canvas.save()
        canvas.drawCircle(100f, 100f, 50f, paint)
        canvas.restore()
    }
}
```

Now the paint object is allocated only once. For the purposes of this existing class, sometimes the paint value would be set to different colors. However, if the assignment is not dynamic, you can take it a step further by evaluating the paint value lazily.

You want to keep your inject balanced and your dependencies light whenever possible. For repositories, services, and other singleton dependencies (dependencies that are single objects in memory, like object), it makes sense to make use of lazy delegation so that there is a singleton instance rather than copies of the same object sitting in the heap.

Consider the code we examined earlier in "Detecting Memory Leaks with LeakCanary" on page 304:

```
class MapImportViewModel @ViewModelInject constructor(
    private val settings: Settings,
    private val app: Application
): ViewModel() {
    /* removed for brevity */

    fun unarchiveAsync(item: ItemData) {
        viewModelScope.launch {
            val inputStream = app.contentResolve.
                openInputStream(item.uri) ?: return@launch
            val rootFolder = settings.getAppDir() ?: return@launch
            val outputFolder = File(rootFolder, "imported")
            /* removed for brevity */
        }
    }
}
```

In this class, the settings dependency is injected using Hilt—you can tell that by the @ViewModelInject. At the time we wrote this example, we were using Hilt 2.30.1-alpha and only dependencies available in the activity scope could be injected into the ViewModel. In other words, a newly created MapImportViewModel is always injected into the same Settings instance, as long as the activity isn't re-created. So the bottom line is: a dependency injection framework such as Hilt can assist you in scoping the lifecycle of your dependencies. In TrekMe, `Settings` is scoped in the application. Therefore, `Settings` is technically a singleton.

Android Jetpack

Hilt is a dependency injection (DI) framework that provides a standard way to use DI in your application. The framework also has the benefit of managing lifecycles automatically, and has extensions available for use with Jetpack components like ViewModels and WorkManager.

The avoidance of unnecessary work expands into every scope of Android development. When drawing objects to render on the UI, it makes sense to recycle already-drawn pixels. Likewise, since we know that making network calls in Android drains the battery, it's good to examine how many calls are made and how frequently they're called. Perhaps you have a shopping cart in your application. It may make good business sense to make updates to the remote server so that a user can access their cart cross-platform. On the other hand, it may also be worth exploring updating a user's cart in local storage (save for a periodic network update). Of course, these kinds of business decisions exist outside the scope of this book, but technical consideration can always help to make for more thoughtful features.

Using Static Functions

When a method or a property isn't tied to any class instance (e.g., doesn't alter an object state), it sometimes makes sense to use *static functions/properties*. We'll show different scenarios where using static functions is more appropriate than using inheritance.

Kotlin makes it very easy to use static functions. A `companion object` within a class declaration holds static constants, properties, and functions that can be referenced anywhere in the project. For example, an Android service can expose a static property `isStarted`, which can only be modified by the service itself, as shown in Example 12-1.

Example 12-1. GpxRecordingService.isStarted

```
class GpxRecordingService {

    /* Removed for brevity */

    companion object {
        var isStarted: Boolean = false
```

```
            private set(value) {
                EventBus.getDefault().post(GpxRecordServiceStatus(value))
                field = value
            }
        }
    }
```

In Example 12-1, `GpxRecordingService` can internally change the value of `isStarted`. While doing so, an event is sent through the event bus, notifying all registered components. Moreover, the status of the `GpxRecordingService` is accessible from anywhere in the app as a read-only `GpxRecordingService.isStarted` property. But remember to avoid accidentally saving an `Activity`, `Fragment`, `View`, or `Context` to a static member: that could end in a hefty memory leak!

Minification and Obfuscation with R8 and ProGuard

It is a common practice to *minify*, or shrink, release builds for production so that unused code and resources can be removed. Minifying your code allows you to ship smaller APKs to Google PlayStore more securely. *Minification* shrinks your code by removing unused methods. Minifying your code also gives you the power of *obfuscation* as an additional security feature. Obfuscation garbles the names of classes/fields/methods and removes debugging attributes in order to discourage reverse engineering.

For Android users, R8 is now the default minification tool provided by the Android Gradle plug-in 5.4.1+. ProGuard, R8's stricter and more powerful predecessor, had a heavier focus on optimizing heavy reflection like the ones found in Gson. In comparison, the newer minification tool R8 does not support this feature. However, R8 is successful in achieving smaller compression and optimization for Kotlin.

Configurations can be done through `proguardFile` (you will see an example at the end of the section). R8 reads the rules provided for the `proguardFile` and executes shrinking and obfuscation accordingly. You can then assign a *proguardFile* to a certain flavor and build type in *build.gradle*:

```
buildTypes {
    release {
        minifyEnabled true
        shrinkResources true
        proguardFile getDefaultProguardFile('proguard-android-
optimize.txt'), 'proguard-rules.pro'
    }
}
```

It's common practice to shrink your APK to upload to the PlayStore. However, it's important to be watchful and prevent unintentionally shrinking/obfuscating code that might need to be used by a third-party library at runtime. Kotlin uses metadata in Java classes for Kotlin constructs. However, when R8 shrinks Kotlin classes, it is unable to keep state with the Kotlin metadata. In a best-case scenario, shrinking/ obfuscating such classes might cause wonky behavior; in a worst-case scenario, it might cause inexplicable crashes.

To demonstrate a scenario where ProGuard accidentally obfuscates too much application code, we observe some wonky behavior on the popular open source library, Retrofit. Perhaps your application works perfectly fine in debugging mode, but in release mode, a networking call inexplicably returns a `NullPointerException`. Unfortunately, Kotlin Gson models go blank even while annotating properties/fields with Retrofit's `@SerializedName`, thanks to Kotlin reflection. As a result, you must add a rule in your proguard file to prevent the Kotlin model class from obfuscating. Oftentimes, you may end up having to include your model classes by adding them directly in your `proguardFile`. Here is an example of adding model domain classes to a `proguardFile` so that release builds don't accidentally obfuscate the aforementioned classes:

```
# Retrofit 2.X
-dontwarn retrofit2.**
-keep class retrofit2.** { *; }
# Kotlin source code whitelisted here
-keep class com.some.kotlin.network.model.** { *; }
-keepattributes Signature
-keepattributes Exceptions
-keepclasseswithmembers class * {
    @retrofit2.http.* <methods>;
}
```

A good piece of advice is: always test the release build!

Summary

This chapter covered the following important performance optimization tips:

- In the Android view framework, deeply nested view hierarchies take longer to draw and traverse than flatter hierarchies. Consider using `ConstraintLayout`, where you can flatten nested views.
- In the Android view framework, it is better to move programmatic draws and animations to drawable resources to offload the work on the RenderThread at runtime.

- Using JSON and XML formats for network data payload is horrible for compression. Use protocol buffers for much smaller data compression.

- Avoid unnecessary work whenever possible: make sure you're not ringing off unnecessary network calls for constant updates, and try to recycle drawn objects.

- Optimizations in performance and memory can come from taking an honest look at the code you write. Are you unintentionally creating objects within a loop that could be created once outside a loop? What expensive operations could be reduced to less-intensive operations?

- You can use a ProGuard file to make your application as small as possible and add custom rules for shrinking, obfuscating, and optimizing your app.

Let's face it: Android can be a challenge to keep up with. It's OK to take information in stride as it becomes relevant for you. Such a strategy guarantees learning opportunities that stay with you for a long time. No matter where you're at in your journey, one of your best resources for both Kotlin and Android (besides this book) is the open source community. Both Android and Kotlin are living, breathing communities from which you can ascertain the newest and most relevant information. To keep yourself current, you can turn to additional resources like Twitter, Slack (*https://oreil.ly/m853Y*), and KEEP (*https://oreil.ly/KZPlx*). You may well also find that you can return to this book to revisit popular, evergreen problems that show up in Android from time to time. We hope you enjoyed this book.

Index

A

Activity component, 62-66
    back stack, 65
    fragments, 64
Activity context, 59
Actor model, CSP, 225
Alarms, 297
Analysis Panel, 289-291
Android applications
    Activity component, 62-66
    back stack, 65
    basics, 55
    bound services, 68-70
    broadcast receivers, 72
    components of, 62-73
    content providers, 71
    environment, 55-62
    fragments, 64
    services, 67-70
    started services, 68
Android fundamentals, 53-79
    Activity component, 62-66
    Android stack, 53-55
    application architectures, 73-75
    application components, 62-73
    application context, 61
    application environment, 55-62
    applications, 55
    broadcast receivers, 72
    component context, 59
    content providers, 71
    context, 59-62
    hardware, 54
    intents and intent filters, 57

    kernel, 54
    Local Model, 75
    Model–View–Intent, 76
    Model–View–Presenter, 76
    Model–View–View Model, 77
    MVC, 74
    patterns, 76-78
    runtime environment, 55
    services, 67-70
    system services, 55
    widgets, 75
Android Profiler, 277-304
    about, 277-280
    Analysis Panel, 289-291
    CPU Profiler, 286-296
    CPU timeline, 287
    Energy Profiler, 297-299
    Memory Profiler, 299-304
    method tracing, 291-295
    network calls and, 283-286
    Network Profiler, 280-286
    recording a Sample Method Trace, 295-296
    thread activity timeline, 287
    viewing network calls with Connection
        View and Thread View, 281
Android profiling tools, 275-309
    Android Profiler, 277-304
    CPU Profiler, 286-296
    detecting memory leaks with LeakCanary,
        304-308
    Energy Profiler, 297-299
    Memory Profiler, 299-304
    Network Profiler, 280-286
Android stack, 53-55

applications, 55
hardware, 54
kernel, 54
runtime environment, 55
system services, 55
any() function, 37
application environment, 55-62
application context, 61
component context, 59
context, 59-62
intents/intent filters, 57
ApplicationContext, 61
ArrayList, 162
ART, 55
asSharedFlow(), 263
async, 150
async coroutine builder, 133-134
atomicity, 82
automatic cancellation, 191
await(), 179

B

back pressure, 111-113, 224
back stack, 65
Binder, 55
Bitmap pooling, 321
blocking call, 109
BlockingQueue, 204
Boolean functions, 37
bound services, 68-70
broadcast receivers, 72
buffered channels, 210
BufferOverflow, 269

C

caching, 321
Call Chart, 288, 292
Call.enqueue(), 178
callback-based API, 240-245
callbackFlow builder, 245
callbacks, 115-128
app creation, 118-126
example-of-purchase feature, 116-118
logic implementation, 123
memory leaks and, 126
structured concurrency and, 125
threading model limitations, 126
view, 119-123
ViewModel, 118

CancellableContinuation, 178
cancellation, 171-187
automatic, 191
coroutine, 174-176
coroutine lifecycle, 172-173
delay, 182
failure, 171
handling, 183
task delegated to a third-party library,
174-176
CancellationException, 181
catch operator, 256-259
declarative style, 256
emit a particular value, 258
example, 257
exception transparency, 256
channel.receive(), 206
channels, 201-233
about, 202-204
buffered, 210
communicating sequential processes,
212-227
conflated, 209
fan-out and fan-in, 222
hot, 232
limitations of, 230-231
performance test, 223-224
produce builder with, 211
rendezvous, 204-207
select expression, 219-221
unlimited, 208-209
ChannelT(Channel.CONFLATED), 209
children CPU time, 289
CircleView, 323
class initialization, 12-13
classes, 12-24
class initialization, 12-13
companion objects, 19
data classes, 20
delegates, 18
enum classes, 21-23
lateinit properties, 15-17
lazy properties, 17
properties, 14
sealed classes, 23
CloseableCoroutineScope(..), 170
cold flows, 240-251
concurrently transforming a stream of values, 245-248

creating a custom operator, 248-251
  interfacing with a callback-based API,
    240-245
collect, 238
collections framework (Kotlin), 29-52
  Boolean functions, 37
  creating containers, 33
  example, 35, 44-51
  filter functions, 38-40
  flatMap, 40
  functional Android, 36
  grouping, 42
  iterators versus sequences, 43
  java interoperability, 30
  overloaded operators, 32
  transformation functions, 37-44
communicating sequential processes (CSP)
  about, 201
  back pressure, 224
  deadlock, 227-230
  example, 212-227
  fan-out and fan-in, 222
  final thoughts, 226
  first implementation, 214-219
  model and architecture, 213
  performance test, 223-224
  putting it all together, 221
  select expression, 219-221
  sequential execution inside a process, 226
  similarities with the actor model, 225
companion objects, 19
concurrency, limiting, 216
concurrent programming, 81-99
  atomicity, 82
  dropped frames, 85-87
  Executors and ExecutorServices, 93-95
  job managing tools, 95-99
  JobScheduler, 96-98
  Looper/Handler, 91-93
  memory leaks, 87-90
  thread managing tools, 90-95
  thread safety, 82-84
  threading model, 84
  visibility, 83
  WorkManager, 98
conflated channels, 209
Connection View, 281
ConstraintLayout, 314
  achieving flatter view hierarchy, 312-316

containers, creating, 33
content providers, 71
context, 59-62
  application, 61
  component, 59
context preservation, 241
Context.getApplicationContext() method, 61
Continuation Passing Style (CPS), 147
Controller, 74
coroutine.start(), 232
CoroutineContext (see context)
CoroutineExceptionHandler, 186
coroutines, 129-155
  async coroutine builder, 133-134
  cancellation, 173, 174-176
  cooperative with cancellation, 180-182
  CoroutineScope and CoroutineContext,
    138-144
  example, 130-132, 150-153
  Job, 173
  lifecycle, 172-173
  structured concurrency with (see structured
    concurrency with coroutines)
  suspending functions, 145-149, 167-170
CoroutineScope, 139, 169
coroutineScope, 189, 250
CPS (Continuation Passing Style), 147
CPU Profiler, 286-296
  Analysis Panel, 289-291
  CPU timeline, 287
  method tracing, 291-295
  recording a Sample Method Trace, 295-296
  thread activity timeline, 287
CSP (see communicating sequential processes)

D

daemon, 73
data classes, 20
deadlock, 85, 227-230
declarative style, catch operator, 256
delay function, 131, 182, 224
delegates, 18
DEX, 55
Dispatcher, 167
Dispatchers.Default, 142, 150
Dispatchers.IO, 142
Dispatchers.Main, 141
display buffers, 87
downstream flow, 241

Drawables, 316-321
DrawableStates, 320
dropped frames, 85-87

E

emit, 264, 268
Energy Profiler, 297-299
ensureActive, 175, 183
enum classes, 21-23
equals, 20
error handling, 251-255
    exception transparency violation, 255
    separation of concern, 254
    try/catch block, 252-254
exception handling, 191-198
    exposed exceptions, 193-195
    materializing exceptions, 259-262
    unhandled exceptions, 196-198
    unhandled versus exposed exceptions,
        191-193
exception transparency, 256
exception transparency violation, 255
Executors, 93-95
Executors.newSingleThreadExecutor(), 122
ExecutorServices, 93-95
explicit intent, 57
exposed exceptions, 191-195
extension functions, 10-12
extension properties, 11
extraBufferCapacity, 269

F

failure cancellation, 171
fan-in, 222
fan-out, 222
fetchImage, 148, 260
fetchProfile, 153
filesystem caches, 322
filter functions, 38-40
filterNot function, 38
finish() method, 63
Flame Chart, 290
flatMap, 40, 48
flatter view hierarchy, 312-316
flowOn, 241
@FlowPreview, 247
flows, 235-274
    catch operator, 256-259
    cold flows, 240-251

error handling, 251-255
example, 237-239
exception transparency violation, 255
hot flows with SharedFlow, 262-273
materializing exceptions, 259-262
operators, 239
separation of concern, 254
terminal operators, 239
try/catch block, 252-254
use case: concurrently transforming a
    stream of values, 245-248
use case: creating a custom operator,
    248-251
use case: interfacing with a callback-based
    API, 240-245
forEach method, 35
ForkJoinPool, 94
fragments, 64
function types, 6-8
functional Android, 36
functional programming
    Android and, 36
    procedural versus, 35
Future.get(), 133

G

garbage collection (GC), 301
generators, 43
generics, 8
getDataFlow, 238
GoogleLocationProvider, 298
GPX Record, 299
GridLayout, 314
groupBy function, 42

H

HandlerThread, 163-167
hardware, 54
hashCode, 20
heap dumps, 278, 300
higher-order functions, 7
Hilt, 325
hot channels, 232
hot flows, 262-273
    create a SharedFlow, 263
    register a subscriber, 263
    send values to the SharedFlow, 264
    SharedFlow as an event bus, 270
    SharedFlow to stream data, 264-269

StateFlow, 271-273

I

identifier field, 15
in-memory caches, 322
IntentFilter, 58
intents/intent filters, 57
interface with a callback-based API, 240-245
invariants, 103-107
    mutexes, 104
    thread-safe collections, 104-107
isActive, 174
iterating over a channel, 205-207
iterators, sequences, 43

J

java interoperability, 30
Java Native Interface (JNI), 55
job managing tools, 95-99
    JobScheduler, 96-98
    WorkManager, 98
Job.cancel, 184
job.cancelAndJoin(), 179
job.join(), 210
job.start(), 172
JobInfo, 96
Jobs, 297
JobScheduler, 96-98
joinToString function, 47
JSON, 321

K

kernel, 54
Kotlin (basics), 1-27
    class initialization, 12-13
    classes, 12-24
    companion objects, 19
    data classes, 20
    delegates, 18
    enum classes, 21-23
    extension functions, 10-12
    function types, 6-8
    generics, 8
    lambdas, 9
    lateinit properties, 15-17
    lazy properties, 17
    null safety, 3-5
    primitive types, 2
    properties, 14
    sealed classes, 23
    unit type, 5
    variables, 8
    variables and functions, 8-12
    visibility modifiers, 24-26
kotlinx.collections.immutable library, 31
kotlinx.coroutine library, 138

L

lambdas, 9
lateinit properties, 15-17
launch {..} function, 172
Layout Inspector, 312
LayoutInflater, 316
lazy initialization, 17
lazy properties, 17
LeakCanary, 304-308
LinearLayout, 314
LiveData, 77, 90, 266
Local Model, 75
logic implementation, 123
Looper class, 163
Looper.prepare(), 91
Looper.start(), 91
Looper/Handler, 91-93

M

map function, 38-40
mapIndexed.mapIndexed, 40
mapOf function, 33
materializing exceptions, 259-262
memory leaks, 87-90
    in app creation, 126
    LeakCanary detecting, 304-308
Memory Profiler, 299-304
method tracing, 278, 291-295
minification, with R8 and ProGuard, 326
Model, defined, 74
Model–View–Controller (MVC) pattern, 74
Model–View–Intent (MVI) pattern, 76
Model–View–Presenter (MVP) pattern, 76
Model–View–View Model (MVVM) pattern, 77
MutableSharedFLow(), 263
mutexes, 104
MVC (Model–View–Controller) pattern, 74
MVI (Model–View–Intent) pattern, 76
MVP (Model–View–Presenter) pattern, 76
MVVM (Model–View–View Model) pattern, 77

N

network calls
  about, 283-286
  minimizing asset payload in, 321
  viewing, 281
Network Profiler, 280-286
  and network calls, 283-286
  viewing network calls with Connection
    View and Thread View, 281
NewsDao, 265
nonblocking call, 109
null safety, 3-5

O

obfuscation, with R8 and ProGuard, 326
object-oriented programming (OOP), 34
offer, 113
OkHttp, 322
onCreate, 15, 63, 67, 78
onCreateView, 15
onDestroy, 63, 67
onDraw, 323
onResume, 78
onStartJob, 98
OOP (object-oriented programming), 34
operators, 239
  create custom, 248-251
  terminal, 239
overloaded operators, 32

P

parallel decomposition, 189
parent context, 144
patterns, Android, 76-78
  Model–View–Intent, 76
  Model–View–Presenter, 76
  Model–View–View Model, 77
performance optimizations, 311-328
  achieving flatter view hierarchy with Con-
    straintLayout, 312-316
  Bitmap pooling and caching, 321
  minification and obfuscation with R8 and
    ProGuard, 326
  minimizing asset payload in network calls,
    321
  reducing programmatic draws with Drawa-
    bles, 316-321
  reducing unnecessary work, 323-325

  using static functions, 325
performance test, 223-224
POJOs (plain old Java objects), 20
primary constructor, 12
primitive types, 2
private visibility modifiers
  in Java, 24
  in Kotlin, 25
procedural programming, 35
produceValues(), 211
profileDeferred.await, 151
programmatic draws, 316-321
ProGuard, 326
properties, 14
protected visibility modifiers
  in Java, 24
  in Kotlin, 25
public visibility modifiers
  in Java, 24
  in Kotlin, 25
PurchaseViewModel, 118

Q

query(), 72
quitSafely, 163

R

R8, 326
RAM, 300
RelativeLayout, 314
RenderThread, 293
rendezvous channels, 204-207
  iterating over a channel, 205-207
  other flavors of channel, 207
runBlocking, 130, 134
runCatching, 193
runtime environment, 55

S

Sample Java Methods, 292
Sample Method Trace, 295-296
sealed classes, 23
select expression, 219-221
self CPU time, 289
send...(), 92
sequences, iterators versus, 43
Service, 59
services, 67-70

bound, 68-70
    started, 68
SharedFlow
    architecture, 264
    buffer values, 269
    creating, 263
    as event bus, 270
    hot flows with, 262-273
        (see also hot flows)
    implementation, 265-266
    implementation testing, 266
    replay values, 267
    sending values to, 264
    streaming data with, 264-269
    suspending/not suspending, 268
singleton objects, 19
Stack, 111
started services, 68
StateFlow, 271-273
static functions, 325
streaming data, SharedFlow and, 264-269
structured concurrency
    app creation and, 125
    coroutines and (see structured concurrency
        with coroutines)
    parent–child relationship in, 137
structured concurrency with coroutines,
        134-138, 157-200
    automatic cancellation, 191
    cancellation, 171-187
    cancelling a task delegated to a third-party
        library, 174-176
    causes of cancellation, 184-187
    coroutine cancellation, 174-176
    coroutine lifecycle, 172-173
    coroutines which are cooperative with can-
        cellation, 180-182
    delay cancellation, 182
    exception handling, 191-198
    exposed exceptions, 193-195
    handling cancellation, 183
    parallel decomposition, 189
    supervision, 187-189
    supervisorScope builder, 189
    suspending functions, 157-171
    unhandled exceptions, 196-198
    unhandled versus exposed exceptions,
        191-193
subscribe method, 251

supervision, 187-189
SupervisorJob, 187
supervisorScope, 189, 194
suspending functions, 145-149
    and coroutines, 167-170
    example, 150-153
    HandlerThread, 163-167
    java.util.concurrent.ExecutorService
        approach for, 160-163
    lower-level constructs of, 146-149
    structured concurrency with coroutines,
        157-171
    traditional threading versus, 171
synchronization, 84, 104
system services, 55

T

terminal operator, 236
ternary expression, 6
thread activity timeline, 287
thread managing tools, 90-95
    Executors and ExecutorServices, 93-95
    Looper/Handler, 91-93
thread safety, 82-84, 101-114
    atomicity, 82
    back pressure, 111-113
    blocking call versus nonblocking call, 109
    defined, 82
    example of thread issue, 101-103
    invariants, 103-107
    mutexes, 104
    thread confinement, 107
    thread contention, 108
    thread-safe collections, 104-107
    visibility, 83
    work queues, 110
Thread View, viewing network calls with, 281
thread, defined, 82
Thread.setUncaughtExceptionHandler, 135
Thread.sleep(), 122
threading model
    basics, 84
    limitations of, 126
threading, suspending functions versus, 171
ThreadLocal, 107
ThreadPoolExecutor, 94, 126, 161
toString, 21
total CPU time, 289
Trace Java Methods, 293

Trace System Calls, 293
transformation functions, 37-44, 39, 247
    Boolean functions, 37
    filter functions, 38-40
    flatMap, 40
    grouping, 42
    iterators versus sequences, 43
TrekMe, 276, 279
try/catch block, 252-254
tryEmit, 264, 268
type inference, 3
type system, 2-8
    function types, 6-8
    generics, 8
    null safety, 3-5
    primitive types, 2
    unit type, 5

U

UncaughtExceptionHandler, 196
unhandled exceptions
    about, 196-198
    exposed versus, 191-193
Unit, 5
unit type, 5
unlimited channels, 208-209
upper bound type, 34

upstream exceptions, 256
upstream flow, 241

V

View, 74
ViewModel, 90, 118, 120, 307
@ViewModelInject, 324
viewModelScope, 147, 170
visibility, 83
visibility modifiers, 24-26
VSync, 317

W

whileSelect, 250
widgets, 75
withContext, 167
work queues, 110
WorkerPool, 108
WorkManager, 98

Y

yield(), 175, 183

Z

Zygote, 56

About the Authors

Pierre-Olivier Laurence is the lead software engineer at Safran Aircraft Engines, near Paris. He started learning Java and Linux systems over a decade ago, which quickly led to full-time Android development. A frequent collaborator on the TileView open source library since its inception, Pierre recently created a version of the library that's 100% Kotlin, leveraging the power of Kotlin coroutines for truly impressive performance gains. An early adopter of Kotlin, Pierre has maintained several open source Kotlin projects since the language was introduced in 2015. With an eye toward personal development, Pierre is an avid reader of O'Reilly books and looks forward to mastering even more technologies in the future.

Amanda Hinchman-Dominguez is a Kotlin Google Developer Expert, an Android engineer at Groupon, and active in the global Kotlin community, both as a speaker and as a community organizer. Starting out in academia, she obtained a B.S. in computer science at Grinnell College. Working across web, mobile, and native-desktop development, her roots in metaprogramming research and community-based learning heavily influenced her direction in both her interests and her career. Her passion for Kotlin naturally shifted toward Android development after some years in the industry, and she hasn't looked back since.

G. Blake Meike is a senior software development engineer at Amazon and has more than 10 years of experience with Java. He's developed applications using most of the GUI toolkits and several of the Java mobile device platforms.

Mike Dunn was a coauthor of *Native Mobile Development* (O'Reilly). He was the principal mobile engineer at O'Reilly Media. He contributed to Google's Closure library and provided extensions for Google's next-gen Android media player, Exo-Player.

Colophon

The animal on the cover of *Programming Android with Kotlin* is a coppery-bellied puffleg (*Eriocnemis cupreoventris*), a hummingbird found in Colombia and Venezuela. They live in tropical and subtropical forests and grasslands, and are threatened by habitat loss.

The puffleg averages 3.7 inches in length, including a 0.7 inch beak and 1.4 inch tail. Their feathers are mostly metallic green, though they have coppery bellies. They have white leg puffs that are said to resemble woolly pants.

Like other hummingbirds, the puffleg is solitary aside from mating. The female builds the nest and raises her chicks alone. The average clutch consists of two eggs. Chicks leave the nest when they are around 20 days old.

In its range, this hummingbird is uncommon and only found in fragmented populations. In both Colombia and Venezuela, many forests have been converted to agricultural fields, leading to habitat loss. Its conservation status is Near Threatened. Many of the animals on O'Reilly covers are endangered; all of them are important to the world.

The cover illustration is by Karen Montgomery, based on a black and white engraving from *Wood's Natural History*. The cover fonts are Gilroy Semibold and Guardian Sans. The text font is Adobe Minion Pro; the heading font is Adobe Myriad Condensed; and the code font is Dalton Maag's Ubuntu Mono.

O'REILLY®

Learn from experts.
Become one yourself.

Books | Live online courses
Instant Answers | Virtual events
Videos | Interactive learning

Get started at oreilly.com.

Milton Keynes UK
Ingram Content Group UK Ltd.
UKHW030757050324
438909UK00003B/16